1

Or Not To Retire?

Also by Sam Venable

An Island Unto Itself
The Story of Little Pecan

A Handful of Thumbs and Two Left Feet

Two or Three Degrees Off Plumb
Sam Venable's Unique Look at Life

One Size Fits All and Other Holiday Myths
A Walk Through the Four Seasons with Sam Venable

From Ridgetops to Riverbottoms
A Celebration of the Outdoor Life in Tennessee

I'd Rather Be Ugly than Stuppid...and other deep thoughts

Mountain Hands
A Portrait of Southern Appalachia

Rock-Elephant
A Story of Friendship and Fishing

You Gotta Laugh to Keep from Cryin'
A Baby Boomer Contemplates Life beyond Fifty

Someday I May Find Honest Work
A Newspaper Humorist's Life

WARNING! This Product Contains Nuttiness
A Fun Look at the Bizarre World in Which We Live

How to Tawlk and Rite Good
A Guide to the Language of Southern Appalachia

"Talk Is Cheap" comedy tour holiday edition DVD,
recorded at the Museum of Appalachia in Norris TN

To Retire?
Or Not To Retire?

A Geezing Humorist's
Quest for Answers

By Sam Venable

Illustrations by R. Daniel Proctor

For Benny and Ella Kate,

the newest additions to our family

Table of Contents

ACKNOWLEDGEMENTS

Most of these essays originally appeared as Sam Venable's columns in the Knoxville News Sentinel. They have been edited for book use and may differ somewhat from their original form. The author thanks News Sentinel editor Jack McElroy and publisher Patrick Birmingham for granting permission to republish this work. In addition, his appreciation goes to illustrator R. Daniel Proctor and cover photographers Paul Efird and Mary Ann Venable, as well as design expert Sam Hill, for their excellent graphics contributions to this effort. Thanks also to Fisher Tire Company, Knoxville, Tennessee, for photo location. And as the author has said in previous book forewords, he is deeply indebted to readers. Without them, he would have been forced to find a real job oh-so-long ago.

What a truly depressing thought.

Until 2014, the word "retirement" rarely appeared in my column, and then only if I was referring to some old fart who had called it quits.

Venable males never retire, mainly because we don't live that long. My own father was but 57—still actively engaged in his classes at the University of Tennessee, his church, his community and his family—when he died of a heart attack in 1972. It's a bit macabre, but I always figured his eldest son would check out under similar circumstances. Not as young as 57, perhaps; but surely I'd just keep striking letters on a keyboard until I keeled over.

I suspect that'll still be the case. I'll write until the very end. For better or for worse, writing is as much a part of me as skin and bones. I just do it now on my schedule and my terms, not someone else's.

The main reason I exited 2332 News Sentinel Drive was economic. I can't explain it, nor can my accountant, but it was more financially advantageous for me to retire rather than work fulltime (which, harrumph, has forever been an oxymoron in my case.)

Also in this chapter are examples of how we freshly minted retirees struggle with the bizarre new world around us—a world dominated by doctors and bureaucrats who don't know the word "quit." Not to mention loving spouses who routinely terrify us with three words: "home improvement project."

Oh, for my old loafing spot back in the newsroom!

Chapter One
TAKING THE PLUNGE

Hanging it up—sorta

My first day on the job at the Knoxville News Sentinel was March 5, 1970. The last came exactly 44½ years later. On the evening of September 5, 2014, I exited the building as a retiree.

(Cue first jokester: "How did Venob know he retired? He didn't strike a lick of honest work in nearly half a century!")

Point well taken. Whether as the newspaper's outdoors editor (1970-1985) or metro-humor columnist (since 1985), I enjoyed the most wonderful non-job career in the history of employment.

I was 22 years old, with reporting stints at two other Tennessee dailies, when News Sentinel sports editor Tom Siler took the riskiest gamble of his professional life and brought me aboard. Tom gave me a desk, showed me how to fill out an expense report, then said, "Hit the road and start writing about the woods and waters." A decade and one-half later, editor Harry Moskos said the same thing but on a broader scale: "Write whatever's on your mind."

That's it. No limits. No agendas. No parameters. Just go write. I tell you from the bottom of my heart it was unmitigated joy.

So why did I leave?

Two reasons.

The first was a matter of mathematics. There were significantly more numbers on my side of the financial ledger as a retiree than as an employee. Such are the vagaries of longevity in the newspaper industry.

But it led to Number Two: Retirement doesn't mean quitting. When ink flows through your veins instead of blood, there's always "just one more" story to tell. It'll be that way 'til they seal my coffin.

Three yellowed, frayed quotes describing this truism hung above my desk for eons.

One was from Ellen Goodman of the Boston Globe: "Being a columnist is like being married to a nymphomaniac. Every time you think you're through, you have to start all over again."

TO RETIRE? OR NOT TO RETIRE?

Another was from Russell Baker of the New York Times: "The job of a columnist is to wait until the battle is over and the real reporters have done their work, and then go onto the battlefield and pick the pockets of the wounded."

And finally there was a simple command from Joel Vance, an old friend from outdoor magazine days: "Write it, damn you, write it! What else are you good for?"

The News Sentinel graciously extended a contract for two columns per week. So I was right back in my same old Local page spot on Sundays and Thursdays. Plus an occasional outdoor piece for Sports.

As I teased with colleagues, this arrangement was the ultimate win-win. Readers who happily follow my drivel still have a Venable opportunity two days a week. Conversely, the ones who don't share my opinions have two fewer opportunities each week to gripe about "what blithering nonsense that asshole regurgitated today."

See? Worked out great for everybody.

How did I get into this nutty business in the first place?

Blame the chemistry department at the University of Tennessee and its cruel insistence that I master complex equations and formulas before graduating in forestry and wildlife management.

I was nearly into my junior year, on the brink of academic ruin, when a fraternity brother suggested a radically different route. I quote him verbatim: "Venable, you're so full of bullshit, you'd make a great journalist." I took one course and fell head-over-notepad in love. Go figure.

I didn't know how to type. Had never worked on a high school newspaper or yearbook staff. Barely knew what appeared in newspapers beyond the confines of the sports section and funnies. But I immediately realized the future and I had just shaken hands.

How things turned out so well for a goof like me is one of life's most baffling mysteries. As a journalist, I had the worst timing this side of a rusty sundial. Three examples will suffice.

On April 25, 1969, a savage crime—still unsolved, btw—occurred on North Broadway. A man walked into a Kroger store, shot the manager dead, then calmly walked out.

Where was I, then the Knoxville Journal's lead police reporter? Touring the "under-construction" City Safety Building with Harry Huskisson, chief of police, that's where. Interior wiring hadn't been completed. There were no telephones, no walkie-talkies. Neither of us had a clue what was going on until we returned to our respective staff cars in the unpaved parking lot and were met with frantic, in-dash radio messages: "Where are you?" I don't know who peeled out faster.

On the morning of September 11, 2001, I hunted wood ducks and teal on Fort Loudoun Lake. I came home to work on the next day's ho-hum column. Neither the radio nor TV was on. I didn't know anything about the terrorist attacks until someone finally telephoned from the office, wondering if Venob was ever going to weigh in.

The day UT basketball coach Bruce Pearl was fired, I was in Jefferson County, poking around in the woods, cellphone tucked safely into the console of my pickup. I didn't find out until late afternoon, then burned a new lane down Interstate 40 to the office.

Yet on all three occasions—and countless more like them—Venable's words were on the page when the press rolled. As far as readers were concerned, I'd been right there, Johnny-on-the-spot, from the get-go. Chain-smoked cigarettes (before I took the pledge in 1979), gallons of black coffee (no way I'll ever give this up) and a cavernous reservoir of adrenaline will see you through any crisis.

I don't know if journalism takes normal people and turns them into Type-A freaks, or whether Type-A freaks naturally gravitate to newsrooms. Writers everywhere understand what I'm talking about. When you're zoned on deadline, someone could cut off a hand and you'd never notice until the keystrokes abruptly ceased falling.

It sounds trite, but where did all those years go?

How did I come up with hundreds of thousands of words annually for more than four decades?

Why do I enjoy writing as much now as I did when I took that first class?

How was I so abundantly blessed with a wonderful wife, kids, grandchildren, friends and co-workers to share this incredible journey?

Beats me. I'm just thankful. And grateful that readers and bosses always afforded me such an extraordinarily long leash. They have been generous with praise, restrained in criticism. It is an honor to serve.

And I'm going to keep right on serving as a r-e-t-i-r-e-e—you don't know how strange it feels to type those letters—with "just one more" story to tell.

See you in the newspapers.

Eat it only if you dare

I've got piles something awful. They're driving me crazy.

No, not piles of the hemorrhoid variety. The piles I'm talking about are stacked on an eight-foot table in my garage. Boxes. Bins. Bags. Papers. Photos. Books. Magazines. Letters. Folders. And much more.

This is detritus from four-plus decades in newspaper offices. I emptied my News Sentinel drawers, lugged everything home and made plans to index, sort and file.

The planning continues.

There will be order to this chaos. Eventually. I'm a pile person. I know which pile contains this, which pile contains that. It'll just take a while for office piles to become home piles—"a while" meaning any time between today and infinity.

The vast majority of this stuff is marked with a date. Newspaper freaks are strict about that. Whether researching or writing, there's nothing more frustrating than not having a specific point to start from.

But in this case, many of the dates relate to food. As in long-past-prime. How embarrassing. Why in the world did I buy something to eat, then promptly remand it to the black hole of my desk?

Hate to waste it, but for the life of me I simply cannot force myself to ingest something the manufacturer says is "best before" a certain date. And why such precision?

There's a can of soup that supposedly went bad September 5, 2012.

A box of oatmeal that went kaput May 22, 2013.

Raisins that croaked December 3, 2013—at, I am not making this up, "21:56."

Huh? Four minutes before 10 p.m.? Does that mean they were OK at noon on December 3, 2013, but lethal at midnight?

By contrast, a bottle of saline solution for my contact lenses merely expired "10/12." Apparently the health and safety of our eyes can't hold a flame to our digestive tracts.

All those items (and others equally out-of-date) are destined for the trash. But I found one non-food relic that will stay. It made me chuckle the day I discovered it and again just now when it resurfaced.

It's the Wall Street Journal, January 15, 2014. It was lying upside down in our break room. I glanced at the costumed, long-bearded person in a front page photo and exclaimed, "Uncle Si from 'Duck Dynasty?'"

Nope. When I turned the paper over and read the caption, I discovered it was a robed Egyptian priest emerging from a voting booth in Cairo.

Wonder if he knows the mallard comeback call?

I need a password password

If I have to come up with one more new computer password, my head's going to explode.

I mean it. Ka-blooey! Gray matter and skull fragments mixed right in there with bushels of capital letters, lower-case letters, underscores, slashes, numerals and all the other "secret" keystrokes that take civilization one step closer to extinction.

My wordsmithing infrastructure changed drastically when I retired. Passwords I invented, used, re-invented and re-used for decades had to be re-re-re-re-invented. I'm dang-near out of options, let alone notepads to keep track of them.

Unless you're the one person in 10 million whose brain is wired like software, there's no way to remember all that password garbage. So you do what the other 9,999,999 of us do.

You write it down. With a real pen. On real paper.

Then you stick it into a file folder, along with reams of other "secret" passwords for bank accounts, prescription drug accounts, medical accounts, insurance accounts, accounting accounts, ad infinitum, until the folder swells to the size of an unabridged dictionary—which, by the way, is a book people don't use anymore because they can look up definitions online. Assuming they remember the password.

Where does this highly classified file folder (marked "PASSWORDS") reside?

Where it can be easily found, of course. On top of the desk. In the first drawer. Beside the computer. It's as obvious as that "secret rock" beside the front porch where jillions of homeowners "hide" a key.

Keeping up with passwords has overtaken keeping up with the Joneses. However frustrating, this has woven itself permanently into the fabric of our lives. And it's only going to get worse because crooks keep coming.

In August 2014, the New York Times reported the latest online security breach. Something like 1.2 billion log-ins and passwords were stolen by a Russian crime ring. (If my prose suddenly contains words featuring one vowel for every 38 consonants and ending in letters like "-itsky," cancel your subscription immediately. If you can find the password.)

But there's hope. According to a recent report in The Week magazine, fingerprint sensors, already available in Apple's iPhone, are the way of the future, along with "biometrics and one-time secure keys."

Brilliant! The bad guys may ultimately figure out how to copy my fingerprints and biometrics, whatever those things are. But they'll never suspect that rock by the front porch where I'll be stashing my one-time secure key.

Leaving one job for another

Over the course of my journalism career, I quit several jobs to take better ones.

Sometimes the boss got mad when you gave him the news—like how dare you attempt to get ahead in this business?! I thought indentured servitude was no longer in fashion, but I guess I was wrong.

Other times, thankfully, the departure was much more pleasant. Let me tell you about one I shall never forget.

Around noon one day in mid-February 1970, shortly after our final daily deadline, I walked into Lee Anderson's office at the old Chattanooga News-Free Press and gave him two weeks' notice that I had accepted the outdoor editor's job at the News Sentinel and would be moving back to Knoxville.

I was stammering, sweaty-palm nervous.

When you're 22—gosh, was I ever that young?—and you're leaving an editor you admired, respected and enjoyed working for, the guy who had hired you less than a year earlier on a wing-and-a-prayer recommendation, anybody would be nervous.

Lee listened patiently as I stumbled through my speech. Then he stood up, smiled, walked over and shook my hand.

"Sam, we've enjoyed having you with us," he said. "You're always welcome here. If things don't pan out with the new job, you don't even have to call. Just come back to work."

They can't teach warmth like that in management seminars or Human Resources 101. It has to come from the heart, and Lee Stratton Anderson has the biggest heart in Hamilton County.

The reason I relate that memory is because Lee has just retired too. He started at the Free Press as a part-time police reporter at age 16 and leaves as associate publisher and editorial page editor. Here is an icon in Tennessee journalism.

A few years ago, I was booked to perform my standup shtick at a convention in Chattanooga. The sponsors asked if I wanted to invite any special guests. Naturally, I picked Lee. He sat on the front row and howled.

As we visited backstage after the show, Lee said, "How come you weren't that funny when you worked for me?"

"Because I was young and scared to death of every editor in the place, that's why!" I replied.

I mentioned our long-ago farewell. Lee flashed his trademark grin.

"Sam, my offer still stands," he said. "You're welcome to come back any time you want. We'd love to have you."

He paused momentarily, furrowed his brow, then asked: "By the way, how much was I paying you back in 1970?"

"Oh, I dunno," I answered. "Maybe $7,500 a year."

"It's a deal!" he exclaimed. "Yes, come back tomorrow! I'll look for you at 8 a.m.—and I'll be happy to offer the same salary!"

Enjoy your retirement, ol' friend. You've earned it. And thanks so much for the great memories.

Trust an expert in these matters

I spent a long newspaper career honing special skills. Not note-taking, word-crafting and other boring stuff. I'm talking skills that truly matter when the chips are down.

TO RETIRE? OR NOT TO RETIRE?

I speak, of course, of the ability to quickly concoct an excuse, flimsy or otherwise, for any and all vocational situations. Thus, you can imagine my interest in a recent study of this talent.

It was a survey by the Harris Poll for CareerBuilder.com, an online company specializing in human resource matters. Researchers asked more than 5,300 employees and hiring managers to name the best work-related excuses they've either given or received.

Some was run-of-the-mill stuff, such as a faked illness (28 percent), a doctor's appointment (21 percent) and bad weather (11 percent). Ho-hum.

Ah, but a few offered truly innovative gems. Among them:

- "I just put a casserole in the oven."
- "I woke up in a good mood and didn't want to ruin it."
- "I was at a casino all weekend and still had money left on Monday morning."
- "I have a gall stone and want it to heal holistically."
- "I caught my uniform on fire by putting it in the microwave to dry."

Not bad. But there's always room for improvement. Here are a few that might work on bosses in the Knoxville-East Tennessee area.

- "I had to testify to the NCAA and the cops about possible (insert specific sport) violations at the University of Tennessee."
- "I've been stuck in traffic at Exit 407 on I-40 the last three days, but at least I can see the roofline of Bass Pro by now."
- "Black Friday black eyes."
- "Wrenched my back helping post 'In God We Trust' signs on (insert specific public building.)"
- "Doing my civic duty to clear liquor stores of excess inventory."
- "I'm still jogging off (insert specific holiday) calories. Only 36 more miles to go."
- "I thought my car battery had died. Silly me. I raised the hood only to discover the pea-pickin' thing had been stolen—and the auto parts store says it'll be three days before they can get me another one."
- "I fell while climbing the maple tree in my backyard to shake out the last few leaves."
- And the Number One excuse, which applies across the board: "Two words—deer season."

Housecleaning on steroids

Nearly half a century of my labor just vanished.

This occurred when a truck from the University of Tennessee Library rolled down my driveway, laden with dozens of boxes crammed with newspaper tearsheets, magazine articles, book manuscripts, notes, photos, audio tapes, negatives, slides, award certificates and letters—both of the "attaboy" and "you asshole!" variety. I trust the vehicle had an adequate suspension system.

Proving how deeply the standards of this institution have fallen, UT began seeking my "papers" several years ago. I always told friends it actually was a quest for toilet tissue. But after retirement I finally hopped to the task.

On one hand, it's a stroke to the ego to think your alma mater values the vocational flotsam from one of its least-promising graduates. On the other, it's like ripping organs out of your body.

I'm the kind of guy historians love and wives hate. My DNA has packrat genes woven throughout. Conversely, Mary Ann suffers from a chronic case of "throwawayitis." Nonetheless, once I began fetching dusty boxes and yellowed file folders from shelves, drawers and closets throughout our house, I had to confess the woman may be right.

Lordy! I had no idea how much had accumulated since January 3, 1968, the day I reported for my first newspaper job at the old Knoxville Journal. Combing through the mess was both fun and bittersweet.

I chuckled at mid-1970s photos of myself in a leisure suit and matching bruise-colored polyester shirt. Felt a glimmer of the rush that swept over me in December 1969, when my first magazine article was published by Sports Afield. Dabbed an eye over stories about golden moments shared with outdoor buddies, human and canine, now asleep in the soil.

And I laughed aloud at my Number One newspaper prize: My first bylined story in the Journal—along with a correction that ran the next day. When your career launches with a dud, there's nowhere to go but up.

Frankly, I'll be surprised if UT archivists keep even 10 percent of this junk. Their idea of what's historically, educationally and journalistically important surely differs from mine. After their winnowing concludes, I'll have to decide if the leftovers go back on my shelves or into a shredder. Mary Ann will be consulted. Maybe.

My only hope is that way off in the distant future, some desperate graduate student will leaf through this collection. If he/she comes away thinking: "Damn! That Venable goof sure had a fun job, although it's hard to believe he actually got paid to write this crap," I shall be smiling from the boneyard.

Death by a thousand metal pieces

Right now my garage looks like a hardware store after its potbellied stove exploded.

This is what happens when you attempt to organize the nail-bolt-screw leftovers after 48 years of marriage, two houses and God-only-knows how many home repair, honey-do list and do-it-yourself projects gone awry.

Heed the voice of experience, America. Avoid this exercise in futility at all costs! Instead, just throw everything away and buy more when needed.

I blame my wife for this insanity. She is afflicted with "organize-itis." This is an irrational condition that manifests itself in the maddening desire to put everything in its place.

I should have known better. I should have put her off—as I've done successfully for the past four-plus decades and counting—anytime she requested the nails-bolts-screws be indexed and filed. But no. In a moment of retirement-fueled weakness, I acquiesced. Now I'm paying the price.

For untold nights, I have attempted to separate finishing nails from common nails, roofing nails from coated nails. Not to mention carriage bolts from stove bolts, machine bolts from anchor bolts. And drywall screws from sheet metal screws, deck screws from flat-head screws.

These are screws, nails and bolts of every size under the sun, too. And I'm not talking carpenter language like "10-penny." I speak in layman's terms of "itty-bitty" to "great ol' big."

I do not separate in the folly of "one nail here, another nail there." I separate (aka "fling") "two %$#-ing handfuls here, four %$&#-ing handfuls over yonder."

Gone are dozens of crumbling paper bags and broken cardboard boxes dating to the Nixon administration. In their place are enough shiny new plastic bins to make my carbon imprint look like Big Foot's.

Maybe way off in the future, someone will invent a nail-bolt-screw sorting machine, like those change counters in grocery stores. Just dump everything in, push a button and collect the collated results.

I can only hope and pray.

Not to be understood by any man

My wife says she retired to drive me crazy. I used to laugh. Now, I'm not sure her intentions were all that comical.

As I type these words, two guys are in our downstairs bathroom, banging and sawing. They're enlarging a door that leads to the laundry closet just east of the bathroom.

Fine by me. The laundry closet always has been a tight fit, even for the few times His Rotundity attempted to squeeze his frame into that area. No doubt the various plumbers and electricians who have visited through the years also will be delighted with this enlargement.

But the downstairs bathroom project transcends the mere widening of one door. Instead, it's only one small element of a greater equation. Hence my opening paragraph.

The clothes washer and dryer have been pulled out. Plus the water heater, which is being replaced. Also MIA is the downstairs toilet. It, too, has been given the heave-ho; a replacement unit waits in the boat shed for installation.

Also marking time in the boat shed is replacement toilet Number Two. It will go upstairs, along with new tile for upstairs and downstairs bathroom floors. Still to be delivered is the tile for a new upstairs shower.

Did I mention the upstairs shower unit will be demolished in coming days? If not, forgive me. I'm so discombobulated with the ongoing demolition-construction cycle, I've forgotten which is which. Or even what month this is.

Why are perfectly functional toilets and showers being yanked and replaced and floors retiled?

Surely you jest. This is a question that men, including yours truly, may ask until the end of time, yet never fully comprehend. The Y-chromosome is incapable of deciphering an answer.

On the other hand women, universally, require no explanation. "Just because" is the only rationale they need. Thus the work continues.

At least the sweat of my own balding brow is not required, as if I could do anything but get in the way.

There is one wonderful aspect of this project, however. One glimmer of hope I shall treasure and remember until they deposit me in the dirt.

We live in a log house. Sitting on the front porch at this very moment are a clothes washer, a dryer, a toilet, untold feet of dusty duct, two folding doors, plus various bits of cast-off hardware.

Soon as I can hunt up a three-legged dog, a pot of plastic flowers for the toilet and a '49 Ford pickup to mount on cinderblocks, I will have scaled the highest rung on the Southern Appalachian redneck status ladder.

I'm not used to being this popular

Lately I've begun sharing something in common with people who just won the Powerball. Unfortunately, it's not money. I'm still broke, still got a pile of bills to pay. But, wow, do I ever have a bunch of new friends!

Friends who call on the phone at all hours.

Friends who are vitally interested in my well-being.

Friends who send volumes of letters every day.

Holy hernia! Sometimes I think about wearing my back brace before carrying all this bulk-rate material from mail box to recycle bin. No telling how many forests were shorn to produce the paper.

This is what happens when you become eligible for Medicare.

There are roughly 1,260 life-health insurance companies in the United States. I believe half have made a personal sales pitch to me. Except most of their mailings don't look like ads.

At first glance, you'd swear these were official documents from Uncle Sam, making an earnest effort to include Citizen Sam in the ranks of the covered. Some even have ominous messages WARNING! me there is only ONE! enrollment period, and I have a TINY WINDOW! of opportunity to take advantage of this IMPORTANT PLAN! So I need to fill out the information box and mail it back IMMEDIATELY!

Whew. It's enough to give you a serious case of the puckers—until you learn to look for the fine print on every parcel: "This is an advertisement. Not affiliated with or endorsed by any government agency."

Getting into the Medicare system wasn't initially easy or simple, however, even for someone like me who spent a career cutting through governmental gobbledygook. Not until I talked with the Knoxville-Knox County Office on Aging did I start getting some straight answers. For that I'm grateful.

But the very thought Mr. Forever Eighteen is (a) calling the Office on Aging for advice and (b) signing up for Medicare?

That's enough to send me to my sick bed.

Beware the Next Big Thing

I retired at the right time.

Not because of the sad economic state of my chosen profession. I remain convinced people will always read in some form or another.

Instead, I got out before the Next Big Thing in men's clothing hit the streets.

That would be the "Suitsy."

This garment comes from a San Francisco outfit called Betabrand, "the online clothing company that lets the Web design the future of fashion."

Betabrand's products are invented by everyday Joes and Janes. New ideas are submitted online. A vote is taken. Approved prototypes get run up the flagpole for funding. If enough units are ordered, the product goes into production.

That's how the Suitsy was created. The inventor, real estate developer Jesse Herzog, calls it "the greatest workplace creation since the water cooler."

With all due respect, methinks Jesse Herzog has been sipping something besides water.

Why? Because the Suitsy is a Onesie for adults. Yes, those all-in-one baby suits pulled over the tyke's diapers.

Here's the official description: "Imagine looking professional but feeling like you're in pajamas. The Suitsy is a jacket connected to a shirt connected to pants. A zipper is hidden behind the shirt-button placard (with false buttons) and pants zipper. Fake shirt-cuff material extends from the end of the jacket sleeves to give the impression of a complete dress shirt worn underneath. It's as if a jumpsuit and business suit had a love child."

Agreed, I'm the least-qualified guy on Earth to offer fashion advice. I spent nearly half a century in the newspaper business, and the vast majority of it was in blue jeans and tennis shoes.

But there was a brief period in the 1970s when I took leave of my senses and joined other men wearing what was then the Next Big Thing.

The leisure suit.

This hideous garment was made of 100-percent polyester. It glowed in the dark for two reasons: (a) color patterns ranging from chartreuse to sky blue and (b) the static electricity it generated. Each leg ended in bell bottoms large enough to conceal a bushel basket. Its wide collars could double as tablecloths. It was worn with a swirled, multicolor polyester shirt that looked like a week-old bruise. And beads. Not to mentioned stack-heeled, two-tone shoes.

I still shudder at the memories.

Thus, I appeal to my brothers still laboring in the vineyard. If you're dumb enough to buy a Suitsy, never have your picture taken wearing it.

Not unless, sigh, you wish to give your children and grandchildren enough laughing material to last the rest of your life.

Does Medicare cover free love?

Crank up the VW van! Road trip, here I come!

Uh, but not just yet. I need to polish off this tasty glass of Metamucil, swallow my blood-pressure and cholesterol prescriptions, wrap Ace bandages around both arthritic knees and find my reading glasses. Then, by crackies, I'm off to the big hippie gathering in the Cherokee National Forest.

As you surely have heard, upwards of 10,000 free spirits are expected to descend on the Cherokee, near South Holston Lake in Sullivan County. It's the annual meeting of a group called the Rainbow Family of Living Light.

Bring 'em on, I say. In 1969 or right now, I stand resolutely behind the principles of peace, love and good times.

Well, yes, now that you mention it, I may have to use a cane or walker to make the aforementioned stand. So will many aging baby boomers. But it's the thought that counts.

Quite a few things have changed since Way Back Then, of course.

Vietnam is now a valued business partner with the United States, especially among astute CEOs who managed to avoid visiting that region when Americans carried M-16s instead of iPads.

What's more, "the lottery" can now be your ticket to riches, not the next bus to Fort Benning.

Then there are "flower children"—those cute little nieces and nephews who sprinkled rose petals down the aisle at your daughter's wedding.

The more I think about it, the more I realize a number of terms need updating. So in the event you're planning to join thousands of other old hippies, consider a few important changes.

Tie dye. Then: clothing accented by bright, swirling patterns. Now: an accident that occurs when coloring Easter eggs with grandchildren while wearing your Sunday suit.

LSD. Then: a powerful hallucinogenic drug. Now: acronym for "Lose Something Dear?"

Bad acid. Then: poorly made LSD. Now: painful reaction to a spicy meal consumed after 9 p.m.

Hip. Then: astutely aware, aka "cool." Now: leg joint that needs replacing.

Joint. Then: a marijuana cigarette. Now: regions of knee, elbow and shoulder that need replacing along with hip.

Get stoned. Then: become physically overtaken by ingestion of drugs. Now: what you paid a landscaper $25,000 to do to your patio.

Free love. Then: abundant sex, anytime, anywhere. Now: Viagra on your company's medical plan.

I'd love to elaborate further, but I just realized the moon is in the seventh house and Jupiter has aligned with Mars. I gotta split.

Hopefully not my pants.

Terror of 'The Itch'

Except for noise, claustrophobia, lack of movement and—be still my soul—The Itch, an MRI is a piece of cake.

That's "Magnetic Resonance Imaging" for those not fluent in med-speak. It's a wonderful diagnostic tool, allowing doctors to see what ails their patients. An MRI does for internal organs what an x-ray does for bones. It uses magnetic waves to painlessly slice through your body, one thin layer at a time. The resulting image paints an accurate picture of what's happening down deep. Sorta like exploratory surgery without a scalpel.

But as marvelous as this instrument may be for the "MRI-er," it's no picnic for the "MRI-ee." If you've ever been there, you know whereof I speak.

It's loud, for one thing: "Whack! Bang! Clack! Wang-wang-wang!" Reminds me of Jacob Marley's rattling chains in "A Christmas Carol." Or maybe the constant slamming of doors in a haunted house. Fortunately, they offer ear plugs to dull the din.

Something else I always ask for is a shield for my eyes. That's to control claustrophobia.

Certain people, and we know who we are, freak out in close quarters. Thus, the eye cover is a blessing. It keeps you from seeing the insides of the narrow tube into which you have been drawn.

What's more, you gotta remain motionless during an MRI. For all its space-age technology, this gizmo has a lot in common with a slow-shutter camera. Move your torso and the image blurs.

But everything pales in comparison to The Itch. This never fails. The more you prepare for it, the worse it gets.

Once I'm in position on the carriage, I go through a physical checklist. I rub my forehead. Scratch my nose and chin. Massage my cheeks. Anything and everything to make certain no square inch of facial real estate remains untouched.

Just as my body is drawn inside the tube, of course, The Itch appears. For the next 20 minutes, it specializes in torture.

It doesn't matter how many times I blink under that eye cover. Or twitch my nose. Or jiggle a cheek up and down. The Itch laughs fiendishly, then grows in intensity.

Here's how I described the sensation to a turkey-hunting buddy: "You know when a gobbler is slowly strutting toward you, in open woods, 30 yards out of shotgun range? And you dare not breathe, let alone move a muscle? And then a mosquito lands on your nose and starts drilling?"

He understood completely.

I have nothing to hide

I've got nothing but time on my hands these days. Such is the life of a surgical patient on the mend.

Ironically, the word "nothing" in the previous paragraph is key to this discussion. It describes my state of dress. Or undress, if you will.

As anyone who ever underwent any kind of surgical procedure knows, the first thing that happens is you take off your clothes. Doesn't matter if you're in for an infected toenail, a five-bypass heart realignment or, as in my case, a herniated lumbar disc, everything comes off. Down to, and including, your wedding ring.

In its place goes one of those hospital gowns with the back seam torn out.

You should count your sartorial blessings at this point, for apparently the gown stays on only during the transfer of patient to the operating room. I wasn't conscious after that so I can't speak with authority. All I know is that my wife and daughter both said I was nekkid as the proverbial jaybird under the sheets when I was wheeled back into my room.

They refrained from laughter. Mostly.

So did the nurse who showed up with a catheter the next day when Mr. Winky went on strike.

Oh, well. I've been down this road before. As the recipient of several surgeries in the past, I'm well aware of the exchange that occurs when you check into a hospital: You give them your insurance card; they give you an envelope for your pride.

In other words, just grin and bare it.

Recently the News Sentinel carried a travel story about an upcoming winter Caribbean cruise. On first blush, it sounded like the perfect gift for folks longing to escape cold weather and soak up sunshine during the holidays.

On second blush, there was more to blush about. Not to mention more sunshine to soak up. That's because this trek is offered as "clothing optional." The specific term used by the travel industry is "nakation."

Yes. Everyone is in their altogether.

Starting price for these seven-day cruises is $1,000 per person. Definitely cheaper than a hospital stay of similar length. But though I'm now a veteran of the buff bum brigade, I'm still thinking "no thanks."

Even if I had regular surgery for the rest of my life, I'd never get comfortable being unclothed in public.

And the first time one of my shipmates approached with anything looking remotely like a catheter, I'd punch 'em in the nose and jump overboard.

My brain and I are feuding

If I can keep from pulling out my hair and cutting off my arms, I just may recover from back surgery.

Crazily enough, there are no problems with my spine right now; that region of my anatomy is recuperating quite nicely and on schedule. Instead, it's my noggin that ails me. Specifically, the gray matter residing therein.

Six-plus decades of abrupt and strenuous lugging, tugging, grabbing, lifting and hauling must cease. I'm being forced to recalibrate my thinking. My brain and I constantly feud on how best to accomplish this mission.

Two examples:

A week or so ago, I purchased a case of wine. The kind people at the liquor store—as they have done since my recent infirmity—loaded it into the truck for me.

Drove home just fine. Dear wife (ever-so-strong of back) wasn't there to tote the box to storage. Any rational person would have waited until she arrived. I am not rational.

"I'll put on my back brace and slowly, carefully pick up this box myself," I thought.

That's what I did—in the process tweaking something that sent me into the recliner for the remainder of the afternoon.

"Why was it so all-fired important that you hauled the box by yourself?" my brain inquired.

"Just was," I stubbornly replied. "I've always operated on the motto of 'Get 'er done, right now.'"

"Well, if you simply *had* to move that wine, why didn't you open the box, remove two bottles, take them to the shelf, then repeat the process until the box was empty? I'm your brain, for Pete's sake! Use me!"

"Hmmm. I'll remember that next time."

A couple of nights later, I was preparing to grill pork chops for dinner. A new, 20-pound bag of charcoal sat in the garage.

In days of yore, I would've jerked that bag to my shoulder and carried it to the grill. Ah, but I'm now Mr. Rational Thinker!

Recalling the wine lesson, I decided to ferry scoops of briquettes from garage to grill. But first, the bag needed opening. I procured a fish fillet knife from the shelf, made a small incision and began extracting charcoal.

Bah! The job was progressing far too slowly. So I ripped the opening larger with my hands—without taking time to redeposit the knife back onto the shelf.

You know where this is going, of course.

Yep, I (a) plunged the blade into my arm and (b) immediately invented several colorful phrases that were broadcast far and wide to my rural neighbors.

Speaking of color, the blade apparently had just enough charcoal dust on it to give me a tiny black tattoo. No doubt my brain will call it a personal badge of idiocy.

Hard to focus on this subject

I don't look so great right now.

Oops, wait. That's not exactly what I meant to say.

"Don't look great" in this context means I can't see well at the moment. Sorta like how a friend of mine, born with a defective olfactory system, always describes her condition: "I don't smell very good."

The reason for my current condition is because I just got a new set of bifocals. Adjusting to them is about to drive me nuts.

Actually, driving is what forced me into this predicament in the first place.

TO RETIRE? OR NOT TO RETIRE?

Not long ago I was in Cookeville, Tennessee, to participate in that city's annual storytelling festival. As usual, I wore contact lenses. Between the interstate haul, a morning show, an afternoon show and a face full of pollen, my peepers were quite weary by the end of the day. Just before turning east toward Knoxpatch, I popped out the contacts and put on my old bifocals.

Whoa! Welcome to Fuzz City!

I could drive safely enough, but everything in the distance was seriously blurred. Thus, I soon was in Doc Cornea's office for an examination.

"Your contacts are just fine," Doc said afterward, "but the prescription in those glasses is way out of whack. Your eyes were having a hard time refocusing."

Thus, I now own spankin' new bifocals. And I'm learning how to see all over again. Geezers everywhere can relate.

Even with seamless glasses, there's a sweet spot between the far-away and close-up region of each lens. Trying to find it gives new meaning to the word "gyration."

You weave in place, leering like a fool.

You bob your noggin up, down, left, right.

You try to tackle stairs and wind up either high-stepping or tripping.

You reach out to pick up an object and grab air.

Having broken in new bifocals in the past, I realize this is all part of the adjustment phase. Everything will eventually fall into place. Hopefully I will not fall in the process.

Perhaps it would be best to warn others. I got to thinking about that recently when I saw two different vehicles being operated by beginners. One was a sedan, the other an 18-wheeler. In both cases, signs announcing "Student Driver" were plastered fore and aft. I noticed other motorists were giving them wide berth.

Maybe something like that should come as standard equipment with new eyeglasses for seniors. After all, they do give us a free carrying case.

Why not one of those sandwich-board signs that drapes across our shoulders? It could proclaim, "Old Goat Wearing New Bifocals—Maintain Safe Distance."

Probably wouldn't hurt to have 911 on speed dial, either.

Geezerdom trumps New Age

Whew. Just in the nick of time. I was about to remake myself into Today's Well-Groomed Man. But then I read the fine print and decided I'd be happier as Yesterday's Same Ol' Slouch.

This occurred when samples of "New Clinique for Men" skin care products showed up at the News Sentinel. Features editor Susan Alexander sent 'em to me.

In a situation like this, two thoughts immediately come to mind.

Did Susan give me this stuff because it begs for a dose of my elfin charm, sunny disposition and journalistic wit? Or because it comes with a hidden hygiene message, like when you unwrap numerous gifts of fancy soap and deodorant on Christmas morning?

While that internal debate raged, I perused the printed information accompanying these unguents, salves and lotions.

"There's a Science to Looking Good," the headline proclaimed.

Great! Science was always one of my favorite subjects in high school and college. In fact, I originally majored in forestry and wildlife biology at the University of Tennessee—before discovering journalism and abandoning hope of ever finding honest work.

So I read further: "New Clinique for Men marries dermatological know-how with common sense to bring men a curated portfolio of specialized skin care including cleansing, moisturizing, exfoliating, shaving and targeted grooming products."

Whoa. My guard immediately went up.

Aren't "common sense" and "a curated portfolio of specialized skin care" mutually exclusive terms?

While I do have a portfolio of investments, it's quite meager. I have no idea if it's been "curated." Isn't that what they do to country ham?

Still, I continued to research the packet. That's when I discovered one of the products, a "dark spot corrector," contains some weird ingredients including cholesterol, "squalane," barley extract and wheat germ extract.

Huh? I take daily medication to control my cholesterol. Wouldn't it be counterproductive to add it directly to my hide?

Barley extract, however, is vastly different. I have long recommended one, two, maybe even three 12-ounce cans of it at any sitting. Four is pushing it, though. You might wind up "squalane" during karaoke. Not a pretty image.

But then the "exfoliating tonic" and "face bronzing gel" ended my brief foray into New Age grooming.

At my advanced stage in life, I don't want the prefix "ex-" applied to anything I do. As for face bronzing? Been there, thank you.

That's what we used call "standing too close to the Coleman stove when it finally ignites."

A tale of two ears

The dead Dutch artist Vincent van Gogh and the living Tennessee writer Sam Venable have something in common—besides liberal application of the letter "V" in their respective names.

We both lost part of an ear.

True, there are distinct differences in these "ear-ectomies." Starting with the ears themselves.

In van Gogh's case, it was the left lobe. In mine, it was the right top.

Our carvings were done in much different manners and settings, too.

Art historians aren't sure whether van Gogh razored his own ear in maniacal frustration or whether the deed was done by his French friend and fellow artist, Paul Gauguin, who wielded a sword with the same aplomb as paint brushes. Either way, the slicing occurred in the heat of rage.

My ear-lopping was via scalpel, under calm conditions, in my dermatologist's office. Doc Derm has been harvesting hide off me for decades. It's the price I pay for a lifetime in the blistering sun, stinging sleet and frigid wind.

Thankfully, this excising always has been accomplished in the name of prevention. Whether with blade, freezing agents or high-powered ointments that briefly turn my face into a potato chip, Doc has managed to keep all my skin ailments filed under the heading of "pre-cancerous." For that I am most grateful.

My van Gogh journey began several years ago when a tiny "antler" sprouted atop the aforementioned right ear. My wife says it's punishment for hunting deer lo these many winters. She could be right.

Doc Derm identified it immediately. He froze it off a time or two. It kept growing back. A few days ago he dug it out. This is the dermatological version of grubbing an oak stump that persists in sending up shoots.

As surgical procedures go, it was a piece of cake. Doc and I had a good visit while he worked. There was no pain at all after the initial stick of a deadening needle—although the "crunch" as Doc snipped cartilage sounded more like he was repairing a boot. It was stitched and dressed in no time.

There are pros and cons about the healing process.

Doc promises there'll be no scarring, which I consider a negative. I'd much prefer a deep crater, outlined with a jagged arc. This would give me great redneck cred when knife fights are mentioned.

But on the plus side, I now have a permanent reply when Mary Ann starts issuing chore decrees: "Sorry, dearest, but I can't hear a thing you say. Don't you remember? I've got no ear."

Reckon van Gogh used the same excuse the rest of his life?

What were we talking about?

One of the benefits of geezing is that there's a lot of company.

Heck, I never knew so many retired old croaks lived in K-town until I joined their ranks. Any time we get together, we address the usual subjects for guys our age: forgetfulness, the nuttiness of modern life, aches and pains, that sort of stuff. As long as we haven't sunk to discussing bowels, I consider us ahead of the curve.

Herewith a few recent examples.

Chuck Reeves was saying it's a sure sign of aging when you start fixing bacon for breakfast, open the microwave and find the potatoes you'd prepared for supper the night before.

For the record, I pointed out an even surer sign is when you shrug "meh" and eat those cold, crusty 'taters along with your bacon.

That reminded Frank Jones of two friends who'd lost their spouses and went on a "his-and-hers codger date" to combat their mutual loneliness.

"Turned out to be a great evening," he related. "They were having fun, laughing, chatting and dancing. As they swirled around the floor, the guy blurted out, 'Betty, will you marry me?' To his amazement, she said yes.

TO RETIRE? OR NOT TO RETIRE?

"Next morning, he woke up and thought, 'I believe I asked Betty to get married, but I can't remember her answer.' The only decent thing to do was call her. She said, 'You sure did ask me, and I said yes—and I'm so glad you called because I couldn't remember who I'd gone out with!'"

Jim Rich chimed in about the plethora of "all natural" chicken products in grocery stores these days.

"Does this mean there are unnatural chickens?" he wanted to know. "Would an unnatural chicken moo instead of cluck? When I was a boy, our family raised lots of chickens to feed our family of nine. In all those years, I never saw an unnatural one. Must be a new development on the agricultural scene."

My report also came from the grocery store. I'd gone shopping with my wife to lay in supplies for a big dinner we were hosting. One item Mary Ann wanted was some fancy bread which, naturally, was on the bottom shelf. She headed out to the produce aisle while I—riveted spine, cortisoned knees and beer gut—got down on all fours and probed around. Fighting my way back upright, I let out the obligatory "uuugh!"

Whereupon a gentle voice behind me spoke: "Do you need help?"

I turned and there stood a sweet little lady, the kind I used to help across the street when I was in Boy Scouts. Even worse, she said, "Your face looks familiar. Don't you write a column for the News Sentinel?"

Gaak! My mind was clouded by embarrassment and shame. But I recovered in time enough to say, "Yes, ma'am, I sure do. I'm David Hunter."

In journalism school they teach the all-important five W's of news gathering and writing: *Who? What? When? Where? Why?*

Good points, for sure. These essential bones make up the skeleton of any readable story. But I always thought there should be a sixth: *Whoo-hoo!*

Sorry; I can't help it. I don't know if smart-assery was woven into my DNA at the moment of conception, or if a lifetime chronicling the human condition and all its whacko foibles opened up a dimension of observation other writers missed. Many times when I approached a subject, the nuttiness factor screamed at me: "Why does nobody else think about this?"

Actually, they do. Hang around any newspaper coffee pot for a few minutes, and you'll see what I mean. The one-liners flow almost as freely as the sheep-dip "joe" newsroom coffee machines are famous for delivering. But after the hoo-haas fade, everybody goes back to their sacred five W's.

Not I.

As long as there are sure-nuff scientific studies about how dogs align themselves by magnetic field when peeing and pooping, or shoplifters wear innovative clothing to carry purloined goods, or irate women duke it out with catfish and mounted deer heads, this ol' boy will never run out of material.

"Whoo-hoo!"

Chapter Two
CAN'T SPELL 'WEIRD'
WITHOUT 'WE' AND 'I'

Did they get research on their shoes?

I have scooped a lot of pooch poop in my day.

Over a period of 20-plus years, there always was a dog—sometimes more than one—in the kennel behind my house. At one point, in fact, an English setter, a pointer and a Labrador retriever simultaneously were on the Venable dole. So trust me when I say I have vast experience in canine excrement.

Yet not once during all this time did I ever take notice how my dogs aligned themselves when, uh, "producing." Which proves I don't know beans, not to mention Bowzer butts, about high-level scientific research.

Not so at the University of Life Sciences in the Czech Republic city of Prague. There, and I swear on six cases of Alpo I'm not making this up, scientists recorded precise observations of dogs as they attended to their business. The dogs' business, you understand.

And?

I quote directly from a PBS Newshour broadcast: "After examining 70 dogs (made up of 37 breeds) over two years, 1,893 defecations and 5,582 urinations, researchers found that under 'calm magnetic field conditions,' dogs preferred to 'excrete with the body being aligned along a north-south axis,' avoiding east-west altogether.

"Dogs were observed in a free-roaming environment," the report went on, "meaning they were not leashed and not influenced by walls or roads that would influence linear movement. Why do dogs prefer the north-south axis and avoid east-west? That was not clear, according to the study."

These findings beg two important questions:

1. Who cares?

2. C'mon guys. Seriously. What were y'all smoking?

The brainiacs have a quick answer for No. 1. According to an article in the Science Times, "the study is important because it could, ideally, open up new horizons in magnetoreception (I didn't make up that word, either) research."

As for No. 2, I can only surmise—and here I stress this is merely a guess on my part—"Maui Wowie."

Imagine hitting the books for years to earn an advanced degree in the field of veterinary medicine, being hired by a prestigious university, and getting the first phone call from your father: "Mom and I are so proud of you, son! What exciting research project are you working on now?"

"I'm watching dogs pee and take a dump."

I don't know what else might be said during the conversation, but I'll guarantee after it concluded, dear ol' dad looked over at the missus and sighed: "Bad news, Gladys. The kid's back on drugs."

Please use words we all understand

Shortly before his untimely death, Wilbur Curtis, this column's longtime correspondent from Holston Hills, telephoned with an odd question—especially for someone like Wilbur, who was a knower of much stuff.

"How much is a mess?" he asked.

Wilbur went on to say he'd bought a mess of green beans to take to a friend, but then the friend proved what a mess he is by asking how much of quantity, green beans or otherwise, constitutes a mess.

Typically, this column does not mess with frivolous questions. But the more I thought about Wilbur's inquiry, the more I realized "mess" is one of those Southern Appalachian words that (a) flows off the tongue smooth as honey, (b) covers a wide variety of sins and (c) defies quantitative analysis.

In other words, "mess" can mean anything you want it to.

The "mess" of fish you give to a neighbor can be as few as five small bluegills or an 18-foot johnboat filled to the gunnels with four-pound catfish. All depends on whether he needed enough to feed himself or supply the main ingredient for his Optimist club's fish fry on the Fourth of July.

Also, it doesn't matter if the neighbor is completely lucid or nutty as a pecan tree. He can be described as a "mess" (pronounced "MAY-yess" in this particular usage) either way.

What's more, it is perfectly permissible to decline his kind offer to eat some of the fish being prepared by saying you don't "mess" with fried food.

Nobody asks for an explanation. Everybody comprehends.

"Mess" shares much in common with "passel," "tad," "smidgen," "right smart of," "nigh 'bout," "fair to middlin'" and other inexact—yet very logical and easily understood—figures of Southern Appalachian speech.

Frankly, I wish people in other parts of the country would use words like these when they speak. Presidential candidates, for instance. I have listened to many presidential debates. The only thing I ever learn is that hot air is a great source of energy.

Both sides sling numbers, figures, sizzling accusations and bold declarations like they're working the chow line on corned beef hash day. As soon as they hush, fact-checkers swing into action, proving the just-spoken numbers, figures, sizzling accusations and bold declarations have less substance than pocket lint.

So why even worry about precision?

The first candidate who acknowledges we have a "mess" of debt solvable by a "right smart of changes" in the tax code and an end to a "passel" of wasteful spending gets my vote.

Who knew smoking was so costly?

Until a few days ago, I never realized how expensive smoking truly is.

You'd think I'd understand by now. After all, the U.S. Surgeon General's report was issued way back in the 1960s. Ever since, we've been up to our trachea tubes in warnings and advisories from both the medical profession and the government, spelling out the multiple perils of tobacco.

But until I saw a recent news story in the Crossville (Tennessee) Chronicle, later picked up by the Associated Press, it never dawned on me what a serious dent smoking can make in a person's billfold.

In case you missed it, this bizarre incident occurred at the Camelot subdivision in Cumberland County. According to police reports, a man and woman showed up at their neighbor's house. They shot the breeze for a few moments. After a bit, the woman asked her husband to go back to their house for her cigarettes. Soon as he exited, the woman asked her neighbor if it was OK to swim in his pool.

Naked.

Sure, the guy replied.

She peeled to her altogether, leaped into the water and swam around for 20 minutes.

Proving what a swell neighbor he was, the guy remained at poolside, no doubt to make certain she didn't drown. He even fetched a towel so she could dry off. Then she dressed and left.

When the guy went back inside his house, he discovered a handgun, jewelry and medicine were AWOL. To the tune of $1,195.

Oddly enough, you don't have to own a swimming pool for this to occur. Personal case in point: On seven different occasions, I've been approached by my neighbors. And wouldn't you know it, the same thing has happened every dadburn time!

It goes like this —

1. The woman forgets her cigarettes and tells her husband to go back home for them.

2. She asks to swim naked.

3. I tell her I don't have a pool.

4. She says that's OK; the lawn sprinkler will work just fine.

5. She shucks her clothes and frolics in the spray while the sprinkler arcs back and forth.

6. I stand by, making sure she isn't bitten by mosquitoes or ticks.

7. I procure a towel and help her dry off.

8. After she leaves, I notice some of my personal stuff is missing.

At this point, I'm out three lawn mowers, two chain saws, a bass boat, assorted garden tools, four rings, a pair of wristwatches, six pocketknives, two televisions, three cameras, all the framed pictures from the wall, plus books, silverware and dishes.

Whew! If my neighbors don't stop smoking soon, it's gonna drive me into bankruptcy.

Women with wicked weaponry

Gosh, what a slow learner I am. After nearly seven decades on this orb, I'm just now realizing how dangerous wild animals can be.

I don't mean elk, bison and bears that routinely have their way with dumb tourists who approach too closely. Not cute squirrels, raccoons and chipmunks, either. Just ask anybody who's been bitten or clawed by one of these furry terrors.

I'm talking about a wild animal (a) after it is dead and (b) in the hands of an angry woman. Now there, children, is a cocked pistol!

Not long ago I wrote about a Texas woman who assaulted her sister-in-law with a catfish caught earlier in the day. According to police reports, the two gals got into a shouting match, and before anybody could say "deep-fried or oven-broiled?" one picked up Mr. Whiskers and whacked the other squarely across the kisser.

That prompted a follow-up when a News Sentinel reader reminded me of a similar incident several years earlier near Kingsport. Yep, another catfish assault involving women.

This time the weapon was cooked, not raw—which I noted took tremendous skill. Anybody can wield a dry, stiff catfish. But a greasy one, fresh from hot oil? Whew! You gotta have some kind of hands!

All of which brings me to the latest woman-with-dead-animal attack. I swear on a stack of Gander Mountain catalogs I'm not making it up. In fact, I'm looking at a copy of the police report as we speak.

It's from Cromwell Township, Pennsylvania. The investigating officer was Trooper Sondra L. Haberl. The report was posted online by the New York Daily News.

Haberl's findings, validated by Pennsylvania Police Sgt. Harold Rinker, stated that Stacy Varner, 47, of Orbisonia, Pennsylvania, and Glenda Snyder, 64, of Mount Union, Pennsylvania, squared off with mounted deer heads. If that's not the genesis of a country music song, there ain't a cow, or catfish, in Texas.

Seems these women were helping Snyder's son move. Among his belongings were the aforementioned deer heads. Snyder claimed Varner—she's the son's ex-wife, adding further credence to the country music angle—wasn't being careful enough with them. And before you know it, the antlers were clacking.

Snyder suffered a scalp laceration. Varner was not injured. However, both were charged, Snyder with harassment and criminal trespassing, Varner with assault.

Hmm . . .

I'm typing these words in my home office, a Neanderthalic, testosterone-dripping he-haven decorated with the preserved remains of ducks, fish and upland birds. Also deer: two eight-point shoulder mounts, plus 19 individual sets of antlers.

If Mary Ann was ever in a testy mood and took command of this place, she could hold off the Russian army.

Careful what stars you wish on

Whether the venue is a duck blind, a bass boat or a deer stand, I spend more time waiting for dawn than your average Joe. Thus, I see lots of shooting stars.

What beauties they are! On the awesomeness scale, it's hard to match these split-second darts of light as they cleave the heavens.

Some people say shooting stars portend good luck. Maybe. Maybe not. Over the years, I've experienced successful outings, also pitiful busts, after viewing these things. In any event, rare is the shooting star that fails to evoke "oohs" and "aahs" from witnesses.

But now I'm not so sure. Based on what I've been reading about shooting stars, my next reaction might be more on the order of "Yuck!" or "Bleech!"

This revelation came after perusing an interview with Italian astronaut Luca Parmitano. It appeared in the London (as in England) Independent newspaper.

Parmitano spent 166 days at the International Space Station. His mission included two space walks. In an online Q&A, Parmitano discussed many facets of daily life out there in the wild blue yonder.

But the number one question, the one Parmitano says he gets asked most often, concerns No. 1 and No. 2.

Specifically, "how to?"

I'm not making this up. Neither is the Independent's reporter, Oscar Quine.

"The best way to describe (a space toilet) is if you imagine a vacuum cleaner, which has a tube on one end and a bucket on the other end," Parmitano said. "When you go for a No. 1, it goes down the tube and gets recycled to water so you can drink it."

OK, that operation I can handle—I think—assuming the process works effectively.

As for No. 2?

"It ends up in the bucket," Parmitano said. "We put the human waste in there, and it makes a fantastic shooting star. If you see a shooting star and then you make a wish, and if it doesn't happen, then you know why."

I surfed the Internet on this issue and discovered—aaak!—earlier interviews from other astronauts who concurred. One Canadian rocket jockey said when the bucket gets jettisoned, it perishes in instant, fiery splendor. All of which means some of those gorgeous light shows might be high-flying You-Know-What.

(Pardon me; I just felt a smidgen of hurl in the back of my throat.)

I'm all for space research. More power to the brave men and women who explore this final frontier. Too, I realize certain bodily functions must be handled appropriately.

But to paraphrase Perry Como's hit song from 1957, ain't no way I'm going to catch a falling star—let alone put it in my pocket and save it for a rainy day.

Learning by the seat of my pants

Please don't bother me right now. I'm busy studying overalls online.

Until a few days ago, I didn't realize how useful this line of clothing truly is. I have owned and worn overalls for years, mainly for yard work and for hunting. They can take a lot of abuse, not to mention dirt, and keep on keepin' on.

But while perusing the News Sentinel a few days ago, I discovered a new function for overalls.

Shoplifting meat.

According to police reporter Don Jacobs, a father and son team from Maryville were charged with attempting to heist a computer tablet from Kohl's in Farragut.

True, a computer tablet likely won't taste great on the grill, no matter how much barbecue sauce is applied. But police said subsequent investigations revealed these two have a lengthy record of arrests and convictions for walking out of stores with unpaid merchandise crammed into their overalls. Mainly meat. In fact, police records state that the pair have been legally banned from entering several retail establishments.

We're talking hundreds of dollars of beef tenderloin and steaks, all ferreted out of local stores inside of their overalls.

Please understand that I have no intention of starting a life of crime. At least not now. But you never know what the future holds. Times could get tough, forcing a lowly scribe to purloin loins to feed his family. Never hurts to be prepared on all fronts, I say.

Thus, I began searching the Internet for accessories. Among some likely candidates I discovered were:

- Scent-Lok Full Season Velocity, seven-pocket overalls with carbon alloy fibers (to hide the smell of stolen meat, perhaps?) for $99.95.
- Walls Legend overalls with Drytec water-repellent finish—inside, hopefully, in case I pee my pants during a getaway chase—for $88.25.
- Three different blue models: Liberty rigid denim ($40.49), Dickies indigo bibs ($31.49) and Five Brothers dark washed denim ($31.49).
- But then I hit pay dirt with L.C. King coveralls, manufactured by Pointer Brands in Bristol, Tennessee. (Be proud, children; if you're delving into crime, at least have the decency and pride to wear homegrown duds.)

These babies come with standard "full cut and pleated back for extra room, side openings, an oversized utility back, watch pocket, rule pocket and hammer loop." All for a mere $94.40.

Just to make certain they fit properly before ordering online, I may go to a store and try on a real pair. And, hey, if I make my exit without stopping at the cash register, just tell the cops I'm following an old family tradition.

A double helping of pain relief

The next time you're at the supermarket and see someone trying on paper plates, do not be surprised.

Yes, trying on. As in fitting. Like clothes. This is going to be huge, guaranteed.

"I guess nobody has ever thought of it before," says inventor Kurt Alexander. "My doctor said it was a great idea. So did my pharmacist. Somebody has already suggested I put this thing on Pinterest."

"This thing" is Alexander's homemade remedy for reducing the agony of shingles.

Alexander is service manager and training coordinator for Braxton-Bragg, a Knoxville company specializing in stone and concrete tooling. Recently he came down with shingles, a chicken pox virus disease characterized by an excruciatingly painful rash.

I know all about shingles myself, having suffered through a dose of them in the late 1990s. The outbreak occurred on my head and extended down to my face, stopping—thank you, Sweet Jesus—just before entering my eyes. Even though this was before Dick Chaney's now-infamous quail hunt, I described the sensation as being hit in the face with a load of No. 8 shot.

Alexander's case erupted in a more traditional location: right shoulder blade and the right side of his chest.

His description of the pain was classic: "Take four strands of barbed wire, wrap 'em twice around your body, pull tight, pour kerosene on top of everything and then put on a shirt made of wet burlap."

The friction of the shirt across his skin was terrible. So terrible that Alexander started going shirtless in his office while doing paperwork.

But duty required he also go out in public. So one day, while gritting his teeth against the agony, he came up with a brainstorm.

"I kept thinking there had to be a way to keep the shirt fabric off my skin," he said. "Then it dawned on me that a paper plate might work. It had to be just the right size to cover the infected area but not stick out too far, like an ice cream dish."

He experimented with several brands and styles before finally settling on one. Then he taped two plates—one in front, one in back—inside his shirt.

Voila! Instant relief!

Over a period of three weeks, Alexander even refined the original plan by punching breathing holes in the rim of each plate.

"Yeah, I kinda bulged a little front and back," he said with a laugh, "but it sure relieved the pain. All joking aside, there's gotta be a way to make a woven, open-mesh plastic cup just for shingles patients."

I can just see the advertising slogan now: "Chinet. It's not just for picnics anymore."

The lies of size

Among the varied pieces of clothing in closets and drawers at my house are two marked "M." As in medium.

One is my varsity football jersey from my 1964 senior season at Young High School. The other is a pair of swimming trunks I purchased last summer. Both fit my torso.

True, the football jersey was worn over shoulder pads back in the day. If I climbed into a set of shoulder pads right now and then attempted to stretch this jersey over the resulting mass, the poor thing surely would be reduced to shreds.

The reason I bring these two items to your attention is to illustrate how sizes have changed through the years as America's waistline expands.

Without getting into embarrassing details, let me simply state for the record that Sam Venable of the early 21st century casts a broader shadow than Sam Venable of the mid-20th. Yet what passes for "M" still fits both Sams.

All of which is the most egregious sleight-of-hand since alchemists were turning lead into gold.

The last time I was a legitimate "M," an unknown Georgia peanut farmer was being mentioned as presidential material.

I breezed through "L" in roughly the same amount of time it took Jimmy Carter to serve his one term.

Ever since, I've been a card-carrying "XL."

Shirts, coats, slacks, doesn't matter. No need to measure. Just find the right color, make sure the label says XL and head for the checkout counter.

But this isn't your father's S-M-L-XL any more.

I made this discovery on the swimsuit shopping trip. By rote, I grabbed a pair of XLs off the rack. They seemed rather bulbous, so I ducked into a changing room.

Blithering bloomers! These would have been loose on Chris Christie! Even "L" was too baggy. Not 'til I scaled down to "M" did some semblance of proper fit occur.

It's been like that ever since. Depending on how many sausage biscuits I consume for breakfast, I vacillate between "M" and "L," which is sartorial fiction in its purest form.

I'm not the only person who has noticed this change. Social scientists have, too, including researchers from the National Health and Nutrition Examination Survey and the Centers for Disease Control and Prevention.

In 2009, CNN Health noted, "People's perceptions of overweight have shifted, and 'normal' is now heavier than it used to be. As the American population has become generally more overweight, brands from the luxury names to the mass retail chains have scaled down the size labels on their clothing."

Gotta admit I enjoy being an "M" or an "L," even if it is total fabrication. We chubs like to think of this as our not-so-little secret.

Just imagine the licensing potential!

The University of Tennessee has announced a $100,000 study to reinvent the condom.

According to news reports, UT polymer chemist Jimmy Mays received a grant from the Bill and Melinda Gates Foundation's Grand Challenges in Global Health initiatives. The ultimate goal is to develop a newer, thinner, stronger condom and make it available to the masses.

This is serious business. Perhaps revolutionary. If initial testing proves fruitful, it might lead to an additional $1 million grant into perfecting a manufacturing process. In the end, this could help control the spread of disease worldwide.

Fine. More power to Mays and his Tennessee colleagues.

But at the same time, this riveting news boggles my professional smart-ass mind. So today I'm happy to shout: "Let the locker room jokes and sophomoric one-liners begin!"

The ink was still wet on this story when both my telephone and email lit up with messages. Yes, of course; they came from legions of my crude friends—a redundancy in and of itself—who couldn't wait to hardee-harr-harr. Herewith some of their more printable thoughts and suggestions:

"Well, it's about time they redesigned those things. Maybe now I can find one that's big enough."

"Where do I sign up as a test volunteer?"

"Will they come in orange and white? What about Smokey Gray?"

"A new condom design featuring The Rock and the Power-T: a marketing match made in heaven."

"Forget those stupid foam fingers. If we ever get back to being Number One in any sport, we'll have the best symbol in the world!"

"Look for polymer chemical majors to quadruple by next semester. Heck, I may go back to college myself."

"Will this do for Tennessee what Gatorade did for Florida?"

"Will they use one of these new devices to replace running through the 'T' at the start of home football games?"

"Think of the halftime formation possibilities for the band!"

"I ain't ever eatin' a hot dog at UT again."

"So much for 'respecting her in the morning.' Just say you're 'engaged in high-level scientific research'."

"How about including architecture students on a new design?"

"UT has been screwing over students, faculty and fans for years. This just makes it official."

Dead Donald will always be 'late'

"I've always said the dead walked among us," Knoxvillian J.L. Stepp told me the other day as he produced a newspaper clipping. "This proves it."

The article described a sure-nuff zombie. His name is Donald Eugene Miller Jr. He lives in Fostoria, Ohio. Miller walks, talks, eats, sleeps and breathes like the rest of us. But there's one distinct difference between he and we: This guy is deader than 40 pounds of doornails.

At least he is in the eyes of the law.

To understand this bizarre case, you must turn back the clock to 1986. That's the year Miller abandoned his wife and kids. Apparently he kicked around for a while in Georgia and Florida, then dropped out of sight completely.

In 1994, eight years after her husband disappeared, Mrs. Miller went to court to have him declared dead. That way, their children would be eligible for Social Security death benefits.

Everything rocked along swimmingly—nobody heard hide nor hair of Dead Donald during the entire time—until 2005, when he showed back up in the flesh. Since then, he has been trying to get declared "living" once more.

But, as his latest court battle attests, that ain't as easy as saying, "Pick up thy pallet and walk."

Probate Judge Allan Davis turned down Miller's latest request, citing a law that puts a three-year cap on changing a death ruling. In other words, once you're dead, you're dead. Even if you're not.

Ryan Dunn, a staff writer for Ohio's Findlay Courier newspaper, quoted Hizzoner Davis addressing Dead Donald like this: "I don't know where that leaves you, but you're still deceased as far as the law is concerned."

All of which begs several interesting questions. To wit:

Since Dead Donald is not living, is he required to pay sales tax on items he purchases? Or does he even have to pay the price itself, considering he's no longer alive?

If Dead Donald is running behind schedule and misses a meeting or appointment, should he be referred to as "the late, late Donald Miller"?

How much of a monkey wrench would be hurled into the legal system if Dead Donald was declared living once more—and then on the way home from the courthouse he suffers a fatal heart attack or gets killed in a car wreck?

Surely there's a TV reality show in this nutzoid situation.

Playing mind games with an idiot

Does this ever happen to you? Or am I totally nuts?

I left the house at dawn a few mornings ago, headed for an appointment 90 minutes away. Barely half a mile down the road, I remembered my coffee-filled Thermos was still on the kitchen counter.

If I'd been well into the journey, I would've said "pshaw-dang," or words to that effect, and kept driving. Too much time and trouble to backtrack. I'd just grab a fast-food cup of joe somewhere along the line.

This close, however, was different.

I wheeled into the next driveway, turned around, scampered back to the house, grabbed the Thermos (giving it a thorough cussing for being

AWOL, of course) and resumed traveling. My lost time was probably two minutes, max.

That's when the mind games began.

"What might have happened if you hadn't gone back?" Part A of my brain asked Part B. "Could those two minutes wind up changing your life today?"

"Huh?" Part B answered. "What are you talking about? What does turning around half a mile from home have to do with changing my life?"

"You never know," Part A said. "Maybe going back for your Thermos kept you alive."

"What?!?!"

"I'm just sayin'," Part A continued. "If you'd gotten on the interstate two minutes ago, maybe an 18-wheeler would've inadvertently swerved into your path. But since you weren't there, the trucker simply pulled back into his lane and kept barreling on."

"OK, fine," said Part B. "Accident avoided."

"Maybe, maybe not," Part A pointed out. "Who's to say that those lost two minutes aren't now going to put you in harm's way?"

On and on Parts A and B bantered and debated. This is what happens when my brain argues with an idiot. It wasn't until Part C (aka "coffee") separated the two that I settled down for what turned out to be a pleasant, uneventful trip.

Still, the what-ifs and who-knows linger. Life is a complex amalgam of fates and coincidences. How these random pieces fall into place is forever a source of fascination and worry.

The late Don Dessart, a dear old church friend of many years, once shared an eerie experience of his during the Korean War.

A young naval officer, Don was staring through a porthole during a firefight. He turned his head ever-so-briefly—and missed being decapitated by a huge piece of shrapnel that somehow threaded its way across the water and into that tiny opening. The brush with death occasionally haunted him thereafter.

Don went on to become an esteemed mathematics professor at the University of Tennessee. If he couldn't come to grips with those odds, what chance does some goof who can barely add, subtract, multiply and divide?

This could make your skin crawl

When most folks cross the river, they leave mementos of their earthly journey in traditional ways.

A favorite ring or necklace, perhaps. Artwork. Photos. Books. Maybe a special piece of furniture or sporting equipment—indeed, any of 10,001 tangible keepsakes.

Others choose to be memorialized by more offbeat methods.

Surely you've heard of caskets custom-painted to match the dearly departed's school colors or favorite sports team.

Also, there's the occasional tombstone engraved with a witty remark, on the order of: "They Were Wrong! I DID Take It With Me!"

I've even read of companies that will load the deceased's ashes into shotgun shells so living friends can enjoy "one last hunt" with their buddy.

But this one beats 'em all. It is now possible to pass down your favorite tattoo to the next generation. And I don't mean in photographs. I'm talking skin that can be framed and mounted on the wall. I'm serious.

When I heard about this service, I was certain someone was pulling my leg—a leg that is still firmly attached to my living, breathing body.

Nope. I did some checking and discovered this isn't an urban myth. There is, indeed, an outfit called the National Association for the Preservation of Skin Art. It is headquartered in Cleveland, Ohio. Its basic membership fee is $115, plus $60 annual dues.

The association offers a skin art registry for "tattooers" and "tattooees" alike. Plus convention listings and profiles of famous needle practitioners.

There's also a lasting legacy option. It's the $2,000 "Final Wish Fulfillment Benefit."

Here's a portion of the process, quoted directly from the association's website: "A preservation kit, containing instructions and all the necessary equipment to recover, temporarily preserve, and safely ship your tattoo to NAPSA, is mailed overnight to the recovery provider. In most cases, your funeral home."

Several months later, the preserved specimen is shipped back to display as beneficiaries wish. Gag! Gross! Bleech!

Then again —

I am typing these words in my office at home. Its walls hang heavy with a variety of preserved skin in the form of ducks, deer heads, fish, antlers, turkey beards and other hillbilly, good ol' boy, Y-chromosome souvenirs from a lifetime in the outdoors. So far be it from me to ridicule NAPSA's bizarre notion, at least in principle.

Any of my family or friends who want one or more of these items after my death are welcome to them. Or my wife can pile 'em in the backyard and strike a match. I care not.

But I'll guarantee this: Ain't nobody gettin' any of my own hide.

These are great pics 'decidedly'

If Steve Nagler ever asks whether you want to see his travel photos, by all means say yes.

Trust your Uncle Passport: This isn't a situation begging for a duck-and-run excuse. None of that "Uh, maybe some other time, pal. Right now, I've got to index and file my paper clip collection."

No, indeed. Nagler's portfolio is well worth watching. It contains some of the finest stuff from far-off lands I've ever seen—and I ain't talkin' snow-capped mountain peaks, beach sunsets, towering waterfalls or floral gardens.

Instead, Nagler's collection consists of posters, billboards and other signs in which the English meaning was, shall we politely say, "lost in the translation."

Nagler is a physicist with Oak Ridge National Laboratory. He's been to China on business several times, cellphone camera at the ready. A few nights ago he shared some of his latest masterpieces with me, such as a can of emergency equipment from his hotel room in Beijing.

On the label were these instructions, verbatim:

1. Take out the fire fighting filter type self-saving breather.
2. Tear at the packing bag of fire-fighting filter type self-saving breather.
3. Wear helmet and pull contractive belt fast.
4. Choose way and flee for your life decidedly.

Nagler concluded, and I concurred, this means that in case of fire, you're supposed to put on the mask and run like hell.

Another series of photos came from signs in the bathroom of a different hotel. They advised how to use a shower mat to prevent falls. Like this:

1. Please put the ground washrag beside the bathtub first, and then put the non-slip mat down the bottom of the bathtub.

2. Please put the suctorial side down, and press it by hand in order to fix it tightly to the bottom of the bathtub.

3. You could take a shower assuring that the non-slip mat is tightly sucked to the bathtub.

Just to make certain guests understood water would be cascading downward during the course of a shower, an additional sign had been mounted inside the tub. It stated, "Caution Wet Floor," and included a stick-figure illustration of some hapless person executing the ol' keister crash. Nothing like extra precaution.

"All of this not only kept me safe," he noted, "but it also expanded my vocabulary. I've found the adjective 'suctorial' to be appropriate on many occasions."

Nagler also showed me a photo from his trip to Sendai, Japan. It featured what appeared to be complimentary bottled water in his hotel room.

Closer inspection of the label, however, revealed this word in English: "Bourbon."

"Although a trifle weak and tasteless, I found it better straight than mixed," he quipped.

The sweet smell of success

If the big cheeses in publishing—at this newspaper and others throughout the country—would listen to a lowly columnist, they would learn how to resurrect our foundering business.

The key is odor.

(Oops, perhaps I should use a more diplomatic term: aroma. Anyhow, you catch my drift.)

Simply infuse the paper with pleasant flavors and watch those circulation numbers spiral upward instead of the opposite direction.

This brainstorm hit me while I was perusing the latest international headlines. From Sri Lanka came word of how a newspaper called Mawbima blended citronella oil with ink to produce mosquito-repelling pages. The story I read happened to appear in the Independent of Great Britain, but it ran in several publications throughout the world.

Here's the skinny: Sri Lankans are plagued by deadly dengue fever, which is spread by the Aedes aegypti species of 'skeeter. The disease infected more than 30,000 in 2013 alone.

Scientists and newspaper production people put their heads together and came up with the ink idea. It debuted on World Health Day, apparently to great success—at least as far as paper sales are concerned. According to the Independent, the paper sold out by 10 a.m., a 30-percent spike.

There was no word on whether citronella ink actually repelled mosquitoes. But I say, "Pfft! Who cares?! Let's make stink with our ink!"

Some possibilities:

• Barbecue. Is there a soul in America whose salivary glands don't pulsate and irrigate when stimulated by a whiff of hickory over slow-cooked pork? Even better, tell the advertising department to link barbecue ink day with printed specials from Buddy's, Chandler's, Calhoun's, Sweet P's and other emporiums of succulent meat. I call that a win-burp-win.

• Fried chicken. See above.

• Cotton candy. Can you say, "Special Tennessee Valley Fair sections"?

• Hot dogs. We already sell game-day football lineups at Neyland Stadium. Why not co-op with tube steak vendors and strike a double blow for Big Orange commerce?

• Flowers. This is a natural for Dogwood Arts Festival editions. But care must be exercised, lest we aggravate sensitive noses into a sneeze-a-thon.

Bite my tongue. What was I thinking? Of course we aggravate sensitive noses!—and then run special discount ads from drug stores and allergy treatment centers!

I now repair to my cubicle to await a letter from corporate HQ. And it better smell like greenbacks.

It sure was a weird signal

I've seen some strange hand signals while driving.

I'm not talking about the universally recognized, single-digit flashes of irritation and displeasure. These usually need no interpretation whatsoever.

Instead, I mean hand signals delivered in such a bizarre way that their meaning was misunderstood. For instance:

I was navigating a winding mountain road one day years ago. Unbeknown to me, a two-car accident had occurred in a curve ahead. Nobody had been hurt, fortunately, but the roadway was quite restricted by debris. Thus, one of the drivers—or maybe it was a passenger—had walked back a few hundred feet to warn oncoming drivers until law enforcement officers and wreckers arrived.

I use "warn" most advisedly in this context, however. You see, all the guy did was stand there, half-heartedly waving his hand. It was more of a casual "howdy" than a frantic "look out!"

I know this for a fact because I waved "howdy" back to him as I passed—and then nearly plowed into the wreckage.

Why the guy didn't show any more sense of alarm remains a mystery.

Perhaps he was still dazed from the impact. Perhaps his arm had grown weary of waving up and down. Or, more likely, he was a disciple of East Tennessee's famous theory of I-Know-What's-Going-On-So-Everybody-Else-Should-Know-Too. Much the same as motorists who resolutely refuse to use turn signals.

But a few days ago I encountered the strangest and most misconstrued hand signal I ever saw on the open road. It came from the driver in the car ahead of mine, waving for me to pass.

I remember thinking, "Huh? Why is he telling me this? There's a curve up ahead, for Pete's sake. Does he actually think I'd pull around him right now?"

Adding to the mystery was the car's speed. It wasn't setting any kind of record, but it wasn't poking along, either. Just another sedan on a winding, two-lane West Knox County road.

The signal went away for a few seconds. Then it appeared again, just as before.

I was about to seriously brake and write off the experience to Drunken Driver 101 when the "guy" whose "hand" I'd been watching abruptly changed sides of the car and began "waving" out the opposite window.

That's when I realized what I'd been seeing all along was neither a hand nor the driver. Instead, it was the long ears of a dog, flapping in the breeze. Ears that would make a basset hound's look petite.

Whew. Either that dog owner needs to roll up his windows or I need new contacts.

Must have been one bad sunburn

Get out your calculators. We've got some incredible odds to compute.

What are the chances a long-haul driver from Maryville would make an impromptu pullover at a truck stop in West Tennessee and run into an Army buddy he hadn't seen in more than 30 years?

That's the easy math. It gets more complicated as the story unfolds. Let David Hyatt, 57, who drives for Milan Express, tell you:

"I'd just dropped off a load near Martin (Tennessee) and was headed to Jackson to take a break. I was about to pass this dinky little truck stop, and for some strange reason I had to pull in. Don't ask me why. I just had to do it."

There was only one other 18-wheeler in the lot. Hyatt backed in next to it, nodded at the female driver in the adjacent cab and suddenly thought, "Hey, I know her from somewhere."

Yeah, right. A not-so-original pickup line, eh?

"That's what I told her," Hyatt related. "I said, 'Ma'am, I'm not coming on to you. It's just that you look familiar. She said, 'I was thinking the same thing about you'."

Turns out the woman had only been driving trucks for four months, having retired from the Army not long ago.

"I was in the Army, too," Hyatt said to her. "I went in at Fort Gordon, Georgia."

"So did I," she replied.

"Then I got rotated to Germany," Hyatt continued.

"So did I," she said.

"Then I went back to Fort Bliss, Texas, and —"

"So did I."

The two stared at each other for an awkward moment. Then the woman spoke: "Did you get sunburned one time while we were out on maneuvers?"

"Yes!" Hyatt exclaimed.

"Well, I'm the one who took care of you!" she answered.

That's when East Tennessean David Hyatt and Yvonne Christian of Denver, Colorado, who had not seen each other since 1981, finally reconnected.

"She was the medic in Charlie Company," said Hyatt. "We were in the same unit all that time. I got out of the Army after eight years, but she had stayed in a full 30."

The more the two talked, the more they realized how parallel their lives had been.

Said Hyatt: "She has a daughter named Jessica who was born in Germany on December 27, 1974. My daughter was born in Germany on December 28, 1974. Her name is Jessica, too."

The two old buddies exchanged addresses and phone numbers and promised to stay in touch. Then Christian turned her truck toward Mississippi, Hyatt his toward North Carolina.

"The last thing she showed me was the paper from a fortune cookie she had just eaten," said Hyatt, still shaking his head in amazement. "It read, 'You are destined to meet old friends'."

In 2014, the folks at Oak Ridge National Laboratory "had it bassackerds," to quote a localism. They proposed a class to help Southerners lose their accent when making scholarly presentations in and around these parts.

It should have been the other way around. Foreigners who come into our territory are the ones who need "to be learnt."

Actually, this idea began with the best of intentions. What evolved, however, was a "Southern accent reduction class" taught by a "certified speech pathologist and accent reduction specialist." Participants would "learn to recognize the pronunciation and grammar differences that make your speech sound Southern, and learn what to do so you can neutralize it through a technique called code-switching."

Not surprisingly, the class deep-sixed as soon as complaints arose. As an ORNL spokesman explained: "It probably wasn't presented in the right way and made it look like ORNL had some problem with having a Southern accent, which of course we don't."

Problem solved. But the truth of the matter is, you will encounter some rather strange accents and customs in these parts. These are what make East Tennessee and its residents so unique, and why I'm proud to be a native. To paraphrase an old military rule, there's the right way, the wrong way and the East Tennessee way.

Chapter Three
NO PLACE LIKE HOME

Siri don't know beans about tawkin'

The assault on Southerners continues. Amazingly, this time it's not from Hollywood.

Those of us lucky to be born in Gawd's Country are long-accustomed to being portrayed on TV and in movies as incestuous, hot-rodding, Red Man-chewing, moonshine-guzzling rednecks with a collective IQ of 12.

Proving, of course, how little the film industry knows about this region and its inhabitants. Not all of us drink 'shine and chew Red Man. Many prefer beer and Skoal.

Anyhow, this latest Dixie bashing comes from the folks at Apple. (Tell Cuzzin Clem that's a fancy computer company, not the main ingredient in Mama's favorite pie.) According to a recent story filed by Foxnews.com, the voice-recognition application on the Apple iPhone 4S "hates the British and Southerners."

This gizmo is called "Siri." In theory, a user can voice any command and Siri will oblige. So much for theory.

Even though Siri is programmed for French, German and three dialects of English, it doesn't know its app from a hole in the ground when speakers of "accented English" (translation: us'ins) are talking. Said Foxnews.com: "Apparently U.S. English doesn't include Southerners."

"Southerners" in this case means everyone below the Mason-Dixon line—whether possessed of Mississippi molasses drawl or the aristocratic "hoose" (house) and "aboot" (about) of the coastal Carolinas and Virginia.

For example, the news service spoke with a technical editor named Mat Honan, who described himself as having a "very slight" Southern accent.

"I grew up in Alabama and lived in Georgia for some time, too," said Honan, "but it's not like I'm Gomer Pyle."

He is according to Siri. Every time Honan made a request, Siri responded it "didn't quite get that."

Despite the ample brain trust at Apple, this may prove to be an insurmountable challenge. There are so many Southern dialects, even us home folks occasionally get confused.

While deer hunting in the Low Country of South Carolina years ago, I had to rely on a bilingual friend (he spoke fluent East Tennesseeze and backwoods Gullah) to carry on small talk with the locals.

Yet even when Southerners from diverse dialectal backgrounds converse, they usually can make sense with each other. When I worked at a duck-hunting club in Southwestern Louisiana, I once asked my Creole friend Dan Nunez if he spoke French at home, like his grandparents did.

Dan pondered deeply for a minute, then replied: "Well, it's like dis, Venob. I can hear it real good. I just can't talk it worth a damn."

Venob, hillbilly Cajun, understood completely.

And then there was the morning when a badly hung-over guide, rummaging through the club's medicine cabinet, asked if I knew where "dat kao, uh dat kao, y'know, dat kao-close-asshole-stuff" happened to be.

I produced a bottle of Kaopectate, and calm was restored on all fronts. Or rears, as the case may be.

We've been hitched to another list

Given the bleak state of economic affairs in the newspaper business right now, I don't expect any immediate action on this proposal. But, assuming the day eventually comes when a dime can roll across the floor and eight department heads don't pounce on it at once, perhaps we could fill a new position around here.

We need a "list editor" in the worst way. So does every newspaper in America.

Why?

Because "best of" and "worst of" lists continue to proliferate like mold in a summer camp shower stall—and every city wants to know where it stacks up in relation to every place else. Knoxville, of course, is no exception.

In recent months alone, K-town and the immediate surrounding area have been named:

- El Numero Uno in the United States for residents who "age too quickly."

- Also Number One, per capita (and possibly linked with the previous category) for "Cities with Highest Rate of Hamburger Consumption." Oh, how my heart swells with pride. Wait. Or is that my carotid artery?
  - Sixth in the "List of Best Mid-Sized Cities for Jobs."
  - "Most Romantic" in the U.S.
  - Twenty-sixth "Most Unhappy" in the U.S.
  - Twenty-ninth "Sneeziest City" in the nation.
  - Fifteenth of America's "20 Dirtiest Cities."
  - Fifth of Top 10 cities that provide "best value, based on low living costs, strong economies and great amenities."

Along the way, we also were mentioned in "Top 10 Places to Live and Boat" and "America's Best Places to Raise a Family."

But before you high-five everyone in the office about those accomplishments, please remember we also ranked 41st in the "Top 100 Sweatiest Cities." So please keep those armpits at low mast as you celebrate.

You are free to accept or reject the accuracy, of lack thereof, of this information. That's because many of the lists were compiled by corporations with a vested interest in the outcome. My guess is these statistics wouldn't pass muster if subjected to scientific analysis. But who am I to ruin some corporate flack's idea of research?

The reason I bring all this up is because we have just landed on another list. According to the website realage.com, we are the "Third Best City in America for Happy Marriages." For the record, we ranked behind Salt Lake City and Greenville, South Carolina, respectively.

Said a news release accompanying the announcement: "The gorgeous antebellum mansion, Bleak House, was used as Confederate headquarters during the Knoxville campaign of the Civil War. Today, it's where many brides and grooms tie the knot in Knoxville."

Huh? That qualifies us as Number Three in the nation for marriages that stand the test of time?

OK, if they say so. But the same endurance formula didn't work out so well for Johnny Reb, did it?

A few things could get lost in transit

As you, your cousin in Connecticut, late-night comedians, and every radio talk show host between Spokane and Seattle have heard by now, Amazon is working on a project to deliver purchases to America customers via unmanned drones.

Yes, the same kind of aircraft the U.S. military uses to dispatch enemies from thousands of miles afar.

There are numerous hurdles to overcome, not the least of which are traffic control, liability questions and approval by the Federal Aviation Administration. Nonetheless, Amazon execs believe a system could be up and running—or flying, as the case may be—in as little as five years.

Whatever. As one who thought cell phones and bottled water would be huge commercial flops, I have no business questioning the workability of this plan. All I'm saying is that news travels slowly in the hills and hollows of East Tennessee. So don't be surprised some day if —

"Hale far, Lukey! Lookit this here bird I shot! Hit's jest like th'one you kilt last week!"

"Dam'fit ain't, Goober! Whar'd you git it?"

"Same place you did—up on Buzzard's Roost Ridge. Heered th'same thang you did, too: that hum like Bart Cubbins makes when he's had a snoot full o'shine. 'Ummmmm, ummmmm.' Then this bird come a'flyin' overhead. Took both barrels, but I brought 'im down through the trees, dead as a hammer."

"Wuz it carryin' anythin' in its claws? 'Member, mine was a'readin' a book. I know hit's crazy t'think a bird kin read, 'specially a book kivvered in plastic wrap. But it shore was a'totin' one!"

"Naw, this'un didn't have nary book, Lukey. 'Sted, it had a pair o'socks. They wuz kivvered in plastic wrap, too. Whut does a bird need with socks and a book?"

"Beats me, Goober. But hit seems to be a'catchin'. Floyd Hipshire told me his boy kilt one of 'em birds, and hit wuz carryin' some sorta little round thang. Had a label stuck to it that said 'DVD'. Floyd said he believes that's a disease you can git hangin' out with the wrong kind o'women. He heered about it in th'Army. Anyhow, he told his boy not to tetch hit. Jest picked up the whole kit and caboodle in a shovel and buried it down in the holler."

"You reckon this is somethin' the guv'mit is up to, Lukey? I ain't never trusted 'em people since they started shootin' rockets toward th'moon and monkeyin' with the time twict a year. They got my hens so messed up, thar a'layin' aigs that ain't fit t'eat."

"Well, now that you mention not fit t'eat, let me tell you somethin' 'bout 'at bird you jest kilt, Goober. You can forgit tryin' to make a meal offen it. They ain't nuthin' but skin and bones to begin with. They don't fry up worth a flip, neither. Even thar gravy tastes turrible."

Things that go 'boom' in the night

As soon as I heard about those mysterious booms in Hamblen County, I did what any self-respecting, smart-assed East Tennessean would do. I started making wisecracks.

"Gotta be another meth lab blowing up," was the first thought that crossed my mind. But then, noting these sounds are located mainly near the Cocke County line, I switched sources.

"Maybe it's a still. Or perhaps it's the ghost of Popcorn Sutton, madder'n a hornet that city folks are making millions off legal 'shine these days."

The more I thought, the nuttier—not to mention bawdier—my explanations became.

"Perhaps it's ice cracking in hell now that Tennessee actually made it to, and won, two consecutive bowl games."

Also, "what about that attempt a few years ago by the town of Bean Station, in neighboring Grainger County, to set a Guinness record for the biggest pot of pinto beans? Reckon the methane buildup finally reached critical mass at the same moment some fool struck a match?"

Then a rare dose of seriousness overcame me (it'll only be temporary), and I began to wonder: "What's really behind this thing?"

In case you missed the news, the Morristown area keeps getting rocked by noise. According to the Morristown-Hamblen County Emergency Management Agency, more than 250 reports came in one week alone.

"This is at least the fifth occurrence," agency director Chris Bell told me. "People describe it differently. Some say it's like a sonic boom. Others say it's like a dumpster falling or maybe a transformer exploding."

Even with the aid of seismographic instruments, officials have yet to come up with an answer.

Seems there's a similar situation in the town of Moodus, Connecticut. Carla Helfferich, a Connecticut native and science writer at the University of Alaska's Geophysical Institute, described it October 19, 1988, for the Alaska Science Forum.

This phenomenon is officially known as the "Moodus Noises." It's been occurring for centuries. Written accounts date to 1702. Scientific studies were undertaken well into the late 1980s.

"There is a good coupling between the ground and the atmosphere," geologist Tom Statton wrote in Science News magazine. "For reasons not entirely clear, sound passes relatively freely between the ground and the air in Moodus."

Maybe the same holds true for the air in Hamblen County.

But just to be on the safe side, I'd avoid striking matches any time, uh, "recycled remnants" of pinto beans drift in from Grainger County.

Down on the farm in a metropolis

If you were asked to name an area of the country where agriculture is recognized at every turn, would you choose:

1. The vast vineyards and produce farms in California's Central Valley?
2. The endless miles of cornfields in Iowa, Illinois and Nebraska?
3. The wheat lands of North Dakota?
4. The Grand Prairie of Arkansas, rice capitol of the United States?
5. King cotton country in the Rio Grande Valley of Texas?

All are excellent answers. No doubt the chamber of commerce in each region could provide impressive statistics to prove its respective claim.

But Julie Walker, a farm gal from Cocke County who knows a thing or three about coaxing crops out of the soil, wishes to add one more name to this list. (Hint: You wouldn't guess it if I gave you 25 chances.)

"New York City," Walker told me the other day as we stood in one of the fields of her family's farm near Newport, inhaling the aroma of freshly plowed earth—"the most delightful perfume in the world," as she put it.

No, Walker isn't suggesting tractors will soon turn the concrete and asphalt of Times Square into soybean production. Rest assured the bulls on

Wall Street will continue to be associated with the stock market, not rib-eye steaks.

Nonetheless, she has just returned to East Tennessee with a different opinion about the perception of agriculture in the Big Apple (uh, not Winesap or Granny Smith, btw.)

Walker was in New York for the premiere of an independent film about the future of farming. The invitation stemmed from her role as national spokeswoman for AgriVoice, a communications business that monitors the dairy industry.

The coincidences she encountered were the stuff of double-takes, right from the moment she hailed a taxi at LaGuardia.

"The first thing I saw was a toy cow dangling from the cab's rearview mirror," she said with a laugh. "Then the first vehicle that passed us on the freeway was a large trailer hauling alfalfa hay. Since I used to own a herd of registered Holsteins, I notice things like that."

The biggest surprise, though, came a few hours later, after she'd checked into her hotel and started looking for a place to eat.

"By chance, I picked a restaurant called American Flatbread," she said. "The first thing I saw when I went through the door was a big sign that read, 'Thank You, Farmers.' It had a map that listed all the local farms where they buy their meat, vegetables, milk and butter, even their herbs. I'd never seen anything like that in my life.

"What are the odds I could be 800 miles from home and find those things? In Manhattan, of all places!"

It's now the home of sober stats

The drunk tank at Morgan County's ancient jail has reopened for business, and a famous example of misspelling is back on public display. That's what I call progress.

The drunk tank once swelled with riotous revelers who'd enjoyed one, perhaps more, too many. It is a cold, concrete enclosure, outfitted with a single, long platform that once served as bed, sitting room and recovery station, depending on the condition of new arrivals.

"Boy, if these walls could talk!" Sharon Kreis mused aloud as she, Sara Goodman and I perused the joint.

TO RETIRE? OR NOT TO RETIRE?

Actually, these walls still do have a lot to "say." All you gotta do is grab one of the hundreds of dusty ledgers stacked floor to ceiling and start thumbing through the pages. Court records, divorces, car registrations, eviction orders, you name it—if it pertains to anything of a legal nature in Morgan County, it's here.

This is one of the most unusual storage facilities I've ever seen. It came about thanks to a group called Morgan County Archives Committee, which is determined to preserve these records in a more user-friendly way.

State law requires these stats be kept, of course. But in Morgan County, as likely is the case in many others, the old books had been shoved, carted and piled into any available corner or closet. Not until the archives group formed did volunteers begin to preserve them in some sort of order.

Kreis said the drunk tank hadn't been occupied since the old jail was decertified around 2006. It turned out to be a perfect location.

"This place is solid concrete," she said. "I bet it could withstand a tornado. All we had to put in were gauges to make sure the temperature and humidity stay constant."

It's going to take years of work to organize these old papers in acid-free binders. But already, the committee has brought one historic Morgan County classic back to life. That would be the hand-lettered sign over the entrance to the building.

Its bold message reads, "It Does'nt Pay to Do Wrong."

"This goes back to the 1930s, when the jail was new and W.R. Brock was the sheriff," said Kreis. "Supposedly he had a drunk who worked off his time by painting the sign. He put the apostrophe in the wrong place. The sheriff liked it any way. So that's how it stayed."

It wasn't until a 1970s renovation project that the spelling was corrected. Archivists figured the original was gone for good. But a couple of months ago, someone checked under the peeling paint and—ta-dah!—there was the oldie-but-goodie. And there it proudly remains.

If tha'ts not historical accuracy I do'nt know what is.

Makes a shot seem truly enjoyable

Through a series of weird circumstances, my wife and I both have visited several doctors recently. Nothing serious. Just the usual jabs, pokes and other painful intrusions.

Despite the discomfort, though, one thought kept running through my head: It could be much worse. I reached this conclusion after visiting with Museum of Appalachia founder John Rice Irwin.

J.R. is immersed in another book about our area. He doesn't know when it'll be out. In fact, he doesn't even have a working title.

"I started out to write about the 20 most interesting people I've met down through the years," he told me. "After I hit 20, I decided to expand it to 50. Then 100. I'm over 200 right now."

You've heard of several of these individuals. The late U.S. Sen. Howard Baker and author Alex Haley immediately come to mind. But there are countless dozens of others whose only historical legacy is their name etched into a gravestone.

One was "Uncle" Campbell Sharp, whose farm lay to the east of the Irwin place back in the day. J.R. believes he was born around the Civil War and died, in his late 80s, shortly after World War II.

"I was around him a lot when I was a boy," Irwin recalled. "He was a very gentle man, but also physically very tough."

How tough? Hold onto your hemostat.

This guy underwent surgery. Three times. On his kitchen table. Without anesthesia.

"Many times I heard my grandfather tell about those operations," J.R. said. "And I saw the scars on Uncle Campbell's side and back myself."

According to local lore, Uncle Campbell was injured in a fall from his barn. He landed on his back, hitting a stump, "and it set up some sort of infection," said J.R.

"A doctor looked at the wound and said he needed to go to Knoxville for an operation. Uncle Campbell wouldn't hear of it. He said if somebody would show him where to cut, he'd just do it himself."

I was visibly wincing as J.R. continued: "Uncle Campbell got four strong men to hold him down on the table and told the doctor to cut. Later, another infection appeared. So he got the same four men to hold him down again for another operation."

Don't relax yet.

"The wound got infected all over again, but by that time the wheat harvest was on and Uncle Campbell didn't want to bother the men. He got up on that same kitchen table and wrapped his arms around the legs and let the doctor cut a third time.

"That one did the trick. He healed, kept farming, raised a big family and lived to a ripe old age."

Now, then—what was it you were saying about the "good ol' days" of medicine?

It's 'natural' with enough concrete

Years ago, back when TVA and the Army Corps of Engineers were hell-bent to impound every gallon of free-flowing water in the Southeast, I saw a hilarious editorial cartoon. It showed an Army general gazing over a scorched-earth, mud-flat moonscape of tree stumps, abandoned homes and demolished barns, all about to be flooded.

"This," he says with a proud countenance, "is the way God would have made it in the first place if He'd just had the money!"

I was reminded of that old drawing recently when John Zirkle passed along the story of his "enlightenment." It occurred while he and his wife were dining at a restaurant overlooking Douglas Lake.

"We were seated next to two couples from Michigan who were vacationing in this area," he told me. "One of them remarked to their server—a sweet young thing of about 18—how beautiful Douglas was. Then he asked how long the lake had been there."

"She told him: 'Well, I've lived here all my life, and it's been here as long as I can remember.'"

"So it's a natural lake?" the visitor inquired.

"Yep, it sure is," the server said.

"But I thought there was a dam nearby," said another one of the tourists.

"Oh sure, there's Douglas Dam," the waitress smiled. "It's just about a mile from here."

And off she bounced to refill iced tea glasses.

Zirkle didn't have the heart to set her straight. Instead, "I told my wife those Michiganders will surely return up north and regale their friends with stories about Tennessee hillbillies who think because a lake 'naturally' forms behind a dam, it must be a natural lake."

Reminds me of the time I took a South Carolinian fishing for trout in Tellico River. En route, we stopped at a country store to buy a daily permit. During the transaction he spelled his last name, which contained the letter "q," to the clerk.

"Huh?" the young lady replied, her face wrinkling. "A 'q'? I ain't never heard of no 'q.' I don't even know how to make one of 'em."

I intervened: "Honey, just write a 'p' backwards, and it'll work fine."

Done and done. The fishing was superb, by the way.

But just because we live in the Eddjukashun Stait, don't think we're ignert. Not long ago, attorney Robert Godwin told me about researching an old deed that included a two-hole privy which straddled the property line.

"Logically," he mused, "the deed established a mutual easement for each owner to use the hole on the other side of the line 'as needed'."

Makes sense to me.

A morning with the missus

Because I poke around in East Tennessee's more remote hills and hollows with fishing rod and shotgun, I often come across old homesteads, rusty farm equipment, root-bound beds of perennial flowers, family cemeteries and other links to yesteryear.

I tread lightly in the presence of these treasures.

Even though each has a story—make that a wealth of stories—to tell, I've always felt like I'm intruding on someone else's personal, historic space. These are outdoor museums and museum rules apply: Look, but don't touch.

I do, however, take notes and pass along my reflections.

On several occasions down through the years, I've found a name or a date and written about the folks who went before. Whether it's a century-old graveyard for children in the mountains of the Cherokee National Forest or a weatherworn farmhouse in the windswept autumn croplands of Nebraska,

TO RETIRE? OR NOT TO RETIRE?

I am forever intrigued. You don't know the times I've wished I could actually hear those voices from the past.

A few mornings ago in rural Jefferson County, I had that opportunity. I could have spoken to a very real person who, no doubt, could have told me volumes of his family's history. But I declined. Even with a reporter's curiosity, occasionally it's best to remain silent and press on.

Larry Cook and I were "making our rounds" for wild turkeys. That's hunting parlance for checking out a ridgeline here, a few acres of forest there, in hopes of hearing the gobble of a lovelorn tom and settling down to attempt calling him toward the gun.

Going on 40 springs now, Larry and I have combed these woodlands together. Occasionally we draw blood. More often we give the turkeys plenty to laugh about. Invariably we make memories.

One of our listening posts is adjacent to a country cemetery. As we bounced along the perimeter road the other day, we noticed a lone car up on the hill, near a marker. Stands to reason. What better than a sun-splashed morning in May for decorating the grounds?

With no turkeys seen or heard, we drove back out a bit later. The car was still there. An old gravel road winding through the graveyard would take us near it.

As we approached, Larry glanced over to nod to its occupant.

"Oh, my ..." his voice trailed off slowly.

I turned my head. It took all of one second to gather in the scene.

There in the car sat an old man. Silver-haired. Sad-faced. His door was swung open toward the headstone. A lone cup of coffee sat steaming on the dashboard, together with a rumpled newspaper.

Larry and I not only had the same thought, we spoke it in unison: "He's come to have breakfast with his wife, hasn't he?"

The two hunting buddies drove on in silence. It would be nearly a mile before either spoke. And then it was only to note how awful the pine pollen is this year. It's a crime how it makes your eyes water.

Putting the polish on a new plant

When most folks come across a tree, bird or fish they can't readily identify, they usually shrug it off with a casual "Hmm, wonder what that thing was?"

The more inquisitive ones might go so far as to consult a field guide. Every now and then, they take their quest further: to experts in the field. But when the pros have no clue, things start to get interesting.

That's precisely what happened a couple of years ago when East Tennesseans Mark and Marci Dunaway began poking around in the mountains on the Hamblen-Hawkins county line, a tract they recently had purchased.

The Dunaways spotted a yellowish trillium that looked like nothing they'd ever seen, either in the ground or on the pages of a wildflower ID book.

They snapped several photographs, which eventually wound up on the desk of Dr. Edward Schilling, a botanist with the University of Tennessee's Department of Ecology and Evolutionary Biology. He couldn't put a name on the plant, either.

So Schilling and his colleague Dr. Susan Farmer (now with Georgia's Abraham Baldwin Agricultural College), along with graduate student Aaron Floden, drove up for a look-see.

Holy-by-gum-moly!

After analyzing the molecular structure and DNA of the plant, the team realized they were dealing with a previously unknown species of this beautiful group of flowers. Ultimately, their findings passed muster in peer-reviewed scientific journals.

All of which means we now have Trillium tennesseense, named in honor of its home state.

Understandably, you won't find detailed directions to the site of this discovery. Too much potential for poaching. But abundant photographs are available through publications like Blue Ridge Country magazine and appvoices.org, website of the environmental group Appalachian Voices.

Talk about a niche location!

"We found this plant—in fact, several thousand of them in one ravine—growing on a certain type of limestone soil in Bays Mountain," said Schilling.

"As soon as we got off that particular type of limestone, these trilliums disappeared."

T. tennesseense joins about 50 other species of trilliums, Schilling said. Many of them, especially the common yellow and white varieties, are quite familiar to East Tennessee woods walkers.

Around six inches in height, this is a rather short trillium. The base of its flower is "purple-maroon," giving way to more pronounced yellow at the top.

One other distinguishing factor is its aroma.

"A lot of kids wouldn't recognize it these days," Schilling said with a laugh, "but it smells exactly like old-time shoe polish."

Another stinky bug to revile

Verily, a little learning can be a dangerous thing.

The first time I heard the name of a new insect invading East Tennessee, I nearly wept for joy. Anything called the "kudzu bug" because it feeds on kudzu juice has to be good, right?

Here is the South's six-legged salvation, right?

This is the cure we've longed for since kudzu began its stranglehold of Dixie, right?

Wrong. Wrong. And wrong.

"Yes, they feed on kudzu, but not to the point of killing the plant," lamented Neal Denton, Knox County agricultural extension agent. "As I was telling someone the other day, an infestation of kudzu bugs might make a kudzu vine go from growing eight feet per day down to six feet. That's about it."

But they sure are bugging people. Especially people who live or work in white buildings. That, says Denton, is the color they are most attracted to.

Tell me about it. One recent warm afternoon, the outside walls of the News Sentinel's building (white, if you haven't guessed already) were polka-dotted with them. They clustered on windowpanes and around doors. The air was filled with wings.

My colleague Frank Munger walked through a swarm of these critters on his way in. He was still swatting at imaginary bugs ten minutes later.

"They seem to be crawling all over me," he griped.

That's similar to a report I heard from an Oak Ridge resident. She told me the hateful things had gathered "by the thousands" on the side of her white house.

"Be sure to keep them on your side of the river," I told her. (This just in: she didn't.)

Kudzu bugs are roughly the size and shape of a ladybug. Except they're brown instead of red-and-black. They arrive in dive-bombing batches.

Denton says kudzu bugs came from Asia via shipping crates. They were first reported in 2009 in Georgia. Ever since, they've spread across the South like a virus.

What's more—oh, joy!—they stink to high heavens if crushed.

It gets worse.

"Once cold weather arrives for good, it pretty much stops stinkbugs and ladybugs," said Denton. "Not so with kudzu bugs. If the weather warms up for a day, even in winter, they'll start swarming again."

There's not much you can do other than cuss, caulk any cracks in your house or have the exterior sprayed by a pest control company. For the record, I recommend cussing. Loudly.

To put a cherry on top of this misery, kudzu bugs have no natural enemies.

"That's the usual case with an imported species," said Denton. "It takes several years for the predators to follow them."

This is one time we should show no Southern hospitality whatsoever.

A difference of opinion

Professor Venob and his wife often engage in heated autumnal arguments. Both Venobs are resolutely firm in their respective opinions. Neither is likely to be swayed by the other.

This difference has nothing whatsoever to do with politics, nor football at the University of Tennessee. Their issue is much more important.

It's this business of the quality of fall foliage.

Sometimes, Professor Venob maintains the red-gold-orange panorama does not meet the typically high standards of Southern Appalachia's woodlands. His wife will beg to differ. Sometimes, it is his wife who makes this assertion. Naturally, that's when he begs to differ.

(At this point, both the prof and his missus stress there never has been a "bad" display of autumn color in East Tennessee. Nor will there ever be. Perish the thought of such rubbish! Rather, the situation can be likened to beer, prime rib and other pleasantries of life: Some are finer, or perhaps less fine, than others. Now, where were we? Oh, yes; leaves.)

Professor Venob, who was a forestry major at UT before he switched to journalism and abandoned any hope of earning an honest living, knows his trees. Furthermore, he forms his annual opinions with boots on the ground and tires on the road.

He spends a vast number of hours in the hills and hollows of the Tennessee Valley. He logs many miles traversing interstate and back roads. Thus, his expert opinion should always be heeded. Especially by his dutiful bride.

If he decrees the hickories to be spectacular, so be it. Also the dogwoods, poplars and maples.

If his missus happens to disagree, that's her problem.

She is not learned in the ways of trees. Nor of summer rainfall, temperature swings and other factors affecting the autumn showcase. On occasion, he goes so far as to point out her deficiencies in these matters.

As a side note, Professor Venob says sleeping on the sofa ain't so bad, once you get used to it.

All hail the little shack out back

Let Paris have the Eiffel Tower!
Let London have Big Ben!
Let Rome have the Colosseum!
Let Athens have the Parthenon!

Townsend, Tennessee, by gum, can top 'em all—by celebrating the bottom.

The Great Smoky Mountains Heritage Center recently unveiled its tribute to a functional icon of American architecture. I speak of the outhouse.

An example of this humble structure was dedicated in a ceremony replete with the official snipping of a toilet paper ribbon.

TP factored into the special day in another way. Admission to the Townsend center was free for anyone who donated at least one roll of VIP (very important paper), all of which was donated to Blount County's New Hope child advocacy group.

Excellent idea—no ifs, ands or butts.

However, given the cultural and historic roots of this venerable building, wouldn't a basket of dried corn cobs or an old Sears-Roebuck catalog been much more appropriate?

A good time was had by all

During the joint meeting of the Brotherhood of Unruly, Lowdown, Lying Hillbillies Observing Creative Knowledge Every Year (BULLHOCKEY) and the Society of Appalachian Saintly Sisters (SASS) at the Museum of Appalachia's Tennessee Fall Homecoming, the following business was transacted:

• Kenny Shreve, head of the BULLHOCKEY-SASS Fiduciary Fund, proposed changing the group's insurance policy to a new carrier every few months.

When asked why, Kenny replied, "On their TV ads, they all say you can save $300 to $500 a month by switching to them. I figure in less than a year, we'll get ours for free."

Ayes 169, nays 0.

• Vince V. Vawter, BULLHOCKEY's nominee for the Pulitzer Prize in Philosophy, significantly upped his chances with this high-brow question: "Is a pair of movie glasses required to read papers that come off those new 3-D printers?"

Vince was praised for his amazing insight.

• Floyd Anderson, vice-chair of Modern Retail Operations, offered this assessment of a mega-grocery store that just opened near his home in Milledgeville, Georgia:

"They use the latest in olfactory attractions to entice customers. At the dairy counter, you experience the scent of freshly mowed hay. In meats, you are treated to the aroma of steaks on the grill. At the egg case, it's the scent of breakfast frying. In breads, the air hangs thick with the perfume of cookies fresh from the oven. But man! This sure ain't the place to buy toilet paper!"

Floyd was summarily ejected from the meeting.

• Oregon lumberjack Quinn Murk, making his third BULLHOCKEY meeting, gave a rundown of his vocational history:

"I started out as a banker, but then I lost interest. Next, I took a job in a bakery because I kneaded dough. I finally got into logging when someone asked me to cut down some trees and I said I wood."

Quinn received the Gorilla Glue Award for his stick-to-itiveness.

• After praying over the assembled masses, Rev. Melissa Anderson, pastor-in-training at the Holiness Hollerin' Sanctified Church and Reptile Farm, opined that "atheism is a non-prophet organization."

A love offering was taken to further Sister Anderson's education. Also for a few more rattlesnakes.

• Appalachian Hippie Poet Bill Alexander voiced his complaint that "dyslexic musicians write inverse."

All 56 fiddlers and banjo players in attendance quickly caucused and agreed to disagree, concluding they "most certainly were not KO" with Bill's findings.

• SASS librarian Carolyn Cornelius said a new book on anti-gravity was so fascinating, she simply couldn't put it down.

• Billy Bob Fortenberry, professor emeritus of analytic chemistry, said recent discoveries have proven H_2O is hot water and CO_2 is cold water.

Several wiseacres in the rear of the crowd suggested Billy Bob was all wet but were quickly subdued by accurate blasts from Sergeant-at-Arms Allen Longmire's squirt gun. Said Longmire: "I took pity on the fools and only fired LO_2: lukewarm water."

• Prunella Hixson gave a detailed report on her recent physical woes.

"First, I came down with arteriosclerosis, then I got angina pectoris. As I was recovering from those, I was diagnosed with tuberculosis, halitosis and pilosis. Right on the heels of all that came tonsillitis, appendicitis, gastritis, tendinitis and neuritis."

Asked how her health was at the moment, Prunella replied, "I still feel terrible, but I've won the last six spelling bees I entered!"

• Andrea Fritts, chairwoman of the Agricultural and Meteorological Study Group, pronounced the recent heat wave "worst on record." It especially took a toll on poultry producers.

"Many farmers had to feed their chickens crushed ice to keep them from laying hard-boiled eggs," she said. "It got so expensive, several producers gave up on ice altogether. They simply switched to mayo and pickle relish and started selling deviled eggs."

The crowd cackled and crowed in delight.

• Larry Mathis, presiding plucker of the BULLHOCKEY Stringed Instrument Quintet, announced a cruel joke had been making the rounds: "Why did the banjo player climb the chain-link fence? To see what was on the other side."

"As soon as someone explains this to my members," he warned, "we intend to file a lawsuit."

• Paleontologist Bjorn "Big Ben" Bennington posed a most interesting question: "Why is so little known about the urinary functions of pterodactyls?"

With no answer forthcoming, he said: "Their 'p' was silent."

• In similar vein, Cathy Brown, who is pursuing a Ph.D. in prehistoric home economics, asked whether anybody had heard the one about the cannibal who came home late for supper and all he got was the cold shoulder.

No one had—although numerous requests were made for the recipe.

• John Rice Irwin, superintendent of the Hire Eddukashun Kommittee, then took the floor to pose a pair of deep questions:

"If a guy jumps off a bridge in Paris, is he in Seine? Also, are Santa's elves considered subordinate clauses?"

• This ignited a verbal free-for-all between Angie Dunkford, Rupert Thornhill and Bonnie Peters.

"A friend of mine fell into an upholstery machine," hollered Angie, "but he is fully recovered."

"So?" shouted Rupert, "a friend of mine is addicted to drinking brake fluid, but he swears he can stop any time!"

"Big deal!" countered Bonnie. "I've got a friend who stayed up all night to see where the sun went. Then it dawned on him."

It took Sergeant-at-Arms Longmire several minutes of gavel banging to restore calm. As only a few fists flew and knives were drawn but not deployed, he pronounced calm had been restored and the meeting could proceed.

- Debbie "Dill" Pickle, SASS delegate to the Arachnid Awareness Alliance, issued a shocking warning to other women in the audience:

"If a man comes to your front door, says he's from the government and is checking for ticks and asks you to take off your clothes and turn around slowly several times, don't do it! It's a scam! He only wants to see you naked!"

Whereupon Bobbi Buzzfussle moaned aloud, "Oh, no! If I'd only gotten this warning last week!"

- Deacon Douglas Fritts, leader of the Ministry for Mysterious Missions, said he'd just read in the newspapers that the Pope was injured by a fall in his bathtub.

This caused Elder Mark Payne to whisper to those sitting nearby: "Psst! What's a bathtub?"

"I don't know," someone whispered back, "I ain't Catholic."

- Joel Zachry, chairman of the Council on Harmonious Relations, said he and his wife had gotten into a heated argument before leaving home and drove most of the way to the meeting barely speaking to each other.

"Just before we got here we passed a hog lot, and I snapped at Kathy, 'Any of 'em kin to you?' She snarled back, 'Yeah. They're my in-laws'."

The Zachrys were ordered to put down the raw onions they were munching, then kiss and make up. After several failed attempts, they agreed to shake on it.

- Baldy Whitlock, chairman of the Oceanic Studies Committee, gave a fascinating session on sharks.

"By using the latest digital and sonar technology, we were able to actually listen as older sharks taught younger sharks how to feed," he began. "For instance, as they came near the shore and approached swimmers, the older shark said, 'Always start your first pass showing just one fin.' The younger sharks did as instructed.

"When they regathered, the elder shark said, 'Now make your second pass showing two fins.' Once again, the youngsters followed his advice.

"As they were preparing for the third pass, the teacher said, 'This time, show three fins.'

"By now," Baldy noted, "the younger sharks were getting frustrated, not to mention hungry. One of them asked, 'Why go to all that trouble showing fins? Why not just attack those swimmers right off the bat and start feeding?'

To which the old one replied, 'They taste a lot better after you've scared the shit out of them'."

Sergeant-at-Arms Longmire was ordered to duct-tape Baldy's mouth for the remainder of the session.

- "Aunt Fritzi" Holmberg, chairwoman of the Office Products Civil Disobedience Caucus, reported that "after careful analysis, we have determined you can push the envelope all you want, but it'll still be stationery."

Several members took copious notes.

- Lt. Col. Roberta Thigwhistle, representing the Military Appreciation Committee, said her group is looking for a soldier who survived both mustard gas and pepper spray to honor at their upcoming banquet.

"This way," she said, "we will truly have a seasoned veteran."

- Continuing the discussion on honors, Homer N. Jethro brought this item to the floor:

"As we all know, Granny Jones, Hootin' Holler's most illustrious moonshiner, passed away last summer. Not once in 65 years of production was she ever caught by the law. I think we oughta erect a statue of her at BULLHOCKEY-SASS headquarters."

Pug Thigwhistle leaped to his feet and shouted, "I second the motion! Granny may have been just a plain ol' whiskey maker, but we loved her still."

Two jars then were passed: an empty one for donations, a full one for sampling Granny's last run.

- Jacob Williams, chairman of the Grounds Keeping Committee, announced that a gaping hole recently had been discovered in the wall of the Big Busts and Bare Butts nudist colony bordering the BULLHOCKEY-SASS property.

"Have you reported this to law enforcement authorities?" Charles Sherwood asked.

"No," Jacob replied. "I'm looking into it myself."

Several members immediately volunteered to assist in the investigation.

- Jacob also reported the recent vandalism of the BULLHOCKEY-SASS outhouse, resulting in complete destruction of the facility.

When asked about any results of his investigation into the matter, Jacob said, "Unfortunately, I have nothing to go on."

TO RETIRE? OR NOT TO RETIRE?

• Loreen Woodcock, Cheerwomin of the Readin' and Ritin' Good Konference, reported that a number of grammar fundamentals were being incorporated into the English classes she teaches.

"Fer'nstance," she said, "I insist that all verbs has to agree with their subjects. Also, always avoid aggressive and annoying alliterations. Third, don't never use no double negatives. Finally, prepositions ain't good words to end sentences with."

By voice vote, Loreen was thanked for her exxce . . . uh, magniff . . . good presentation.

• There being no further business, the meeting was adjourned. Granny's refreshments were served well into the night. No arrests had been reported by press time.

If I could return to Earth in the 22nd century, no doubt I'd be awestruck by all the common gizmos and gadgets that hadn't even been invented in my day. Just as long as nobody required me to use them.

I'm a card-carrying technophobe. Which makes me a laughingstock, not only among younger people but also many in my generation.

It's not that I can't learn new tricks. I simply chose not to. Plus, I'm blessed with a wife who never met a new digitized device she doesn't learn to operate quickly. She is my enabler. As long as I can holler, "Honey, how th'$&#%! does this piece of $#&%&! work?" all is right in my little world.

Am I hardheaded? Perhaps. Stubborn? Maybe. Content? Yes!

True story: My bass boat came equipped with a fancy depth-finder. This is an excellent tool for locating rocks, bridge abutments, channel drop-offs, creek bends and other fish-holding areas beneath the surface. But I rarely turn my unit on because I get confused which buttons I'm supposed to punch. Big deal; I generally fish in shallow water anyway.

If I did come back 100 years from now, I suspect I'd find a number of hardheaded, stubborn, yet content folks just like me. They may have lived on the razor-sharp cutting edge of technology in their younger years but eventually realized how dull it soon became. Age has a habit of doing that, especially to lazy, enabled cretins. And we know who we are.

Chapter Four
VENTING ABOUT VEXATIONS

A redneck lost in high tech

There are lots of newfangled devices I can happily live without during my remaining time on this planet.

One is the $1,500 Google Glass, an ultra-high-tech computer worn on the noggin like eyeglasses. It is all the rage among geeks these days.

No more stepping into the path of oncoming vehicles because their heads are down while their fingers and thumbs furiously peck out texts on a tiny keypad. No, siree! Their faces will be gazing straight ahead!

Of course, their eyes will still be glued to a monitor, this one even tinier than a keypad. Perhaps more advanced models will come equipped with a sensor that screams "eeee-iiii!!" shortly before colliding with a bread truck.

Another digital doohickey I don't have to worry about buying is the iPad Commode Caddy, offered by mail order giant Hammacher Schlemmer for $100.

I quote directly from the company's ad: "This is the bathroom stand that replaces a traditional basket of magazines by accommodating both an iPad and a roll of toilet paper. Ideal for browsing one's digital reading material while indisposed, it places an iPad 32 inches from the floor on top of a flexible 10-inch gooseneck that provides optimal positioning for reading."

This ad was forwarded to me by a trusted colleague. Hate to admit, but my first reaction was to assume it was a spoof from The Onion. Not until I called up the Hammacher Schlemmer website and saw it with my own eyes did I realize this was real. Then I immediately fell to my knees and prayed for the future of civilization.

Techno-bashing Neanderthal that I am, however, there is one gizmo I wish somebody would invent: A compact, easy-to-use, 24/7 personal instant replay machine.

Perhaps this would lessen the "discussions" my wife and I have about something from the past—meaning anywhere from 45 minutes to 45 years earlier.

Hardly a week goes by that Mary Ann and I don't disagree about some little family snippet of who-did-what or what-happened-when. I suppose this occurs with most couples, especially after they've been together as long as we have. It's nothing major, but it blows my mind how we can remember the same events so differently.

A personal instant replay machine would solve the problem. Just hit the rewind button and let the record speak for itself.

Or maybe not. During a 2013 baseball game in Cleveland, Ohio, instant replay proved conclusively that the umpires botched a huge call. Yet the stubborn umps refused to amend their initial decision.

I'm not so sure most husband-wife "ironclad recollections" wouldn't turn out the same way.

Will the real me please stand up?

You're at work and get a phone call from the police.

Your house has been broken into, a cop says. So have nearly all the houses in your neighborhood. For that matter, almost every house in town.

So you drive home and look around. Nothing seems to be out of place. Nothing's missing, at least not that you can detect.

"Are you certain we got hit?" you ask the investigator.

"No doubt about it."

He continues: "We don't know who did it—probably won't ever find out, to be perfectly honest—but there are fingerprints all over this place. Just wait. In the coming days and weeks, you'll probably discover how much stuff was taken from you. Hope it's not too serious and doesn't ruin your life."

Gulp . . .

That's the unsettling feeling more than 100 million consumers—present company included, unfortunately—experienced when news broke about a huge security breach at Target and Neiman Marcus stores. Seems our credit card information—including name, street address, e-mail address and phone number—got hacked. Trillions of pieces of personal data then were available for sale on the international black market.

Well, #$%*! Welcome to the nightmarish side of technology.

Mary Ann, chief financial officer in the House of Venable, tracks our credit purchases. Always has, even before the Target disaster. Nothing is awry at this point, she reports. Whew.

Maybe, knock-on-wood, nothing will be. Just the sheer volume of this purloined information likely means most of us won't be affected. We're all swimming along like a huge school of minnows, hoping dumb statistical luck keeps us from winding up in the belly of a shark.

In my particular, aka threadbare, case I almost want to laugh. The thought that someone halfway around the globe would pay bootleg prices to become me is hilarious.

Just in case it happens, though, here are a few cross-references for anybody tempted to do business with the new Sam Venable:

Check for my appendix operation scar. Ditto the ones from two back surgeries. There's also evidence on my right arm from a nitric acid burn in high school chemistry. In the web between my right index finger and middle finger is a scar from a spurring I took from a wild turkey gobbler that wasn't as dead as I assumed when I picked him up, also another on my left arm from a similar thrashing several years earlier; I am a slower learner in this regard. Ask what condiments I like, and don't like, on hamburgers and hot dogs. See if they know some of the weird middle names in my family. Quiz 'em about the title of the first magazine story I sold nearly half a century ago.

If the new Sam Venable passes all those tests, at least I hope he's a few inches taller and 20 pounds lighter than the fireplug original.

Always look for the silver lining, I say.

One more reason to be wary

First, a disclaimer. The following critique of a new consumer product comes from the same guy who thought social media and grocery store sushi would be flash-in-the-pan fads. You have been warned.

Nonetheless, I'm quite leery of computer-chip implants that allow users to activate computers, dial telephones, start car engines and unlock doors at the wave of their hands.

I'm not pulling your leg or your arm. The technology already exists. It is sure to be refined in the near future.

TO RETIRE? OR NOT TO RETIRE?

Already, a Seattle, Washington, company called Dangerous Things (didn't make that up, either) is selling these gizmos. They're about the size of a grain of rice and are surgically tucked into a fold of skin between the thumb and forefinger, transforming the wearer into a sure-nuff Robert Robot.

No more keys. No more codes. No more passwords to remember—or forget, as the case more accurately may be. Instead, you just wave your hand across a sensor and—presto!—open sesame.

Some of this high-tech gadgetry has marvelous medical potential. Perhaps it could bring life back to withered limbs. Or allow the blind to see. In that regard, I say full speed ahead and don't spare the hosses.

But for everyday use by me and thee? Thanks, but no thanks.

I have enough trouble with the computers, large and small, that rule my life on a daily basis—such as the machine I'm typing on as we speak.

Most of the time, it performs its tasks without complaining. But "most" doesn't cut it any more than a human heart or set of lungs that work "most" of the time.

On those not-infrequent occasions when it does go on the fritz, my world turns into a personal hell.

The machine might freeze up. Or else it abruptly shuts down. Or else it suffers from any of 10,001 digitized ailments that, in geek speak, means it has a migraine or the runs or the pukes. Or all three.

This condition is frustrating enough when I can tickle keys or push buttons. Imagine the angst if my only recourse is to keep waving my hands over and over, eliciting no more response than what happens in a public restroom when you're trying to activate one of those stupid "motion" paper towel dispensers.

Speaking of which: Why, pray tell, do different brands of towel dispensers have sensors in different places? On some, you wave in front. On some, you wave in back. You wind up standing there, dripping all over the floor and your pants, moving your hands around like the Village People singing "Y.M.C.A."

Trust me. If God didn't want us to use our hands the old-fashioned way, He wouldn't have given us middle fingers.

Trying to unlock a mystery

Unlike the chorus of a 1971 pop song by "Melanie," I have neither a brand new pair of roller skates nor a brand new key.

I do, however, have old keys. By the multiplied bunches. With such a mass of metal, I'd surely qualify for the Janitorial-Night Watchman Hall of Fame.

I know this for a fact because I just walked in from the garage. There, I gathered 13 individual key rings that were dangling from nails on a shelf support post.

They contained a total of 45 keys. I counted them twice, just to make sure.

In the console of my truck, I found yet another key ring. It held five. Plus a single key attached to no ring whatsoever.

It all adds up to the grand sum of 51 keys.

Of those 51, I can immediately and correctly identify the use of six. Repeat, s-i-x.

These are my go-to guys deployed on a frequent basis for various locks and ignition switches in my pickup, camper-top, Mary Ann's car, bass boat and trailer hitch. I know each one in an instant. No guesswork necessary.

Of the remaining 45, I suspect eight or nine could be properly ID'd if tested in rarely used locks in truck, car, boat and around the garage. I didn't take time to experiment, although these keys do look vaguely familiar upon second glance.

Another two or three, I think, went to old newsroom desks, either at the News Sentinel or maybe even back to my days in Chattanooga.

One ring contains two keys. Somewhere along the line, I used a black marker to identify them as "ST" and "OLD," respectively.

I know what "OLD" means—the word definition, you understand—but have no idea which ancient lock was involved. Alas, "ST" is a complete mystery, except it likely is much newer than "OLD."

The others? Beats the heck out of me. You could put a cocked pistol to my head, give me a 1,500-count, and I'd still have no clue.

So why keep them?

What?! Are you daft? As any hoarder will attest, the correct lock may turn up at any given moment!

How would you feel if this situation occurred and you didn't have a key to fit it—even if you didn't know which key it was? Certainly makes sense to me.

I'll tell you what else makes sense: Carrying jingly, jangly, bulging keys is a royal pain. That's why I hang 'em on nails in the garage where they can mature into a state of total uselessness.

This phobia gets worse.

You know that single, ring-less key I mentioned in the fifth paragraph? It goes to my truck ignition. I always carry it solo. By itself. No chain, no fob, no nothing. It's easy to find. Never gets lost.

Don't you know Mr. Freud would've had a field day with data like this?

The few, the proud, the cursed

My computer diva wife says this can't happen. It's nothing more than coincidence, she insists.

Hogwash, say I.

Agreed, Mary Ann knows a thing or three about the digitized devils that have ruled humanity, in offices and in homes, for the past 30-plus years. Also agreed, she is retired from a career in software instruction.

Nonetheless, I'm certain she's wrong about my relationship with computers, which can be summed up in three words: They hate me.

Either that or else I exude a strange pheromone that's deadly to high-tech equipment. No other answer is possible. Period. I've made up my mind and will not be swayed.

How else can you explain why I've become a one-man wrecking ball in the presence of these evil things?

Shortly after my retirement, we had to buy a new computer for the house. Our old one just up and quit, perhaps because I breathed on it the wrong way.

Ever since we got the new one, it has been acting oddly—but only when I'm at the keyboard.

When I'm tickling the keys, our computer turns into Eddie Haskell. It toys with me. Mocks me. Refuses even the most simple of commands, like illuminating the screen or activating the speaker. I'm serious. I can push keys 'til my fingertips go numb. Nothing.

But when I finally summon Mary Ann in frustration, it behaves the same way Eddie did on "Leave It To Beaver" when Mrs. Cleaver entered the room.

"Oh, hi, Mrs. Venable. I was just showing young Samuel here how to turn on the speaker. It's really very easy. See?"

Jerk.

It's not just the computer. It's Mary Ann's smart phone, too. I use this device to run credit cards for book sales. When I can get it to work, that is. Most of the time, it sits in my palm like a stone, resolutely refusing to cooperate.

I brought it home a few days ago and barked, "This $#&! thing is broken!"

Mary Ann swiped the screen once. It flickered to life immediately.

I'm certain I heard Eddie's voice in the background: "Oh, hi, Mrs. Venable. I was just showing young Samuel here about the airplane mode. I tried to tell him it wouldn't accept credit cards this way."

Yet my crowning achievement occurred a few nights ago. Mary Ann was watching a Netflix movie in the loft of our house. I was in the kitchen reading a book. An honest, paper-page book, not Kindle. After a while, I walked upstairs to join her.

So help me, the movie started pixilating. Right-by-gosh-then. It didn't stop until I walked away.

If the federal government wants to purchase my powers to disarm enemy computers, I'm in. But they better make contact via real letter. Email will fail. Guaranteed.

Plagued by more nutty instructions

I was preparing to butter a roll during lunch a few days ago when an odd thing caught my eye.

Instructions. On a pat of butter. I am not kidding.

This tiny rectangle of delicious lipids was sealed in a foil wrapper. On the bottom layer, where the edges of the foil overlapped, were the words "PULL OPEN"—along with an arrow indicating which direction to pull.

I did as instructed.

The flap unfurled, exposing the opposite side of the foil. Sure enough, there was another good ol' "PULL OPEN" and a corresponding arrow.

"Wow!" I thought to myself. "What a brilliant person I must be! All my life I've been opening pats of butter and never once did I have to be told how!"

Then a frightening thought occurred.

"Yikes! What if I hadn't paid any attention to the instructions? What if I had opened the foil top-to-bottom instead of side-to-side? Would the butter police come rushing into this restaurant, whisks pulled and ready for action? What sort of jail sentence do butter law violators face?"

Maybe instructions like these have been printed on butter packs since long before Mrs. O'Leary's milk cow kicked over that lantern. If so, I've never noticed them. Still, I couldn't help coming away from an otherwise pleasant meal with the discomforting notion that Americans have been dumbed-down once again.

This is somewhat like those little packets of moisture-absorbing crystals that come inside medicine bottles. The ones that say "DO NOT EAT."

At least that's vaguely understandable because people are, in fact, consuming the remainder of the medicine bottle's contents. But what about when this same packet shows up in a shoe box along with your new sneakers? That makes about as much sense as a label on the shoelaces stating: "NOT FOR FLOSSING TEETH."

I don't know why these nutty warnings and admonitions bug me so. I realize we have become a nation of "sue-ers," ready to pounce on the faintest hint of a manufacturing error. And this is simply the corporate CYA response.

Still, I have to shake my head in mirth, if not dismay, when I pick up a product that is riddled with stupid instructions. Such as a box of birthday cake candles that clearly states, "PRODUCES FLAME AND HOT WAX."

Then again, some of these lame instructions don't go far enough.

Not long ago, I picked up a three-pack of bath soap. Sure enough, it came with the standard rules: "WET BAR, LATHER, RINSE, REPEAT."

But if somebody is so dense they have to be told how to use soap, why don't the instructions also say, "REMOVE WRAPPER FIRST"?

A dress code mystery has been solved

I have long marveled at acts of defiance over the laws of gravity.

How does a megaton jetliner move through thin air? How does the Leaning Tower of Pisa stay upright? How does Dolly Parton keep those huge—well, you get the idea.

But a much larger mystery involves "gangsta" pants worn by certain young men. Yes, those XXXL shorts that look like chest waders gone bad. The ones that reveal approximately 54 square yards of underwear material and dangle precariously above high-topped tennis shoes.

Every time I see a kid wearing an outfit like that, two thoughts immediately cross my mind.

1. Thank you, Lord, for not allowing such a hideous style to come into vogue when I was young and impressionable.

2. How do those crazy things stay up?

Concerning Number One: I understand the youthful need to be cool, especially in matters of attire. What's more, I understand the youthful need to express your own individuality by dressing exactly like 50,000 of your closest and dearest friends.

Doesn't matter if we're talkin' baggy shorts or skinny blue jeans so tight they cut off circulation to the lower extremities. Kids are going to wear what's hip, no matter what.

Kids nothing. Adults are just as susceptible to sartorial insanity. Do the words "leisure suit" ring a bell? I rest my case.

But the answer to Number Two has always stumped me. Until a few days ago, that is. Now, I have seen the light! More importantly, I have seen the suspenders.

Yes. Suspenders. Just like old men wear. Except these aren't your everyday geezer keeper-uppers. They're smaller and intended to stay hidden.

This revelation came to me in Sweetwater, Tennessee, while attending the National Muscadine Festival. Among the throngs milling through downtown, swilling fresh "muskydine" juice and eating funnel cakes, were several exceedingly cool teenagers dressed fit to kill.

Between ear rings, nose rings and lip rings, there was enough metal on their heads to start a recycling center. But, as usual, what really caught my eye and piqued my curiosity was the gravity-defying position of the voluminous shorts they were wearing.

One of these kids happen to take a longer stride than normal, causing the tail of his shirt to rise. That's when I saw the suspenders. They were attached to the inside of his pants and came from somewhere higher on his torso. His shoulders, I know now.

You see, as soon as I got home and Googled this awesome discovery, I realized gangsta suspenders have been on the teen market for years. Will wonders never cease!

I don't know whether to be thrilled at finally solving this mystery of anti-gravity—or dismayed I'm the last person on Earth to find out.

Bah! Give me buggy whips!

I'm the last person who should be dispensing advice on how to shop. For anything. Not only do I loathe the notion of shopping for any kind of product or service, I have the commercial acumen of a toad.

To make matters worse, I'm not a forward-thinking individual. You know, those people who see trends so far in advance, they have moved on to even newer horizons when the rest of us dullards are just discovering the "old-new" stuff.

Nonetheless, business experts say 3-D shopping is the next big thing. They say we will punch a few computer buttons and immediately "see" ourselves trying on all manner of clothing. Or experimenting with new sporting equipment. Or driving a new car.

I say baloney. As far as Bidnessman Venable is concerned, this 3-D hokum will ultimately prove to be bad for commerce.

Not because it won't work. Oh, it'll work all right. If it doesn't exist already, the technology will soon be available for John Q. Smith to "see" himself wearing new clothes. Or teeing off with a new driver. Or snoozing on a new mattress.

That's the problem. It'll work too well.

We, meaning thee, me and John Q. Smith, will be "seeing" ourselves as others see us. Not as we see ourselves.

And therein lies a huge, bankrupting rub. Nobody, including thee, me and John Q. Smith, wishes to endure such embarrassment.

Right now, I can look at a handsome, rugged, slim-waisted model in a men's clothing catalog and think, "Wow! I'd look good in that sport coat, too!"

That's Falsehood Number One, oldest trick in the marketing book.

I can even go so far as to try on the same sport coat in a men's clothing store and stare at myself in the mirror.

That's Falsehood Number Two—second-oldest trick because what we see isn't real. We're still imagining.

Not until we have plunked down serious coin for the sport coat, worn it in public and then caught an unrehearsed glimpse of ourselves in the reflection of a glass door do we (1) see the truth, the whole truth and nothing but the truth and (2) internally scream, "Aaak! Who is that walrus wearing such a hideous sport coat?"

By that time, of course, the store has our cash and we have yet another item of clothing to hide in the closet or give to Goodwill.

Not so with 3-D. We'll go straight from the "Wow! I'd look good in that sport coat" stage to the "Aaak! Who's that walrus?" stage. Thus, no sale.

Take it from Bidnessman Venable: This nutty 3-D fad will tank faster than iPhones.

Goose-quill pen not required

Bless you, Kristen Walraven.

Ms. Walraven is a teacher in Pekin, Illinois. She has launched a Saturday program for preschoolers and first- and second-graders. It is called "The Mighty Mighty Writing Club." Her goal is to teach youngsters the basics of writing fluency. As in pencil on good ol' dead-wood paper.

I learned about her work from a Pekin Daily Times story by Elise Zwicky, which had been picked up by the Associated Press. As my ancient eyes crept from paragraph to paragraph, I was tempted to pump a palsied fist into the air and wheeze, "Yes!"

Wait. Before you accuse Ms. Walraven and Old Man Venable of being Luddites when it comes to written communication, the answer is a resounding "no."

Based on what I understand about her program, she is not taking students back to the 1950s, where they will struggle with a No. 2 pencil and lined notepaper to copy the A-B-C-D cursive chart posted above the blackboard. In fact, she's not even emphasizing cursive at all, unless parents want her to.

What she is doing is teaching students to express themselves beyond the "lol" and "omg!" textspeak of the era in which we live. As she pointed out in the article: "I taught for seven years in an elementary school setting, and I observed that students in kindergarten, first and second grade who really struggled with writing fluency also struggled in lots of other subject areas.

"I don't really have a problem with print or cursive, although I know some people think cursive is a dying art form. I find that the majority of kids print. Cursive is a much faster way to write, so I try to promote it for some of the (older) kids who really struggle to copy notes from the smart board or take notes during lectures—but it's like starting from square one to teach some of them how to write in cursive."

To reiterate: I realize that the abbreviated communications used in texting, instant messaging and others of their social-media ilk simplify and speed up the process of relaying thoughts from Trey to Seth, Celeste to Susan. Furthermore, I realize when something simpler and faster comes down the pike, it will be adopted by the masses. That's the way humanity progress.

But it is comforting to know the basics are still important. It's like making sure students know how to add, subtract, multiply and divide the old-fashioned way before they're permitted to start punching a pocket calculator.

Who knows? Maybe if this "writing fluency" fad catches on, it will prevent future generations of Homo sapiens from developing thumbs the size of turkey drumsticks. What a novel concept.

New look at old games people play

This is par for the course, the story of my geezerly life: A list of "Top 10 Summer Aphrodisiacs" has just come out, and hardly anything on it registers with me or my wife.

I was alerted to this racy news in an email from Brook Urick, public relations manager for an online travel dating site called MissTravel.com.

"Between the scantily clad and exotic destinations, summer is absolutely the sexiest season," she began.

Right off the bat, I could tell Brook and I had different seasonal-sexual opinions. I find nothing whatsoever romantic about hot, humid, sticky, sweaty weather. These people never heard of spring or fall? But I continued to read nonetheless.

"Planning a romantic tryst isn't the only way to ignite passion during these sultry months," Brook wrote. "I'm talking about aphrodisiacs."

She went on to say that 22,000 MissTravel members had been polled about the matter, and here's how they responded.

For women, in order from first to tenth: Champagne, exotic accents, burning candles, artisan doughnuts, spontaneity, cashews, musky scents, frozen treats, yellowtail sashimi and infused water.

For men, also in order, first to tenth: String bikinis, green juices, honey whiskey, beach wave hair, freshly baked blueberry pie, minimal makeup, tonka bean perfumes, fireworks, bacon.

I ran the women's list by Mary Ann. She answered just about like I figured she would.

"Champagne is fine, and so are cashews—but certainly not together! If I smelled a burning candle, I'd think the house was on fire and would grab some water, infused or otherwise, to extinguish it. What's more, the very thought of musky scents and raw fish make me want to throw up; the only doughnuts I'm familiar with come from Krispy Kreme; and the only 'exotic accent' I've ever heard from you is Southern Appalacheze."

Hmm. Definitely not good odds for whoopee.

As for me, bikinis, blueberry pie and bacon are right on the money. But most everything else in between? Yuck. I might as well hop into the shower and turn on the cold water full blast.

Green juice—like what squirts out of a caterpillar when you step on it?

Honey whiskey—the stuff you sip to help fight a terrible cold?

Tonka whatever—isn't that a kid's truck?

There's nothing wrong with fireworks, of course. The louder the better. Let 'em roar! That way, when I ask Mary Ann at bedtime if she wants to sleep or what—and she hollers back through the din, "What?"—I'll know I'm already partway to first base.

Here's the ultimate in redundancy

Some of the funniest reading I've enjoyed lately has nothing to do with the funny pages, joke books, humor magazines or my favorite go-to for hilarity—politics.

Instead, it's the "readable voice mails" my computer spits out.

I don't know how this started. Could be one of the "customer services" my computer-geek wife recently activated. All I know is every now and then my computer says it has captured the visual version of a voice message on my phone.

Such redundancy is like wearing suspenders with a belt. Why my computer thinks I need a duplicate of recorded telephone messages is beyond me. But mine is not to wonder why.

What's so side-splitting, though, is the marked difference between words spoken over the phone and words printed on paper. We're talking alpha-versus-omega to the 100th power.

If you think I'm making this up, please look over my shoulder as I attempt to decipher the "readable voice mail" my computer recently regurgitated. I type directly off the page, including all the incorrect punctuation and grammar, not to mention total lack of sense:

"Hey Sam john (?) time open this morning in regards to your son (?) Justin. Hey I just wanna tell you a couple of things most importantly I seen where you purchase it to your wallet in position (?) although I'd still get the furniture (?) in the last few days so she checks to pods (?) you're probably got some birds around ball bowling lanes and the other thing is pastor-it's (?) your last call of the white board did not expect to hear from you. He asked about you a lot. So okay. I'll see ya."

You are free to dig furrows in your scalp, the same as I did when the printed message appeared.

I'd already killed the audio by the time the printed version showed up. So I can't tell you what was spoken, word-for-word. But here's the gist of it: A friend had called to report good trout fishing on the Holston River; he also saw several flocks of ducks. I swear on a stack of Bibles. How that equates to "I'd still get the furniture" is well above my pay grade. Maybe Justin, the son I never had, might know.

Some of my other "readable voice mails" aren't quite as convoluted. But they're funny nonetheless. Such as (again verbatim): "Hey call Warren. It's about her (?) was returning your call."

That was from one of my former News Sentinel colleagues. She was returning my earlier call. Neither she, nor I, mentioned anybody named Warren.

Mary Ann, the aforementioned computer-geek wife, says such gobbledygook can be minimized if the software is "trained" to recognize words and phrases of individual callers.

What? And spoil this fun? Absolutely not!

Never know when I'll get the urge to "purchase it to your wallet in position" again. Maybe I'll just put it on Justin's tab.

Scouting was tougher 'Way Back When'

It's gotta be easier than ever to be a Boy Scout these days, for a variety of reasons.

First, there aren't as many little old ladies to walk across the street.

When I was a kid, helpless little old ladies—old men, too—were everywhere. Any time you approached a street corner, there was always some she- or he-geezer standing there, chewing her/his gums and mumbling about the dangers of navigating sporadic traffic moving at the breakneck speed of 14 mph.

These days, street corners have been replaced by interstate entrances and exits. And there are no geezers, she or he, needing assistance.

Instead, there are people of my own mature stage in life. Our only concern is exiting or blending into traffic that is moving at the speed of nuclear fission.

Camping equipment is a lot better these days, too.

Back in my Pleistocene scouting era, we had to limp along with World War II surplus gear handed down from our ex-GI dads.

I'm talking canvas backpacks that weighed 85 pounds empty. Stiff, ill-fitting leather boots and musty tents that were respectively "insulated" and "waterproof" in name only. Dented canteens that imparted a permanently foul taste to the water and likely galvanized our internal organs from metal ingestion.

Today, all Dad has to do is walk into any full-line sporting goods emporium, plunk down his credit card and outfit Junior with $4,500 worth of form-fitting, lightweight, day-glow, tough-as-nails synthetic boots and rain suits Junior will outgrow in eight months.

But by far, the greatest advantage for today's Scouts is fire-making.

When I was a teen, our greatest challenge was generating a roaring blaze—on which we could scorch a yummy can of ancient C-ration mystery meat—by rubbing two sticks together.

This was a cinch, of course, provided one of them was a thick, wooden, strike-anywhere kitchen match, a box of which had been secreted into the confines of that 85-pound backpack. As we young Scouts grew, so did our ability to make fire magically erupt in piles of green wood, thanks in no small part to the discovery of charcoal lighter fluid.

But those innovations can't hold a flame, literally, to what's available today.

I speak of the Bison Airlighter, "a cordless fire-starting machine that jets out a four-inch butane flame and constant stream of blowing air."

For a mere $80, plus $20 for a three-pack of butane refills, Junior can produce a campfire at the snap of his fingers "instead of hovering over a pile of kindling and twigs and gently blowing."

And just think how yummy those scorched $50 freeze-dried meals will taste!

Staying 'a head' of all the others

Oh, what cruel fate our daughter suffered as an infant! When she came into this world on June 4, 1974, Megan had blond hair—and I'm not necessarily speaking of color. Instead, I'm talking about amount.

Hair. As in one.

OK, maybe that's a bit of an exaggeration. Megan did have a tiny tuft of golden fuzz atop her noggin. It was barely visible if you turned her head just so and the lighting was at the proper angle. However, every time she was bathed and those little "hairettes" matted down, she looked balder than the proverbial cue ball.

This was quite a change from her brother, born one year earlier. Clay arrived with a thick, dark head of hair. Wet or dry, his carpet was always on display.

Time has a way of taking care of these things as infants grow into toddlers, then young children, then teens, then adults. Megan's hair filled out just like it was supposed to do. It's as blond as ever. Clay's thick hair still is dark but seems to be following the follicle path charted by his father. It now is streaked with salt and pepper.

The reason I bring up this nugget of family history is to underscore the backward, uncivilized era in which our two kids were born.

If Megan had arrived now instead of 1974—and if her parents had forked over $29.95, plus shipping and handling—she could be sporting a flowing mane any Hollywood starlet would envy.

That's what you get with "Baby Bangs, the first and only ready-to-wear hairstyle headbands ever made."

Yes. We are talking wigs. For baby girls. I swear on a case of Garnier fructis shampoo I'm not making this up.

This isn't replacement hair for a child undergoing the trauma of chemotherapy. Or one whose hair, for medical reasons, refuses to develop properly. Instead, this is fake hair for infants whose parents are too impatient—dare I say vain?—to let Little Precious be seen in public without glowing, luxurious locks.

I have just downloaded a bunch of images from the manufacturer. It offers hairstyles in five distinct patterns. Color options range from blond to natural brown, medium brown, light brown, golden auburn and natural black.

Actually, using the adjective "natural" in this context is a bit of a stretch because these wigs are made of "monofiber Kanekalon, the most realistic man-made hair fiber available." But why fret over details?

Oh, well. Far be it from me to tell today's parents not to rush their infant girls into adulthood. If they also want to sign them up for Dallas Cowboy cheerleader camp, have at it. Might as well fit 'em for a wedding ring, too.

A win-win solution for our woes

A recent off-the-cuff remark by reader Katherine Thompson set my mind whirring and my fiendish laugh cackling.

Katherine, who lives in Lenoir City, called to complain about a pricey, yet defective, propane grill.

"Five years ago, I paid $700 for that thing," she sighed. "If I knew then what I know now, I would've just bought seven $100 grills. I know I would have come out better."

The main problem, she explained, is overall lack of quality.

"It's simply not well-built, even though it's a famous brand anybody would recognize." (Katherine named it for me; I concur.)

"Since Day One, it has been a huge disappointment. It rusts terribly. I have replaced three burners and two racks. Plus the gas regulator is shot. I had someone fix it, and it worked fine. Two days later, I put on a steak and tried to fire it up. Nothing."

We've all been there, of course. It's a wonder three-fourths of Americans aren't bald because of the hanks of hair yanked out in frustration over gizmos eternally on the fritz.

"What I ought to do is drag it out to the road, chain a sledgehammer to it and charge people $1 to take a whack at it—you know, like they used to do with old cars at the county fair."

"Miss Katherine," I abruptly exclaimed, "you are a genius! Why haven't I thought about this before?

"The 'new and improved' software system the News Sentinel installed shortly before I retired worked as poorly as your grill. It crashed. It hung up. It refused to print. In fact, if the process got any slower, I proposed we go back to Gutenberg and start over.

"Let me know when you drag your grill to the curb, and I'll drive to the office and grab my computer. I haven't been this excited in years!"

I tease, of course, about toting my "new and improved" computer to Lenoir City for demented demolition. It would be much more satisfying to haul everything to the Grand Canyon and give it the ol' heave-ho.

But seriously, why hasn't a business been created for this type of venting? I'll guarantee it would rake in $100 million the first month of operation.

You name the device—phones, TVs, refrigerators, washing machines, dryers, computers, car batteries, lawn mowers, electric razors, sporting equipment, ad infinitum—and I'll guarantee there are vast legions of people who'll vouch their "new and improved" items are little more than high-dollar pieces of (stinky stuff).

I say stack 'em and whack 'em. At $1 per swing, we could erase the national debt in no time.

I'm not a seasoned traveler. Compared to the footloose crowd, I'm only slightly more mobile than a tree. I've got friends who gad about more in any given year than I will in a lifetime.

On business or for pleasure, though, I've trod three continents; logged tens of thousands of miles via car, bus, boat, train and plane; spent nights in sleeping bags, flea-bag outposts, mom-and-pop motels and ritzy hotels; and taken my meals from tin cans, paper plates and fine china.

Yet home is where I hang my hat. Most of my journeys are short. And I've been around enough to form two principles of travel.

These are the Missing Ingredient Theory (MIT), and the Minus One Theory (MOT).

MIT means you won't pack a certain "this" or "that." Guaranteed. Invariably, it will be something necessary for the success of the trip.

MOT means you'll never find what you're looking for in your luggage.

I call it "minus one" because one item will always stay hidden. If you're probing through your shaving kit for a toothbrush and toothpaste, you will find one, not both. The only time the toothbrush and toothpaste will surface simultaneously is when you're searching for a hairbrush—meaning the toothbrush is destined for double duty, and your hair will smell like Crest.

I'd like to elaborate further, but I can't find my notes.

Chapter Five
TRAVELS NEAR AND FAR

A much more plausible explanation

WHITETOP, Virginia—Given the recurring dispute along Tennessee's southern border, it was no great no surprise to discover a similar situation on the northern side of the state.

Except this isn't a dispute in the literal sense of the word. There is no quarreling, no verbal jousting between politicians, no threat of lawsuits. Instead, everybody raises a glass and enjoys a hearty laugh.

You're aware of the Georgia-Tennessee feud, of course. It's been simmering for two centuries. Has to do with water. Georgia claims the original survey determining the boundary between it and Tennessee should have followed the 35th parallel, not dipped slightly below that mark.

This was not a huge deal in 1818. But by the dawn of the 21st century, it had billowed exponentially.

If the line follows the path Georgia insists upon is correct, the border would nick the Tennessee River—and now give parched Atlanta an abundant source of water. Tennessee, naturally, says Georgia is all wet.

The controversy continues to be argued in legislative halls of both states. Up along the Tennessee-Virginia line, however, the debate—if you can even call it that—is far more amicable.

That's what I discovered while bicycling the Virginia Creeper Trail.

This 34-mile route between Whitetop and Abingdon follows the path of an abandoned rail bed. It's a glorious ride, especially the 17-mile leg (all downhill, yesss!) between Whitetop and Damascus. For the moment, though, let us concentrate on a tiny piece of real estate at the northeastern-most corner of Tennessee.

This is aptly called "The Offset," because it veers slightly from the rest of the border.

Why? According to one official trail marker, the original survey line in 1749 followed a latitude of 36 degrees, 30 minutes.

The trail marker goes on: "In 1779, the boundary line was continued, but a discrepancy occurred and a correction was made to bring the boundary to the former line. The land in this area of discrepancy was called 'The Offset'."

How did this discrepancy come about?

According to the marker, legend says the survey crew learned about a whiskey still in the area and took off in search of liquor, "carrying their survey chains with them. After enjoying the fruits of the mountains, they continued running the survey line due west, through about two miles to the north."

I'll drink to that theory any day.

And who knows? Maybe that's what happened on the 1818 Georgia survey, too.

In shadow of 9/11, friends meet again

NEW YORK—Harry Goody and I finally came full circle.

This occurred when I stood at the 9/11 Memorial and slowly ran my fingertips across his name, etched into Panel S48 of the beautiful, yet sobering, waterfall monument.

Most people's eyes well with tears when they visit this horrible/hallowed site. Mine were no exception.

Harry was among the estimated 2,735 World Trade Center employees who perished in the terrorist attacks of September 11, 2001. He was 50, married with three children, and worked for the New York state tax and finance office on the 86th floor of Tower Two.

Like so many others on that cool, blue-skied September morning, he merely was doing his job, minding his own business. Then his life ended during hell on Earth, the worst day in modern American history.

I never knew Harry personally. Yet he has been my soul brother and traveling companion for years. It happened like this:

The tenth anniversary of 9/11 fell on a Sunday. At our church that morning, parishioners were asked to select a name from the victims list, write it on an armband via Sharpie pen and wear it several days in reflective tribute.

I picked Harry Goody for two reasons. "Harry" is the first name of my friend and former editor, Harry Moskos. "Goody!" was a favorite expression of my late mother-in-law, Opal Steinhoff.

As I discovered via Internet, he and I shared several things in common.

Harry had an interest in the outdoors. He owned a mountain bike and often rode it through the "wilderness" of Central Park. What's more, his nickname was "Chucky"—close to the "Chuck" I'm called by a handful of longtime hunting and fishing buddies.

As it turned out, the band was too tight for my wrist. So I wrapped it around my walking stick. It remains there to this day.

Together, Harry and I have hiked hundreds of miles of trails through East Tennessee. He has accompanied me numerous times on overnight treks to the summit of Mount LeConte in the Smokies.

Now here I stood, after an exciting, albeit exhausting, day of touring the Big Apple—Central Park, the Statue of Liberty, the High Line, Trinity Church and other iconic destinations in this dynamic city.

For the first time since 9/11, I was back on Harry's home turf, staring at his name and thousands of others who were killed in the insanity of perverted religious fervor. It was at that very moment a poignant thought struck, ever-so-emotionally.

I had shown East Tennessee to Harry. Now, he had returned the favor.

Thank you, my dear old friend. God bless you and all the others who died so senselessly.

Torturous ride for a great view

NIAGARA FALLS, New York—On October 4, 1901, schoolteacher Annie Taylor made daredevil history by becoming the first person to survive a barrel ride over Niagara Falls. According to legend, the first words she uttered when extracted, bloodied and bruised, from her crude vessel were, "No one should ever attempt this again!"

I'll go Miss Annie one better. No one should ever attempt visiting Niagara Falls via Amtrak.

Come by car instead. Or bus. Or airplane. For Pete's sake, take Pony Express, Conestoga wagon or pogo stick.

My wife and I speak as numb-bun veterans. We rode Amtrak from New York City to Niagara Falls, then back the next day. We could've hitchhiked faster.

TO RETIRE? OR NOT TO RETIRE?

Average driving time for this span is eight hours, depending on traffic and bathroom/fuel/food stops. It took us 15 hours—each way. No joke.

This was at the start of a 12-day journey into the Northeast, mostly by rail. Fortunately, we got our nightmare over with early on. In so doing, we learned an important lesson about Amtrak travel in this part of the country.

East-west "schedules" (insert laugh here) are mere suggestions. They are subject to frequent, lengthy delays. If any timepiece is used for calibration, it most assuredly is a sundial.

North-south routes, on the other hand, operate with Swiss-watch precision. The difference between the two is mind-boggling. We're talking a rusty tricycle versus a $40,000 Harley.

Why? Turns out the east-west tracks are owned by CSX. Its freight trains have priority over passenger cars. Thus, a 120-mph "people train" can be, and often is, sidetracked until 40-mph freight cars chug past. In addition, CSX crews spend each summer repairing sections of track. Stops of 35-45 minutes are constant.

I don't know the ownership of north-south tracks. But, as one Amtrak employee confided to me, most run to and from Washington. Politicians ride them. You do the math.

"If a train runs two minutes late," he said with a grin, "the phones start ringing."

Ah, yes. Makes perfect sense now.

Train woes notwithstanding, we wouldn't have missed Niagara Falls for anything. It was as spectacular as anticipated, certainly matching its ranking among the seven great natural wonders of the world.

We were lucky to catch it on a blue-sky day. The roar of tumbling water was deafening. The mist and wind were like Clingmans Dome in late autumn.

We hiked all over the U.S. side, gasping and snapping photos every step. Then we walked across the bridge into Canada (passports required) and savored an even better view. Gorgeous!

But just like Miss Annie, we don't need to do it again.

A whole different level

INNSBRUCK, Austria—Never let it be said that these people don't have a sense of humor, sadistic or otherwise.

At the base of the Bergisel Olympic ski jump stadium sits stately, flower-decorated Wilten Cemetery, still accepting bodies after more than 500 years. It is the last thing skiers see as they shove off the 164-foot-high tower and go sailing into the void.

"When Pope John Paul visited Innsbruck in 1988," one of the locals told me, "he said, 'Not even with God's help would I go off of that jump.' And he was a skier!"

As is dang-near everyone else. The University of Innsbruck has a medical center in this town. During winter, doctors set an average of 45-60 broken bones every weekend. Said the same local: "Most of (the victims) think they know (skiing) better than anyone else. They are too wild."

Nonetheless, skiing is a way of life in the Alps. Children here first learn to crawl, then walk, then ski. By 4, they can out-ski most tourists ten times their age.

Indeed, outdoor sports rule. Besides skiing, there is fishing for trout ("forelle," best I could decipher) plus hunting for deer, bear and boar from wooden stands that dot the edge of many fields and forests.

You don't just plunk down a few dollars for a license and hit the woods. First, there are stringent tests to make certain you are proficient, accurate and responsible. What's more, one Swiss sporting goods dealer told me, a basic license runs $800-$1,000. Per year. And you thought hunting was expensive in Tennessee?

Another popular outdoor sport is—be still my fluttering heart—hang-gliding. Numerous times I watched hang-gliders launch themselves off mountain crests in the Alps. We're talking leaps of silk-winged faith across thousands of feet of empty air.

Call me wimp. Call me wuss. Call me Chicken Little. I happily concur. There has never been enough beer brewed, nor whiskey distilled, nor a John Ruskin joint ever rolled that would entice me to do something completely stupid as that.

Still, I gotta hand it to the people of Western Europe. They are as physically fit as any humans I've ever encountered. They have the, uh, "aromatic essence" to prove it, too. Underarm deodorant isn't a high priority item. If you, whew, catch my drift. Or theirs.

Big deal. These people continually work out—again, as a way of life. And they don't drive to a health and fitness center to do it.

Instead, they walk. Everywhere.

They walk to school. They walk to the office. They walk to church. They walk to the store—and carry bags for their purchases.

Or else they ride a bicycle.

You don't know the number of suited banker-insurance-business types I've seen pedaling to and from their jobs. Nor the 70- and 80-somethings on Swiss and Austrian sidewalks, calmly rolling a bike through the crowd until there is enough room to mount and pedal away. Instead of vast acres of paved parking lots for cars, they have 100-foot spans allocated to locked bicycles. Trust your Uncle Schwinn: There are footpaths and bikeways along city streets and country lanes throughout this land. It is nothing to see someone(s) walking or bicycling down a country path, miles from civilization.

Some of this activity may have economic roots. If gasoline routinely sold for $7-8 per gallon in the United States, as it does overseas, perhaps John and Jane from Johnson City wouldn't drive that often, either.

Not-so-ironically, these people eat heartily. Dishes of pork, beef, veal, eggs and cheese are included on most menus. Often the meat is pounded, coated with rich seasoning and fried as a "schnitzel" in one form or another. I suspect they ingest more alcohol than your average American. Also, many use tobacco. When was the last time you saw ash trays on restaurant tables in the U.S.?

But they walk-walk-walk and bike-bike-bike as normally as you or I would casually climb into the front seat of a car and turn the ignition key. Rarely did I see a Swiss or Austrian resident running strictly for exercise.

All of which means that when they wind up in the boneyard—Wilten Cemetery, if not somewhere else—it's probably due to sure-nuff old age. Not an early stroke or heart attack triggered by obesity.

Locked in love

SALZBURG, Austria—As visual-water pollution goes, it's rather tame. You can see it on virtually any bridge in this storied musical city.

We're talking padlocks. By the hundreds, perhaps thousands. Each secured to the chain-link grid.

"Young couples put them here to show their love for each other," our local guide explained as we trekked across the Markat Bridge one drizzly morning.

"They ceremoniously toss the keys into the river below to make certain the lock will never be re-opened. At one time, city officials removed them with bolt cutters, but it has grown into such a tourist attraction they have been allowed to stay."

On closer inspection, I noticed that among the sea of key-operated devices dangling from chain-link was the occasional combination lock. I just had to ask: "Does this mean it's an iffy relationship, like maybe one member of the twosome might slip back and remove it on the sly? Or maybe it's the memento of a quickie?"

"Could be," our host replied with a laugh. "Your guess is as good as mine."

My note pad bristles with tidbits of local lore like that. Such is the benefit of taking a guided trip to the Swiss-Austrian region rather than do-it-yourself. I've visited Europe both ways and can attest to the advantages and disadvantages of each.

In 2006, I accompanied my wife, sister and brother-in-law to Germany. We went strictly solo, relying on my sister's substantial pre-journey research, as well as hints from German friends.

You're on no set schedule this way. Plenty of time to select individual sites and explore them to the fullest.

Conversely, on a guided trip, the schedule is much tighter, more rigid. You go with the flow on a predetermined format.

Yes, this does limit your exposure to opportunities you'd prefer to study in greater detail. But such a drawback is more than offset by (a) the travel agency's vast inventory of points of interest, (b) the encyclopedic information and historical context available from seasoned guides, and (c) the fact someone else is driving.

TO RETIRE? OR NOT TO RETIRE?

Trust one who speaks as an auto-accident veteran of Scotland's narrow roadways, circa 2003. It's sooo much nicer to climb aboard a chartered coach and look at scenery instead of trying to decipher confusing road signs and dodge motorcycles zipping through traffic.

No matter how you choose to visit this part of the world, though, it's a lot like German beer: there ain't no bad.

I could have spent the entirety of our 10 days strictly in the Alps. I've seen them frigid and snow-covered, also rocky and barren in the heat of summer. Regardless, their stark beauty and wildness never fails to gladden my soul.

Growing up in the shadow of the Great Smokies, one is lulled into believing no other mountain vistas can compare. Not so. For all its splendor, the hill country of my beloved homeland pales in comparison not only with the Alps but the Rockies of the western U.S. as well.

Just ascending these sharp-edged peaks via cog-train, tram or gondola is a treat.

The lowland valleys, lush with abundant crops of wheat, corn and hay, slowly give way to alpine meadows dancing in wildflowers and tinkling with cow bells. One expects Julie Andrews to burst onto the scene at any moment, filling the crisp, clean air with orchestrated sounds of music.

As meadows yield to forest, one cannot help but notice—and sigh with envy—that the spruce-fir canopy is dense, lush and green, not browned by the swarms of adelgids that have withered coniferous woodlands in the Smokies.

There was plenty to see and do down below, of course. Even a bluegrass fan like yours truly enjoyed the many Mozart highlights of Salzburg. I chuckled aloud at numerous "human statues" posing for tips in the square that features a bronze of the famous composer.

Speaking of music: At Dom St. Jakob in Innsbruck, we were fortunate to drop in during a rehearsal on the church's 4,000-pipe organ. If you can't get religion in a setting like there, there's no hope. Several dabbed moist eyes.

For sure, we were your typical goober American tourists, lunching on high-fat "krainer" sausages from open-air carts and snacking on lush strawberries from farmers' markets. What's more:

• A yodeling, slap-dancing, "Ricola-pipe" folklore show we attended in Innsbruck surely was the Austrian version of the "Grand Ole Opry."

- We snapped dozens of photos at gorgeous floral displays on house porches and city streets alike.
- A publication touting "Vol Beat" temporarily caught my eye—until I opened it and realized that's the name of a heavy-metal band from Denmark. What do you bet they don't even play "Rocky Top"? But at least we had advance warning that the most-photographed "sculpture" in Innsbruck is not artwork at all; it's merely a series of stainless steel vents for the underground parking garage.
- Speaking of that curious species Tourium stupidii, I'm happy to report that none in our party committed the unpardonable sin like a visitor to Lucerne did in 1993. He/she tossed a cigarette from the "Kapellbrucke" bridge, built during the 1300s. The smoldering butt landed on an anchored boat below, setting it on fire. Flames quickly licked upward, turning the historic structure into an inferno.

I thought about that incident when I saw signs in Bern, Switzerland, appearing to warn of piranhas in the River Aare winding through town.

Huh? Piranhas in a frigid waterway swollen with snow melt?

Not quite. Thanks to a local who translated, these messages pointed out there are no piranhas in the Aare, just places where submerged rocks make diving hazardous. Still, I couldn't help but think the same type of signs would ward off jerks, local or otherwise, who befoul Smoky Mountain waters. In that vein, maybe even a few piranhas would help!

Two other notions crossed my mind while in Europe.

First, it's oh-so-easy to fork over money when you have no idea how much is leaving your fingertips.

The currency in Switzerland and Liechtenstein is the Swiss franc. In Austria and Germany, only euros are accepted. Since I could never keep up with exchange rates, I simply deployed local cash and my credit card as if they were play money. Much like Congress does.

Also, despite the constant montage of languages filling the air—German to Portuguese, French to Japanese, Spanish to Italian—I realized there is one common oral denominator. In any language, at any venue, the crying of tired, upset, angry children is a universal sound. And the pained, frustrated, embarrassed expression on parents' faces is a universal look.

No translation necessary.

Food for thought while dining

PORTLAND, Maine—Let the record show that your obedient servant unabashedly confesses his lifelong consumption of animals.

He is a meat-eater and a leather-wearer.

He has acquired the aforementioned flesh directly (with rod and gun and prepared, A to Z, by his own hands) and by proxy (with cash and Visa at the supermarket and shoe store).

He intends to continue these practices for the remainder of his time on this orb.

That being said, your obedient servant cannot help but ponder the paradox of lobsters—yes, even as he drags another succulent morsel through drawn butter.

What other animal, wild or domestic, is so subjected to mockery from the time of its acquisition to the moment of its demise?

Whether here on the coast of this gorgeous state, or far removed from the ocean in the midst of, say, Kansas, lobsters spend their final days as condemned prisoners.

They remain on public display. Their claws are banded shut. They huddle in tiny tanks. They are oohed and aahed over by drooling, leering, laughing diners. They meet their fates in scalding steam.

And it's all such fun.

I hold before me a copy of the "Boothbay Region Dining Guide," a 42-page, beautifully produced magazine touting restaurants, resorts and recipes devoted to lobsters. In the middle is a section titled "How to Eat a Lobster." It features a seven-year-old, gap-toothed Maine lass, the epitome of Norman Rockwell cuteness.

Over the course of 11 photographs, she adroitly rips a freshly prepared lobster into edible pieces, using her fingers and metal tools.

Can you possibly imagine the public outcry if:

This were any other animal?

Customers casually picked between live chickens, live cows and live hogs at a restaurant? "That one looks juicy! Wait, is that one fatter?"

The victim was summarily boiled alive?

A slick magazine depicted anyone, let alone a child, happily shredding the meat with bare hands?

Oh, what hypocrites we humans can be when it suits us and our appetites.

Please understand. I offer not one word of this critique as holier-than-thou. I positively love lobster meat and have for years.

While in Maine, I ingested "lobstahs" whole, cut up and served in lobster-roll buns, mixed with mac and cheese—a local dish I could eat three meals a day. Without question, here is one of the finest, sweetest treats ever to pass the lips. If I lived in this state for more than a few days, my already prodigious gut would billow to grotesque proportions.

Nonetheless, honesty does compel me to think about—and cringe at—the overt cruelty of it all.

Cutting edge of the Alps

LUZERN, Switzerland—One should never travel to this beautiful country without carrying or buying a Swiss Army Knife. Or both.

I have owned and used "SAKs" for decades. Not those monstrosities with 26,378 built-in tools. Instead, my favorites are the tiny ones with a blade, tweezers, toothpick and file-screwdriver. Best all-round gadget ever tucked into a blue jeans pocket.

At first glance, you'd think the two SAK makers were adversaries.

Victorinox calls itself "the original Swiss Army Knife." Wenger boasts it is "the genuine Swiss Army Knife." They may have been competitors at one point, but any rivalries today are cosmetic. Victorinox bought Wenger in 2005, meaning both laugh to and from the bank.

By any name, though, there's nothing a SAK can't do. Case in point:

Mary Ann and I took a cog-rail car up a 48-degree alpine slope to the blustery summit of Mount Pilatus. By chance we met Elisa Wharton, who teaches at the University of Michigan. She had a throbbing finger, the recipient of a giant splinter from a wooden fence at one overlook.

No problem. Venob whipped out his aged, yellow-handled SAK (which had traveled to Europe in checked luggage), "sterilized" it with a squirt of Mary Ann's hand cleaner and gave it to Elisa's boyfriend, Roberto Alaino.

He sliced with the blade and successfully probed-plucked with the tweezers, proving (1) a SAK is ideal for impromptu surgery and (2) Elisa has an incredibly high threshold of pain.

I celebrated by purchasing yet another SAK after descending the mountain. Camo handle this time. Be prepared, I say. A man can never own enough SAKs.

Pilatus was one of two peaks we visited, by rail and gondola. Mary Ann and I may be veteran hikers in the "tame" Smokies, but the Alps are towering, rugged real estate. I much prefer to ascend comfortably nestled on my butt.

The other was Mandlspitze, a rocky perch overlooking the enchanting city of Innsbruck, Austria.

Heights don't bother me. But, gulp, when the crest of a mountain is less than 15 yards wide and there ain't nothing on either side but air for thousands of feet, you step very carefully.

There was a small glacier on the back side of the summit. I watched students playing on the steep snow and said a silent prayer nobody slipped and tumbled into the abyss. I'm still praying now that I don't have nightmares.

You need to stand atop the Alps and gaze into eternity to get a feel for how vast they are.

You need a thesaurus to find sufficient adjectives to describe their beauty.

Most of all, you need to make sure your gondola ticket for the trip back down to Innsbruck is safe inside your blue jeans pocket. Right alongside your Swiss Army Knife.

Adventures on Old Man River

HAMILTON, Illinois—I'm cultivating two new experiences here on the mighty Mississippi River, roughly halfway along its 2,320-mile journey from northern Minnesota to the Gulf of Mexico.

One is decoying ducks while flat on my back inside the tiny confines of a bouncing layout boat. The other is eating carp. Lots of carp. Never let it be said this old dog is averse to fresh tricks.

I drove to Illinois to renew acquaintances with East Tennessee friends who'd moved north. All of us are longtime waterfowlers. We spent several wonderful, windblown, barrel-melting sessions decoying mallards, pintails, teal and other puddle ducks in well-brushed blinds amid inland sloughs.

Then we moved to the broad Mississippi itself and further engagements with tens of thousands of diving ducks—mainly scaup, ringnecks, redheads and canvasbacks—that famously file along this ancient course during migration.

Initially we shot from huge box blinds in shallow water off the main channel. Then one night, friends of friends from Michigan showed up. They were towing an armada of boats—everything from deep-draft, mega-horse 20-footers best suited for the Great Lakes, down to the aforementioned layouts. Over brews, brats and the usual "lemme-tell-you-about-the-time" b.s. of a typical hunting camp, we launched a plan to join forces the next morning and attack on all fronts.

"Wait 'til you try layout boat shooting," said one of the Michiganders. "It's duck hunting like you've never experienced down there in the South."

I wasn't certain how to read the faint smile on his lips. Was it hospitable? Or sinister?

The answer, I soon discovered, was a bit of both.

A layout boat is little more than a floating disc of wood and fiberglass. Imagine an aspirin-shaped kayak. It rides atop the waves, anchored fore and aft. The deck—painted gray and streaked with black to imitate the rolling surface of the river—slopes all around so excess water easily slides off. There's just enough room for a shooter to wedge inside, along with shotgun and an abundant supply of shells.

Layouts are the legal version of "sinkbox" blinds from the late 19th and early 20th centuries. As their name implied, sinkboxes created a hole in the water in which the hunter stood. They were surrounded and supported by large flat aprons of wood, onto which hundreds of cast-iron decoys were set to hold everything in place.

Lethal? You better believe it—to ducks and humans alike. Thankfully on both accounts, sinkboxes were outlawed in 1918. Floating layouts have taken their place, particularly on vast open waters of the North where diving ducks predominate.

"Lay" is the key word in this discussion. Once the layout is securely anchored, a hunter is deposited by the "tender boat" and reclines scant inches above the surface. Long strings of decoys are dropped all around. I'm talking multiple hundreds. Then the tender boat motors away, and the action begins.

In half a century of duck hunting, I've occupied untold numbers of brushed blinds built either at lakeside or on poles in shallow water. In both cases, you're positioned above the fray. Not so in this case; you're eye-level with the 'coys. The accompanying perspective of fowl dive-bombing into your spread, right on the deck, is surreal. Takes some getting used to, frankly. It calls for fast swinging and snap shooting, but only after you've quickly risen to a sitting position. (Note to self: Begin intensive daily regimen of sit-ups before next layout boat expedition.)

As exciting and action-packed as the layout experience was, however, I wouldn't want to make a habit of it. Way-yonder too much like work. Between mountains of decoys and tender boats moving back and forth to ferry gunners and retrieve dead and wounded ducks, here is the outdoor version of a Broadway production. Ah, but when in Rome it has no equal!

The same theory applies to eats. I made this discovery at noon one day when our convoy pulled into a mom-and-pop diner. Listed on the menu for lunch and supper was something called "scored carp."

I thought it was a joke.

I thought incorrectly.

In this region of the Midwest, an area heavily populated by the descendants of Europeans, carp are a valued food fish. I am not pulling your leg. Nor am I tricking your taste buds with hackneyed fiction about "planked carp"—where the fish is nailed to a thick plank, heavily seasoned, baked for hours, then tossed into the garbage and the plank eaten. No, indeed.

Said my buddy Bill Allen: "When I first moved here from Maryville (Tennessee) and discovered scored carp, I thought, 'Have these people lost their minds?' Then I tried it. Holy smoke! It's delicious!"

Several factors contribute to this culinary delight.

First, these carp are netted from cleaner waters than you'd typically associate them with. They are iced quickly. Next, they are scaled, not skinned; the hide itself remains intact.

For the last few days, I've marveled as commercial fishermen performed this task at a cleaning table. Zip! A thick-bladed knife, worked against the grain, sends quarter-sized scales flying in all directions. These experts can scale a seven-pound carp in about the same number of strokes you or I need to shave our whiskers. Then massive fillets are carved off both sides of the carcass.

Now comes the all-important "scoring."

Carp have bones running laterally through the meat. These need to be chopped finely. The fillet goes meat-side up on a cutting board. With a sharp knife, parallel slices are made to—but not through—the skin. About every quarter-inch, best I could tell.

There wasn't time to measure precisely because these guys go at it in a blur: chop, chop, chop, chop, much like a chef reducing carrots and celery to tidbits. After that, the entire fillet is coated with a mixture of salt, pepper, flour, cornmeal and whatever secret seasonings are favored by the particular eatery, then deep-fried.

I'm telling you, children; this is scrumptious. I ate scored carp at a variety of diners along the banks of Big Miss'sip and enjoyed every bite. Of course, anything fried is bound to taste delightful. What's more, alcohol was administered frequently. But it was merely an accompaniment to the feasting, not a numbing force to assuage long-held inhibitions.

Ira Smith, a commercial fisherman who plies the river between Hamilton, Illinois, and Keokuk, Iowa, has eaten scored carp most of his life. He sells his catfish but keeps most of the carp for personal consumption.

I watched him at work one afternoon, deftly reducing half a boatload of what East Tennesseans jokingly call "carpus delecti" into slabs of meat destined for hot-grease induction. At one point, I inquired if he thought the sluggish rough fish from our fetid, muddy, shallow waters would "eat good" like the ones he was preparing.

"Sure," he replied with a shrug. "They're carp, aren't they?"

Lotta faith, that Ira.

A lesson in cultural relativity

BERN, Switzerland—Albert Einstein lived at 49 Kramgasse in this capital city from 1903 through 1905. It was here he began developing the theory of relativity. His old apartment is now a tourist attraction.

I don't know physics from 20 cases of Shinola. But I have come to understand the "relativity" of daily life in this part of the world. Specifically, how it differs from America.

Folks here aren't big on air conditioning. Many hotels, offices and shops don't have it at all. No need for it most of the year. But during the occasional heat wave that strikes Western Europe, I don't see how they survive.

TO RETIRE? OR NOT TO RETIRE?

On three days—two when we were in Switzerland, one in Austria—the mercury flirted with 100 degrees F. There was sky-high humidity to boot. But just like we did half a century ago, these people simply grin, sweat and bear it.

Thank heavens our hotel rooms were cooled. Again, "relatively" speaking.

By city law, the AC in hotels throughout Bern automatically shuts off between 8 a.m. and noon. I had to manually reset the thermostat every evening for a puff of cool.

Sure, this is a small, touristy price to pay for visiting such a wonderful, historic, scenic region. And I gotta admit it makes environmental-economic sense. Why do we Americans keep our houses like igloos when nobody's home?

There's something else we could learn from the Europeans: no littering. As in zilch, ixnay, nada.

During a 53-mile bus ride between Bern and the resort city of Gstaad, through both rural and urban settings, I tried to spy a roadside cup, paper or can. One did not exist. Period.

Astounding! Shame on ugly Americans who can't travel 300 yards without tossing something out their car window.

Oddly enough, there aren't that many trash cans in public places. People simply hold onto their refuse until they come across a container. Only then do they pitch.

One morning in bustling, downtown Bern, I saw a teenager pedal his bike all the way across the street and through a parking lot to deposit his empty Red Bull can into a bin. In Tennessee, I'll guarantee that can would have been mindlessly flung the second it was drained.

Oh, there is trash all right. Except here they call it art.

At a municipal park in Montreux, along the shore of Lake Geneva, Mary Ann and I happened upon a manicured, heavily flowered display of "sculpture" crafted from old tires, wheel rims, toilets, tubs and other human offal. It was comically beautiful.

In the center of it all sat the rusting hulk of a bashed junker car, planted inside and out with trees, shrubs and flowers.

Had there been a sprig of kudzu, I might have wept out of homesickness.

Proof Mother Nature can heal herself

IN THE GREAT SMOKIES—If you want to see a living miracle, with emphasis on "living," lace up your boots and hit the Alum Cave Bluff trail.

You need not trek all the way to the summit of Mount LeConte to see what I'm talking about. Not even to Alum Cave Bluff itself.

In fact, you'll only need to hike—easy strolling, by the way—about 1.5 miles, just a few hundred yards above the aptly named, stair-stepped Arch Rock.

Keep going. Cross the footbridge at Styx Branch, walk up and around the bend, and you're there.

See anything unusual?

I didn't think so. That's what makes this so bizarre.

I almost wish the National Park Service would erect a marker at this point in the trail so visitors would notice and understand. The marker could read something like this: "Twenty years ago, the scenic hollow in front of you was a rocky moonscape. It was the picture of death and destruction. No plants, no trees. The air smelled of sulfur."

Yes, indeed. This was the site of monumental devastation wrought by Mom Nature herself.

Late in the afternoon of June 28, 1993, a cloudburst dumped heaven-only-knows how much rain on a small portion of the Huggins Hell watershed up the mountain. It spawned a flash flood that sent a torrent of boulders, giant trees and mud crashing downstream, clearing everything in its path, right down to bedrock.

All of the above is fact. It has been written about several times, by yours truly and other journalists visiting these mountains. Yet if you had told me in 1993 what the place would look like two decades later, I would have replied with a most-skeptical, "Yeah, right."

But, by golly, the repairs are well underway. Not from the hand of humans, either. This is 100-proof homegrown. What Mother Nature taketh away, Mother Nature giveth back.

The once-scoured gulch is now thick with ferns below and birch, cherry and maple above.

True, the trees still are sapling-sized; it will be decades before they join the mature forest high on both sides of the hollow. But the place is lush, green and placid nonetheless. The gentle creek gurgles along as if nothing more ferocious than heavy dew ever fell on this spot. Songbird sonnets fill the air.

At the lower end of this immense slide is a mountain of logs, rocks, mud and limbs approximately 50 feet tall. I know because I saw it with my own eyes shortly after the incident occurred.

It's still there, of course. If you take off walking down the hollow and plow through the brush, you'll find it. But the emergent vegetation is so dense it's now hidden from view.

Not bad for non-government work.

The pain in Spain was quite insane

EDINBURGH, Scotland—Forget Tennessee versus Florida. Forget Auburn versus Alabama. Forget LSU versus Ole Miss. Indeed, forget the fanatical fervor of Southern football in its entirety.

I can issue this dictum because I recently watched an outpouring of athletic nuttiness that puts 'em all to shame.

It was European football, aka soccer, played in Seville, Spain.

This was their version of the Super Bowl. It was pure-T bedlam—and I was 1,200 miles removed from the action. As noisy as it was where I was sitting, I can only assume in-the-flesh witnesses suffered permanent hearing loss.

My venue for the game was Deacon Brodie's Pub on High Street in Edinburgh. For several days, all the newspapers had been hyping this event, and I didn't want to miss it. Neither, apparently, did hundreds of my closest and dearest Scottish friends.

Frankly, I was amazed so many people remained in the United Kingdom for the game. Accounts varied in the newspapers, but suffice to say between 40,000 and 60,000 emigrated to Seville. For a weeknight event, no less. One fan—I hold a copy of the Edinburgh newspaper as proof—even stood up his bride-to-be and 1,500 guests to fly to Spain for the big match. Said Tay Baig of Glasgow: "The wedding can happen again, but I couldn't miss Seville." And we think Vol fans are bonkers.

Inside smoky Deacon Brodie's, throngs turned out to cheer for the home team—Glasgow Celtic, the reigning Scottish champion. Their opponent was Porto, the Portuguese champ.

To repeat: I am clueless about soccer, even though my son and daughter participated in league play as youngsters. But I'm exceedingly familiar with the basics of human survival.

Thus, I realized it was in my best interest in this environment to (a) order multiple rounds from the bar, (b) cheer loudly when the locals cheered and (c) boo raucously and display internationally recognized signs of displeasure when appropriate.

I accomplished all three tasks with vigor.

Alas, it was not to be. Porto scored late in overtime to claim a 3-2 victory and cinch the European title. There was no joy in Scotville. The next day, local papers blared the sad news with catchy headlines like "The Pain in Spain" and "Killa in Sevilla."

But even though my brief European football-watching experience bore scant resemblance to my many years of Southern football-watching experiences, there was a distinct similarity. It was one every follower of University of Tennessee jockdom will understand and appreciate.

This occurred after the game had ended and the unhappy crowd was dispersing. Along with several disconsolate Scotsmen, I was standing near a long metal trough in a small room toward the rear of Deacon Brodie's Pub. We were returning the beer we had rented. The fellow next to me groaned loudly, shook his head slowly and sighed in melodious brogue:

"Aye, lad we'll get them next yarrr, thaaat's f'surrre!"

You just know Tennessee orange blood flows through that guy's veins.

How do you say 'Go Vols' in German?

BADEN-BADEN, Germany—I was standing on a sidewalk, rubbing my eyes in disbelief. If I hadn't known it was 14 hours by jetliner back to Knoxville, I'd have sworn this was Cumberland Avenue on a football game day in October.

You think K-town owns a patent on orange and white gadgetry? Blodsinn! ("Nonsense!")

In matters of the O and the W, Baden-Baden has Knoxville beat by a metric mile. Perhaps we're twin cities, separated at birth. Either way, I've never seen an area, in Tennessee or elsewhere, as consumed by these hues.

"Oh, yes!" confirmed Arianna Bianchet, who runs an ice cream shop in the tourist town near the Germany-France border. "Orange and white are very fashionable colors here."

You said it, sister.

Everywhere you turn, folks could pass for Volunteer faithful. Except this is a style statement. There's no collegiate connection whatsoever.

I'm not talking pale orange or burnt orange, either. I'm talking brilliant University of Tennessee orange that surely falls in the same color spectrum UT protects with legal fervor.

Where do all these products come from? Virtually every retail outlet in town.

I wandered for two hours in the central shopping district and filled nearly three pages of a notebook with orange and white paraphernalia. Among them:

• Clothing of all descriptions for men, women and children, including slacks, skirts, blouses, thong underwear (imagine Phil Fulmer in a pair ... no, on second thought, don't), tank-tops, T-shirts, golf shirts, dress shirts, neckties, caps, hats (one perfectly grotesque headpiece of dyed marabou feathers was priced at $725), visors, sweat suits, sweaters, jackets, vests, swimsuits. "Tom Tailor" was one brand of men's orange and white striped shirt. It even featured a "T" on the shirt pocket. If I'm lyin', I'm dyin'.

• Footwear and related accessories: stack-heeled shoes, running shoes, flip-flops, dress shoes, socks, orange nylon hosiery and orange toenail polish.

• Orange housewares like lamps, pots, pans, sheets, towels, drinking glasses, pitchers, chairs, candles, tablecloths, coasters, flower vases, serving trays—even a soft-boiled egg dish and matching spoon.

• Miscellaneous items: Pocketbooks (one for a mere $420), earrings, watches, watchbands, dog leashes, motorcycle helmets, gift paper, toothbrushes, notebooks, file cabinets, toys, greeting cards, gym bags. And for the smokers on your list, "Reval" and "Ernite 23" brand cigarettes in orange packages. So help me, the shopping carts in "City Wagener," a high-end superstore, even had orange and white plastic handles.

Oh, yes. There was one more unusual trinket I discovered on my search. It was in a specialty store on a narrow street named "Buttenstrass." This was a sex shop featuring all manner of erotic books, videos and adult toys.

I shan't go into detail about the product, other than to note its resemblance to a certain portion of the male anatomy. Suffice to say it gave new meaning to the term Big Orange.

The late Jim Dykes and I used to laugh about Knoxville's unique "column connection."

Technically, Jim and I were competitors. He wrote columns for the Knoxville Journal; I wrote columns for the News Sentinel. Nonetheless, we were longtime friends who shared a special journalistic link: Both of us were former News Sentinel outdoors editors.

Jim held that beat in the late 1960s. I took over when he switched to general news writing in 1970. Jim eventually left the News Sentinel for TVA and started writing his Journal column as a freelancer. About the same time, I moved from the outdoor beat and began cranking out opinion and humor columns for the News Sentinel. I doubt there's a city our size anywhere in the United States where the two competing faces of their respective daily newspapers both honed their skills in the woods and waters.

You are free to interpret any deeper meaning—assuming there is one—to this vocational quirk.

The outdoors is dear to my heart. Always has been, always will be. The most amazing thing is that I received a good salary, plus expenses, to traipse around in the boonies and reduce my thoughts to paper.

Larceny knows no bounds.

Chapter Six
WOODS AND WATERS

A bogus bovine blind

Green-winged teal arrived with the break of day. The diminutive ducks were everywhere. Twisting, turning in wasp-like swarms. To the right, to the left. Peeping, whistling, chattering. I've never witnessed anything like it in East Tennessee.

It was all we—Larry Cook, Britt Farrar and yours truly—could do to keep our shotguns stoked with steel 4s and refrain from laughing aloud about the gear we were deploying.

Most of our stuff was standard fare. We were positioned on the bank of a standard Jefferson County farm pond. The water in front of us was dotted with standard mallard and teal decoys. We were hailing these flocks with standard duck calls.

But our "blinds" were anything but standard.

There was no brush to shield us from avian eyes. No camo netting. No paint. No trees.

Instead, we were sitting behind fake cows. Repeat: bogus bovines.

This idea didn't come from a "Three Stooges" cartoon, although Moe and Curly might've felt right at home. Rather, these cows were designed specifically for hunting.

They're made by what appears to be a geographically-challenged Pennsylvania company, "Montana Decoys, Inc." Most of the time, they're used by archers stalking antelope in the vast open country of western U.S. cattle ranches. They're silk-screened, lightweight and come equipped with a see-through mesh panel, as well as metal tent-stake legs.

Larry ordered one of these $100 gizmos from an outdoor equipment catalog. As soon as I saw it and realized its potential for stalking waterfowl, turkeys and other game on East Tennessee cattle farms, I did likewise. Britt was so impressed he bought two. Our own mini herd, you might say.

Before duck season opened, I put one of these cows to the test. After spotting ducks in a pond on the far side of a wide-open pasture, I began my approach. It took maybe 20 minutes of stop-start, clump-clump walking behind the "beast." (Cows don't move quickly. Nor do I.) The tallest vegetation was fescue at my ankles.

I finally stopped 15 yards from a trio of unsuspecting shovelers. No doubt I could have gotten closer, but a barbed-wire fence blocked my path. Didn't matter. By then I was convinced, not to mention desperately trying to stifle a howl and praying nobody was watching from afar.

How fooled were these wild ducks?

They never stopped feeding when I poked my head above the cow. Indeed, they showed scant interest when I stepped from behind the panel and into plain view. Wearing jeans and a T-shirt, no less. Not until I clapped my hands and shouted did they leap from the water. I stood there, slowly shaking my head in awe, as they beat a hasty retreat into the sky.

A few days later, I shared the results of my experiment with Robert Roche, a longtime outdoor friend who frequently travels west for ducks and pheasants.

"You better believe those cows are effective," he said. "And I can go one better than that. I've got a handicapped buddy in South Dakota who built a huge one out of two sheets of plywood and attached it to his truck."

And we think golfers are nuts.

OK, so stalking with fake cows seems to work. What about actual decoying with them?

Yowza! The results of the teal episode at the beginning of this essay were outstanding. We finished just shy of a three-man limit. Yet there was a caveat: It took place early on a dark, cloudy morning with ducks coming in low, right on the deck. With high birds under bright sunshine, I'm not so sure.

But there's more than one way to pluck a duck. Our fake cows are black and white. Next time, we're thinking about using similarly colored umbrellas on the back side of them to break up our profile. Seriously.

The first guy who laughs out loud and flares an incoming flight has to buy breakfast for his fellow cattle barons.

Witness to history

I just finished a spectacular fishing trip and never exited the house.

It occurred as I cleaned out some storage boxes left over from my outdoor writing days. Deep in one tomb—among half-century-old negatives and slides, yellowed newspaper and magazine clippings, letters to and from readers, random notes and other drivel—was a long-forgotten collection of manuscripts I inherited from Bob Burch.

Burch (1907-1985) was one of the most widely read and influential Tennessee outdoorsmen of the mid-20th century. At various times in his career, he worked as a sporting goods salesman, marina operator, photographer and author. His last job was information specialist for the old Tennessee Game and Fish Commission, which published reams of his "Burch Bark" columns during the 1950s and '60s.

As I leafed through this treasure trove, one story in particular caught my eye. Written in November 1966, it recalled the day Burch was privy to an important moment in local angling history. He was present when what is believed to be the first fish was caught on spinning tackle in East Tennessee.

Let that sink in for a minute.

Of the untold hundreds of thousands of spinning rods and reels (and millions of miles of monofilament line) deployed annually throughout this region, Burch apparently saw the first one in action.

This took place in 1939 on Norris Lake. Burch and his wife, Vivian, had a cabin near present-day Hickory Star Dock. The new TVA reservoir teemed with trophy bass, both largemouth and smallmouth, plus walleyes.

"Expert and neophyte alike flocked to this mecca," he wrote, "and any and all caught fish."

One day Burch received a (quite rare) long-distance telephone call from New York. Seems a "Mr. Brown" had just come to the U.S. and wished to sample Norris' legendary opportunities. Burch agreed to guide him. The visitor soon arrived.

Aside from the lowly and ever-present cane pole, sport fishing back then was conducted either with fly equipment or cumbersome "knuckle-buster" casting outfits. Not so in this case.

"When he began to assemble the odd-looking gear he had brought along, I had difficulty keeping a straight face," Burch recollected. "The rod, a beautifully finished bamboo, was equipped with big agate guides set in

German silver mountings and appeared to be a cross between a fly rod and a casting rod.

"The reel defied imagination. It looked like a Rube Goldberg coffee grinder."

Just as it is now, "jump fishing" in schools of feeding bass was popular. Burch and his guest putt-putted their small boat into a cove, cut the engine and waited. Within minutes, the surface boiled.

"Slowly and cautiously," he wrote, "we paddled toward the feeding fish. When in range, I let fly with an old, chewed-up Creek Chub Skipper on heavy casting gear. Bingo! A hefty largemouth slurped the wooden imitation."

As Burch wrestled the bass, "Mr. Brown" cast a small, lightweight spinning lure. It fell short of the mark. No strike. Before the school went deep, Burch put three more bass into the boat.

When the next school surfaced, Burch retired his casting rod. From then on he strictly paddled, putting his guest closer to the action. That's when "Mr. Brown" began catching bass with regularity. Mission accomplished.

So who was this newcomer with the "coffee grinder"?

None other than Bache H. Brown, who had begun tinkering with fixed-drum spinning reels in Europe in the 1930s.

Although spinning experiments date back to the late 1800s, it wasn't until the years immediately before and after World War II that improvements were made and the marvel of what became known as "non-backlash fishing" came into its own. Brown was one of the pioneers.

Immediately I set storage boxes aside and began tickling computer keys. Brown's legacy wasn't hard to find. According to the website oldreels.com, "The initial force behind spinning reels in the U.S. was famous sportsman Bache Brown . . . The first spinning reel manufactured in this country was an American version of the French Luxor, which evolved into the Bache Brown Masterreel in 1947."

The website fishingtalks.com, concurred: "The Bache Brown Masterreel quickly became the benchmark of today's spinning reel fishing."

Through further computer searching, I discovered the going rate for a Bache Brown spinning reel back then was around $25, far out of reach of the average angler. But as the post-war economic boom swelled across

America, more and more sportsmen saved their money and acquired one. Repeat: one.

When I think how many multiple, mass-manufactured, inexpensive-yet-high-quality spinning outfits fishermen own today—I counted 11 in two racks in my garage alone; more are stored in the bass boat—it blows my mind.

Same with Bob Burch. As he mused near the end of his 1966 story: "The possibility that this man and his outlandish spinning gear would revolutionize sport fishing in this country never once entered my head."

A lesson in eye tricks

Sometimes your eyes and your brain don't immediately connect. Happens to all of us.

Maybe you're at the airport, waiting to pick up a friend, when another friend walks up. For a moment or two, you don't "see" the second person because he/she isn't who you're looking for.

Or maybe you pluck a red treat from a holiday candy dish and pop it into your mouth, expecting to taste cherry or peppermint—only to discover it's blazing-hot cinnamon.

Thus, you can appreciate my brief mental confusion a few days ago. I was in my tree stand, watching the grown-over edge of a field for late-afternoon deer. In the waning light, I caught brownish, horizontal movement in weeds some 40-50 yards away.

Perfect.

But what materialized a few seconds later sent my eyeballs and my gray cells into total disarray. I definitely could see a white, flicking tail. It's funny now, but I distinctly remember thinking, "That's the littlest deer I've ever seen in my life."

Mainly because it wasn't a deer. It was a bobcat.

I've lived at this place in western Knox County for 18 years and killed heaven-only-knows how many deer from that particular stand. High above, I've also watched great-horned owls, barred owls, red-tailed and red-shouldered hawks, foxes, raccoons, 'possums, songbirds galore, squirrels, chipmunks, rabbits, turkeys, quail, ducks and coyotes too numerous to mention.

Until that instant, however, I'd never seen a resident bobcat.

In fact, this was only the fourth time I'd ever spotted a bobcat in the wild: once while turkey hunting in Georgia, once while deer hunting in Virginia and once, also deer hunting, in Cocke County, Tennessee.

As the beast tiptoed closer to my stand, my eyes and my brain reached friendly consensus and settled back to enjoy the show.

Seconds later, the script got even better when yet another bobcat appeared. Both were adults, but the second one was decidedly larger.

From 15 feet up, I stared in awe as they crept toward the thicket I was in. My gear bag was on the ground near the base of the stand. I was certain its scent would spook them.

Nope. They paid it no heed whatsoever. The smaller one actually hopped upon a fallen pine tree, barely two or three human steps from where I'd gone up the ladder. It sat there like a house cat, stubby tail twitching, white-tipped ears alert, as the larger one investigated a brush pile. I suspect they were team-hunting, one to flush and the other to pounce.

No prey appeared. Moments later, they evaporated deeper into the thicket on silent footsteps.

I let out a slow breath. Wow. What a spectacle.

Perhaps this is the Year of the Bobcat. My former News Sentinel outdoor colleague Bob Hodge saw either one or two—the second could've been a re-sighting; Bob's not 100-percent sure—while deer hunting in Middle Tennessee. His Powell buddy, Mike Brown, also spotted one the same day.

"I watched it sniff around a stump down the hill from me," Hodge laughed. "A little while after it left, the all-clear signal must have sounded because that stump exploded with chipmunks."

Later, via phone, TWRA spokesman Matt Cameron agreed with me that these sightings surely were a fluke, not any indication of a sudden increase in the Tennessee bobcat population.

"Bobcats are among nature's most elusive animals," he said. "Very few people ever see one. They come out occasionally during the daytime, but mostly they're nocturnal.

"We really don't have any way to survey their numbers," he added, "but we believe the population is stable. About the best indication is the number of bobcat pelts that show up at fur sales. It's been running about the same every year."

As for the remainder of my late-afternoon vigil?

No deer, small or large, appeared.

As darkness closed in, my eyes and my brain briefly jousted about another horizontal shape at the far edge of the thicket. But the hands that gripped my muzzleloader weren't buying any of it. Indeed, the short dispute ended when my brain shouted in exasperation, "You're not eyeballs; you're goofballs! That's nothing but a bent-over cedar! You've been looking at it all afternoon!"

About then, belly growls reminded the rest of my body it was suppertime. There being no counter-arguments from any quarter, I unbuckled my safety belt, climbed down and headed for the house.

Hope those bobcats got to enjoy a warm meal, too.

Liars! Liars! Liars!

After reading the results of a recent scientific study, I've come to the conclusion that honey bees, hunters and fishermen share a common trait.

They're all full of B.S.

At least that's the case when it comes to keeping secrets. None of them are above twisting the truth, slightly or forcefully, to throw potential competitors off their trail.

This study was conducted by insect researchers from Washington State University. Their findings were published in the professional journal Current Biology.

Seems that when members of a bee colony find a new source of nectar, they are faced with a dilemma. They need to keep things on the Q.T. from other colonies, while at the same time informing their buddies about the exact location.

I won't go into all the high-brow mumbo-jumbo from the Washington State report, but the bottom line is this: Honey bees tell lies.

Knowing eavesdropping bees are ever-present, they "whisper" to each other that the new nectar source is well-protected by their own kind. Thus, any interlopers might get their butts kicked. Apparently the ruse works. Not wishing to expend unnecessary energy and possibly losing members to all-out war, the other bees stay away.

Brilliant!

It will come as no surprise to veterans of the woods and waters, of course, but hunters and fishermen have been dishing this same brand of malarkey for eons. They were doing it when everybody lived in caves and gathered their groceries with spears. They still do it whether shooting a custom-made .270 Winchester or casting from a $50,000 bass boat.

Sometimes the prevarication is subtle, sorta like what the bees do. Sometimes, it's outright bovine scatology. Each situation varies.

Case Number One: Hiram Hunter is hot on the trail of a spring turkey. He's been oh-so-close a morning or two. He also knows Herman Hunter is after the same bird. They run into each other at the barber shop, and Herman casually inquires if Hiram has had any luck.

Determined to reveal nothing of substance, Hiram has a quick decision to make. Naturally, he's going to lie. But how?

Does he say: (a) the turkeys have been silent all spring, no gobbling activity whatsoever or (b) it's a useless madhouse out there; the woods have been overrun with other hunters? Either way, he's giving the impression there's no reason for Herman to venture outside of his front yard.

Herman listens carefully as the information is offered. Now it's his turn to make an instant decision.

Does he think Hiram is (a) lying through his teeth or (b) truthfully venting his frustration about mobs of other hunters?

See? Decisions! Decisions! Decisions!

Case Number Two: Fred Fisherman has just discovered a trout stream he never knew existed. It's full of rainbows and browns, dumber than bricks.

Uncharacteristically, his ego overrides his native caution. In a fit of lunacy, he shows Floyd Fisherman a cell phone photo of the huge trout he's been catching. Floyd casually inquires where this action is taking place.

Naturally, Fred's going to out-and-out lie.

But does he send Floyd on a wild goose chase three counties to the east? Or does he toss out hints that it's the same "secret" stream Floyd accidentally revealed to him last season?

Again, this is the same principle as the bees.

You know what's even nuttier? It's the name hunters and fisherman have always given to these top-secret spots. They call 'em "honey holes." No joke. Proving that in matters of confidentially, it doesn't matter if you have six legs or two.

Or, as the old saying goes: "All hunters and fishermen are liars except you and me. And I ain't real sure about you."

That is the truth, the whole truth and nothing but the truth.

There's always a catch

Now that fishing season is in full swing, I've decided to make some serious money.

Not by turning pro and competing in bass tournaments, for Pete's sake. That's way too much work. As much as I love being on the water and matching wits with Pisces, doing it 12-14 hours a day, year 'round—in howling gales and under a blistering sun—sure isn't my idea of a pleasant vocation.

Instead, I intend to literally reel in the cash.

I got the idea after reading excerpts from a recent news broadcast by WTVC-TV in Chattanooga. It seems two teenagers, Mark Spicer and Dylan Crumbley, were fishing in Chickamauga Lake near Blythe Ferry when they made a most unusual catch: two cloth bags. The lads ripped 'em open and found wads of greenbacks.

OK, so "greenbacks" is the casual term for U.S. currency, which this stuff was. More than $10,000, the bulk in twenties. But the color of these bills was predominantly red, as in what's left when a dye pack explodes in the aftermath of a bank robbery.

The boys turned their catch over to Rhea County authorities, who suspected the loot came from an earlier bank job in Ooltewah. Said investigator Mike Owenby: "Supposedly one of the suspects jumped into the trunk of a car during the getaway. That's when the dye packs went off."

Owenby said two suspects already under arrest in connection with the heist apparently had weighted the bags with rocks and tossed 'em into the river.

The most important segment of this story, however, didn't appear until the final paragraph. It read, "The teenaged anglers reportedly were using a Rat-L-Trap bass lure."

A-ha! So that's the secret! Just throw Rat-L-Traps and start reeling in the moolah!

But what kind exactly? Ouch. Therein lies a rub that ruined my get-rich-quick scheme. Turns out there are forty'leven varieties of this popular crankbait on the market.

I made a sashay through the Rat-L-Trap display at Bass Pro Shops and found more than 900 individual lures in a vast array of sizes (1/8, 1/4, 1/2, 3/4 and 1 ounce) and colors (gold chartreuse, sunrise perch, lavender shad, fathead minnow, honey craw, fire tiger, silver Tennessee shad to cite just a few of more than three dozen patterns and hues.)

Clearly, several hundred baits in different sizes and colors would be needed to cover all conditions. At $6.49 apiece, plus tax, this would quickly add up and seriously erode my margin of profit.

Well, poot. Guess I'll have to go back to hoping for plain ol' fish, not fortunes, next time I hook up my boat and head to the lake.

Assessing blame correctly

I am atop foggy Mount LeConte, finally off the trail. A chilly, windswept rain pummels the roof of my digs, Cabin No. 6 at LeConte Lodge.

I have removed sodden boots, put on fresh socks and climbed into a pair of camp sandals. Already I am wearing warm, dry pants, under and outer.

I reach into my backpack for more comfortable items that will—huh?

I dig even deeper—aw, c'mon now!

My fingertips rake across the bottom of the backpack—whotth'hell?!

Frantically, I invert the bag and shake it like a sack of potatoes. Only then does the cold, harsh, wet truth soak into my cold, wet, numb skull—Venob, you (bleeping) idiot!

This, dear children, is when I remembered a tiny detail that occurred hours earlier, before Mary Ann and I set off for the mountains. A detail Mister-Boy-Scout-Ever-Preparedness never thought would happen to him.

I'd left most of my upper clothes in the garage. On a chair. The same chair where I had temporarily placed them while adjusting something else in the backpack.

Arrgh! "Temporarily" was now blood-pressure-building "permanent."

At that moment, the only parcel of dry, above-waist clothing I owned was a single, long-sleeved, cotton shirt. Definitely not de rigueur for a damp night at 6,594 feet.

Happily, I was blessed with hiking companions who hadn't suffered pre-trip amnesia. One of them, Alvin Sanders, produced a Pendleton wool shirt and a small bottle of Jim Beam. In that order. On the basis of this humanitarian act alone, I proposed the Episcopal Diocese of East Tennessee grant him immediate sainthood.

How could this be?

After 25-plus years of leading a weekend church outing to LeConte?

After exhorting others about the wiles of weather in the Smokies, even during summer?

After always having a backup plan with just-in-case supplies?

"Senioritis" won't work because Alvin is six years my elder. Nor can I claim being lulled into foolish complacency after many years in the woods. Alvin still has me beat, hands down. A former employee at LeConte Lodge and wellspring of park lore and information, he pounds out more trail miles in any given season than I will log in a decade.

No. Mister-Boy-Scout-Ever-Preparedness is convinced this calamity can only be blamed on one thing: evil clothing. To make certain it never happens again, Mister-Boy-Scout-Ever-Preparedness took corrective action the minute he got home.

He gave those wicked, hateful, low-down left-behind clothes the loud and thorough cussing they richly deserved.

One persistent tick

In the spirit of sportsmanship and great respect for a worthy adversary, I doff my camouflage cap. To a tiny tick.

Not just any tick. Despite its diminutive size, this tick is—or was; more on that in a moment—the meanest, baddest, fiercest, most determined specimen in all of Arachnida. I suspect it smoked unfiltered Camels, rode a Harley and all eight legs were heavily tattooed.

He (she?) and I united in Jefferson County on the second weekend of Tennessee's 2015 spring turkey season.

I didn't make the discovery on my own. Indeed, I wouldn't have found it in a week's searching. My wife got the honor. Happened like this: It was noonish. I'd just come inside the house (after, forgive the bragging, dressing a 19-pound gobbler) and headed for the shower. When I peeled off my camo T-shirt, Mary Ann said, "Ugh! How disgusting!"

TO RETIRE? OR NOT TO RETIRE?

She didn't use to be so crass. But what the heck; we've been married nearly 50 years. My ample real estate looks neither 20-, 30- or 40-something any longer.

Yet it was what clung to the expanse of aged real estate that caught her eye.

The tick was attached just below my right shoulder blade. Not only would I never have found it, I never-ever could have removed it. Not even prior to two back surgeries.

Good wife that she is, Mary Ann gritted her teeth and extracted it from my hide. Ever since, she has been applying antibiotic and anti-itch ointments upon request.

(With one exception. I was at the newspaper office a few days later, and the bite was itching like fire. I stepped into the men's restroom, peeled my shirt, put a blob of cortisone cream on one fingertip and tried to apply it. Not a pretty sight. The only thing that worked was to take a deep breath, "hug myself" and make a quick stab with the fingertip. Thank heavens nobody walked in. Otherwise, we would've had a Page One photo of a hairy, bent-backed, self-hugging walrus.)

But here's why I admire the tenacity of that tick: It had fought through not one, not two, but three layers of camo clothing liberally saturated with permethrin spray.

I've written previously about the godsend of permethrin-laced products. They're the finest stuff ever manufactured for killing ticks. Yes, kill. As in DOA. They still get on your clothes, but after taking a couple of steps across the dried layer of permethrin, they curl up like a Frito. Off they drop. I've watched this process with my own eyes.

I've been spraying my turkey clothes with permethrin for more than a decade. To the best of my memory, this is the first tick that ever survived the outer layer. Let alone layers beneath.

I probably should have had this beast mounted and displayed over the fireplace. Instead, I gave it the royal flush. And as swirling waters carried it down, my sportsmanship wavered momentarily. I suspect the last human sound Mr. Tick heard was maniacal laughter and crude words about his ancestry.

Hope so anyway.

Moose of a fish

"Buddy, that's a mighty nice smallmouth," another competitor said to Eric Himmelreich as they stood in the weigh-in line at a fishing tournament. "What do you reckon it'll go?"

Himmelreich held up the clear plastic bag containing lake water and a trio of bass. He studied intently.

"The biggest one is probably a little over three pounds," he replied.

Good guess—at least as far as weight is concerned. According to records at the University of Tennessee's fish collection, this specimen (officially listed as No. 90.4245) checked in at 3 pounds, 6.5 ounces.

But it sure wasn't a routine smallmouth bass. And therein lies a scientific tale.

Himmelreich, a Knoxville dentist, caught the fish in Watts Bar on a soft plastic crawfish bait. This occurred during a tournament sponsored by the Second District Dental Society. The fish was part of a three-bass tally (6 pounds, 1.5 ounces) that earned Himmelreich the $200 top prize.

However, the instant the weighmaster eyeballed Himmelreich's catch, he announced, "Usually we put all these tournament fish back into the lake. Not this one. It's going into the university's collection. It's a moose!"

No, the critter hadn't morphed from fish into mammal. But its size was spectacular. And its true identity likely would have gone unnoticed except that the weighmaster was none other than David A. Etnier, Ph.D., retired professor of ichthyology at UT and knower of much stuff about things living underwater. As soon as he picked up the bass, Etnier began counting soft dorsal rays and pectoral fin rays. Nothing added up correctly.

Initially, he assumed it was a largemouth-spotted bass hybrid. But back at the lab, where he could check scales and run other tests, Etnier changed his ruling.

"It's a smallmouth-spotted bass hybrid," said Etnier, who also serves as an identification expert for the Freshwater Fishing Hall of Fame. (Who else do you know once resorted to spinal X-rays to determine a hybrid musky's precise lineage?) "I suspect this is a real old-timer, probably 7-9 years.

"Smallmouths and spotted bass do cross with each other on occasion, but I've never seen a specimen larger than this," he said. "I'll guarantee if they recognized records for hybrids, this would be at or near the top."

One chance, one shot, one deer

I was deer hunting and Gordon MacQuarrie was duck hunting, but we both faced the same dilemma: How to make every shot count.

Not that I would attempt to carry MacQuarrie's water, you understand. The king of American outdoor writers, MacQuarrie (1900-1956) remains a popular author to this day. His delightful accounts of "The Old Duck Hunters, Inc., which stands for Incorrigible," still sell briskly for Wisconsin book publisher Willow Creek Press.

Nonetheless, as I settled into my deer stand a few afternoons ago, I couldn't help but think about a MacQuarrie classic called "Bluebill Day."

This article was first published in 1932 by Field & Stream. In it, MacQuarrie describes the afternoon he went waterfowling and didn't bring sufficient ammunition. It was a monumental mistake. Normally meticulous in his pre-hunt preparations, MacQuarrie arrived at his blind with frightfully few shotgun shells. The story recounts how he rationed them to himself, one at a time, until bagging the limit.

I didn't have the luxury of "one at a time."

Instead, I had one. Period. As in uno. Singleton.

I made this shocking discovery moments after plunking down in my stand and placing supplies at the ready.

Grunt call? Check.

Rattling sticks? Check.

Binoculars? Check.

Speed loaders with 100 premeasured grains of Pyrodex-Select black powder? Check.

Saboted bullets? Check.

Percussion caps?

Hmm . . . percussion caps?

Repeat: percussion caps?

Uh, one mo' time: percussion caps?

Arrgh! Where the $#%&! were my percussion caps?

You can have enough powder to blow up Fort Knox! Enough saboted bullets to take on the Russian army! Big deal! Without percussion caps to detonate this firepower, you might as well be holding a broom!

After panicked digging into my daypack, I found the aforementioned single cap. Immediately, my mind began debate. Do I drive back to the house for more? Or roll the dice with one?

It was a little after 3 p.m. on a dark, dreary, temperature-falling afternoon. The deer, if any, would be moving soon. I decided to stay put.

This would be one shot and one shot only. Just like in Daniel Boone's day. No chance for follow-ups if a deer appeared and, heaven forbid, I didn't take it down cleanly.

Thus the vigil began. As minutes ticked by and the cloudy day grew grayer and colder, I began second-guessing.

"This is totally irresponsible!" I fussed silently. "You idiot! You goof! You know better! What if? What if? What if?"

Happily, all ended well.

At 5:15, a deer magically materialized—how do they do that?—40 yards below my stand and began rubbing a sapling. Nice antlers. Broadside. A split-second pause. Safety off. Crosshairs settling. Half a breath. Hold it.

The .50 caliber Knight belched, and my world was enveloped in a dense fog of acrid smoke. When everything cleared seconds later, all I could see was a white belly on the ground. Heart shot. Verily, the buck never knew what hit him.

This would've been a dandy 8-point, except for an entire missing antler. There were four long, beautiful tines on one side, zip on the other. Big deal. I need another mount like the proverbial poke in the eye. Here was an excellent supply of winter meat.

Dark was fast approaching. I hot-footed for the truck. Dragged the deer to it. Loaded everything up and was homeward-bound 30 minutes later. One-shot mission accomplished.

No doubt Gordon MacQuarrie would have approved—and then fussed at me for such slipshod preparations.

A fortunate find

I'll wager serious coin that my four souvenirs from an opening-day dove hunt are the wackiest in East Tennessee.

Two of them were the pair of Eurasian collared doves I bagged in addition to the 15-bird mourning dove limit.

These gray-white speedsters sport a distinctive black neck band; hence their name. They are classified an "invasive species" by state and federal wildlife managers. Translation: feathered kudzu. Natives of Asia and Europe, collared doves were introduced to the Bahamas in the 1970s. They reached Florida by the '80s and since have spread as far north as the Great Lakes.

These birds are long and lean, not squat and dumpy like city pigeons. They're about one-third larger than native mourning doves and have a bat-like wing beat instead of the "flit-flit" of a mourner. Once you've seen 'em fly, you'll know what I mean.

Their call is different, too. It's more like a cuckoo than a dove.

Having previous culinary experience with collared doves, I can assure you they're just as tasty as mourning doves on the grill or in the smoker. Meatier, too.

My other two opening-day souvenirs were acquired during 45 minutes of intense frustration as birds dive-bombed the Monroe County silage fields I was gunning.

One is an empty Winchester 12-gauge shotgun shell, bent at a 10-degree angle. The other is a rusty, two-foot length of ½-inch rebar.

I hated the first, loved the second. And therein lies a story.

This outing began, in full-fledged Southern tradition, with a barbecue lunch. The only thing better than the food were tall tales, laughs and bear hugs among old friends who've been practicing this outdoor rite for nearly half a century. Around 2:30, we headed into the fields.

I set up under a broadly crowned oak 150 yards distant from the main event, my assumptions being (1) shade trumps searing September heat any day and (2) doves flying into and out of the silage fields likely would pass nearby. Both assumptions proved correct.

I was roughly halfway toward the limit when my Benelli autoloader abruptly issued a weak "poof" and refused to cycle a new round. I've occasionally had this occur with reloads but never with factory ammunition.

The bolt was jammed. Not until I used the heel of my boot was I able to force it open. I removed the barrel expecting—and discovering—the worst.

What a mess. The shell's brass was partly detached from the plastic hull. The primer had nearly blown out. The swollen hull was tightly lodged inside the chamber. There was no way this hull, now deformed at the aforementioned 10 degrees, was coming out.

I tried my pocketknife. I tried a branch cut from the oak tree. I tried a volley of cuss words. None worked. My kingdom for a ramrod!

Then I remembered the radio antenna on my pickup, parked near a ditch some 200 yards away. Perhaps it would do the trick.

Approaching the truck, barrel in hand, I spied something even better: a mound of scrap metal, old tractor parts and construction waste the landowner had piled for removal. I probed around and—huzzah!—found that blessed section of straight, heavy rebar. What are the odds of such fortune?

I dropped it down the barrel. Doink! The damaged empty shell dislodged immediately. I was back in business. And as I happily discovered during gun-cleaning duties, the rebar didn't scratch the interior of the barrel whatsoever. It's shiny as a diamond.

The bent hull and rebar now reside in my garage. I'm not sure what their ultimate fate will be. Perhaps I'll build a statue using them as central ingredients.

I could call this masterpiece "An Ode to Exasperation and Improvisation."

Well worth the work

I enjoy eating shellcrackers. I enjoy cleaning shellcrackers. I enjoy catching shellcrackers.

Not necessarily in that order.

Truth be told, angling for these bar-brawling, bull-shouldered panfish is about as much fun as you can have in a boat.

No offense to my bass buddies, but a boss shellcracker can out-duel a largemouth twice its size. And in spring, when these pugilists move into shallow water to spawn, there is no easier form of fishing.

Cast. Watch for float to go down. After spirited tussle that strains an ultra-light spinning outfit to the max, deposit the latest one-pound victim into the ice chest. Repeat. See? Simple.

Ah, but the first chore is finding the elusive beasts in the first place.

I have no idea where shellcrackers, or redear sunfish, (Lepomis microlophus) go after they spawn. Perhaps to deep shelves. Perhaps to mid-lake. Perhaps they sprout wings and migrate to Peru. All I know is you better take advantage of them when they invade the shallows to make baby shellcrackers.

The key, through my experience, is any gently sloping inlet off the main channel—as long as it is littered with pea gravel. Not chunk rock. Not clay. Just lots of gravel.

The days leading up to, and just after, the full moon in May and June are reported to produce the best action. But I say any moment you can fill a cooler with a limit (20) of these delicious fish is time well spent.

Bait? You name it. I use a pinch of nightcrawler, but anything meaty will suffice. Since shellcrackers get their name from crushing the hulls of aquatic snails and eating the muscular flesh inside, one would think shrimp would be a viable alternative. One would think incorrectly. Besides, 'crawlers are far less expensive.

When it comes to platter fare, shellcrackers have no freshwater equal—with the possible exception of walleye and sauger. Rolled in seasoned meal and deep-fried to a golden brown, they will turn even the most finicky fish-eater into a cholesterolic glutton.

Before that, however, they must be cleaned. Which brings us back to the start of this essay.

Because of their large size, 'crackers stand up well to an electric knife. Fillet them just like bass or crappie, peel off the skin and excise the rib cage. Some purists insist on scaling and keeping the skin. I am not a purist.

I've never objected to rendering game and fishing into table fare. The way I see it, if you're going to take an animal's life, at least have enough respect to finish the job.

True, there are fleeting moments when your sporting zeal gets away from reality and underestimates the labor ahead. I think of that sometimes when a two-day limit of ducks demands defeathering or a deer killed just at sunset means you'll be up late.

But what the hcek. Nobody said the results of a hunting or fishing trip were as easily bagged as supermarket groceries.

So excuse me, please, as I repair to the shade—one hand working an electric fillet knife, the other extracting fat shellcrackers from the cooler. Not a bad way to spend a spring afternoon.

Turning back the clock

Ron Jones is among the estimated 80,000 Tennessee bowhunters who hit the woods when archery season opens every September. But he sure doesn't use the same gear as everybody else.

No fancy carbon-riser compound bow for this guy. No aluminum-shaft arrows with plastic vanes and expanding broadheads. No trigger release system.

Instead, he takes the term "primitive weapon" back to its roots.

Almost everything Jones hunts with these days is handmade and 100-percent natural. That includes his longbow crafted from a stave of Osage orange, arrows made from river cane, flint points he patiently knapped during the off-season, fletching from the wing feathers of a wild turkey he called in and killed, bowstring wound from deer sinew—even the buckskin clothes he tanned and sewed himself.

Which begs an obvious question. Why?

"Deer hunting had gotten too easy for me," said Jones, an Oliver Springs resident and superintendent with Wasserman Construction Company in Knoxville. "Technology was taking away from the challenge. I wanted to go back to the way things were 1,000 years ago."

This wasn't an instant conversion. More like an evolution.

Jones grew up in rural Potter County, Pennsylvania. He was hunting by age eight. Over the years, he became attracted to the challenge of archery and initially followed the same path as others.

"I hunted with a compound bow until 2008," he said.

He then drifted into manufactured longbows and recurves. And before you could say "Robin Hood," he wound up turning back the clock by centuries.

Milking the Internet for guidance, he found a series of how-to books published by the Bowyer's Bible. He experimented, made mistakes, learned, adapted, honed his skills.

"I guess in all I've made about 25 bows," Jones said. "Some of them are quite usable. In fact, I've sold a few to friends."

He paused for a grin: "A bunch of others have sailed through the air, followed by appropriate language."

TO RETIRE? OR NOT TO RETIRE?

Obviously, this return to ancient weaponry lowers the amount of venison acquired in any given season. Jones has taken three deer with his homemade equipment: two does, plus an 8-point buck from Royal Blue.

Let the record show that he hasn't totally forsaken more modern weaponry—although the word "more" should be considered in a strictly relative context.

"Sometimes when the rifle season is on, I'll go back to shooting a fiberglass longbow or recurve," he said. "Also, I use a gun during the muzzleloader season."

A scope-sighted, percussion-cap, Pyrodex-belching, in-line rifle like the rest of us New Age "primitives"? What do you think?

When it comes to blackpowder ventures, Jones opts for a flintlock. Which, naturally, he built himself. From scratch.

There is, however, one 21st century trinket Jones has embraced wholeheartedly. He's a big fan of high-tech, digital trail cameras to assist in his scouting.

"I've got several pictures of some really good deer," he said. "I'll be looking for them this season."

A wise managing editor once gave me some good advice about subject matter: "You'll never go wrong with children or animals. Doesn't matter if people go 'aaaaww' about a cute story or get outraged about an injustice. As long as it involves children or animals, they'll read every word."

Here's one more tried-and-true subject. Holidays.

Everybody can identify with them. They love most of 'em and hate a few of 'em, especially if the date brings up bad memories. Nonetheless, people will always read about, and react to, any holiday whether it's widely recognized or not.

April 10, 2016, was National Siblings Day. Frankly, I'd never heard of such an observation. Followers of Facebook certainly knew about it, however. From daylight 'til well beyond dark, they filled their pages with long-ago photos of brothers and sisters.

National Siblings Day is like 95-plus percent of the bazillion holidays not recognized by government edict. In other words, no time off from work like with Christmas, July 4th, Thanksgiving Day and other calendar stalwarts.

I'll lobby for one more to be included. How about coast-to-coast celebrations, testimonial dinners, toasts (translation: free likker) for National Newspaper Columnists Day (a real holiday, by the way) on April 18?

In keeping with the theme, every columnist in America should put in a full day's work. Then they can go back to goofing off the other 364.

Chapter Seven
EVERY DAY'S A HOLIDAY

One small effort to bring change

A few days ago I had lunch with my fellow retired News Sentinel colleague Bobby Wilson. As happens when graybeards get together, Bobby and I quickly lapsed into a session of "remember when ..." We repeated oft-told tales about the crazy, creative characters we'd worked with through the years, noting that their craziness and creativity often were proportional to their intake of alcohol. Usually while on the job.

This time we also delved into memories of newsroom dogma.

Then, as now, many ironclad rules were slow to die, even if ridiculous and outdated. One of these was racial identification in news stories—and I can't think of a better time to share it than the observance of Martin Luther King Jr. Day.

At one time, most Southern newspapers took great pains to point out if a person was black (often the description was "negro," capitalized in some publications, lowercase in others), even if race wasn't germane to the story.

This Jim Crow practice had mostly faded by the early '70s. But some institutions clung on stubbornly. Among them was our sister paper in Memphis, The Press-Scimitar.

Bobby, who worked at The Press-Scimitar before coming to Knoxville, told me a classic story about one staff member's effort to bring change. His name was Jim Willis. Then a general assignment reporter, Willis rose in the ranks of Scripps Howard, eventually retiring as editor of the Birmingham Post-Herald.

"Get Jim to give you the details," said Bobby, offering the phone number.

It was sometime around 1975, Willis recalled when we connected later that day. There had been an altercation at a local TV station involving weather reporter Dave Brown.

"A guy just showed up one day and took a swing at Brown for no apparent reason," he said. "Not long after, he came back to the station and asked to see Dave Brown again. The receptionist recognized him. She called upstairs to alert Dave, and they concocted a story to trap the guy in a hall until police could get there."

The ruse worked. Cops arrived. A mentally disturbed man, last name of White, was taken into custody. End of story.

Literally.

You see, it was at the end of his story that Jim Willis crafted a brilliant sentence. In an effort to highlight the silliness of his paper's race rule, he closed with this gem: "Brown is white and White is black."

No, that alone didn't stop unnecessary racial ID. The edict continued until there was a change of leadership at the paper. "Still," Willis told me with a laugh, "it's the first story that comes up when old Memphis reporters get together."

I suspect Dr. King, who spent his life encouraging people to see beyond skin color, would have loved it.

Now, where did I hide it?

It would be a lot easier to give a gift to my wife on Valentine's Day—any other holiday, for that matter—if I didn't:

1. Acquire these things in advance.

2. Have so many convenient hidey-holes around the house.

Concerning Number One: I don't shop like normal people, meaning at the appropriate time of year. I just buy stuff on impulse, whenever I happen to see it, regardless of season.

If I'm in a store on, say, August 5 and spot something I think Mary Ann would like for her birthday the following July 4, I get it right then. And hide it.

Which leads us to Number Two: Where the %$#! did I stick the %$#! thing?!

Consider a series of events from last Christmas. Throughout the spring, summer and fall, I made book-signing rounds at a variety of retail venues. At several of these places, I acquired trinkets for Mary Ann. Each went into the witness protection program until Christmas Eve.

"Piece of cake," I remember smugly thinking as we drove home from midnight Mass. "I'll send her to bed, and then Santa Sammy will get to work."

Gaa! I nearly tore up the house. For naught.

Seriously. After an hour of furious hunting, I had (a) found nothing and (b) lost every smidgen of Christmas spirit imparted at church.

The worst part about a situation like this is you can't vent audibly for fear of waking Mrs. Claus. Ask any Type-A. There's nothing more frustrating than having to eke a 10,000-megawatt tirade under your breath.

Spent and defeated, I quit. I started upstairs, wondering how I was going to explain this nuttiness in the morning—when it abruptly dawned on me I'd removed everything from one favorite hidey-hole to another a few days earlier!

Yep, there they were. I wrapped, taped and deposited them, with a thud, under the tree.

Which brings me to my, uh, "present present" crisis. Somewhere, I have a Valentine's Day gift for my beloved. I know this for a fact.

I know exactly what it is. I can tell you the day and place I bought it. There are witnesses.

I just can't remember—gadnabberwhipsnitchaphooey!—where I hid it!

Oh, well. At least time is on my side.

There are still a couple of favorite hidey-holes to check. Plus, I've still got more than a week to solve the hateful mystery.

But if—worst case scenario—you encounter some idiot in the wee hours of Valentine's Day, cursing quietly to himself and pawing through mounds of leftover gift junk at an all-night store, don't say a word. Just keep walking.

Cupid Venob won't be in the mood for small talk.

Smut that arrives in the mail

With a slow and wicked smile, Cassandra loosened the straps on her blouse. "Come closer," her hot breath whispered, "let me show you my fruits."

Oops. I didn't realize you were reading over my shoulder. Give me a second to gather my senses.

There. Better now. I'm still torn up, but at least I should be able to speak rationally.

The problem is trashy, unsolicited printed matter that keeps appearing in my mailbox. It's so bad it oughta be outlawed! First Amendment be damned! There are some things people simply should not have shoved in their faces!

What is this awful material that shows up on a daily basis? Hard-core porn? Political half-truths?

Worse than that. It's those—Shhh! Brace yourself and cover the kiddies' ears—spring catalogs.

The first tawdry wave arrived in mid-January. Mostly for fishing equipment from Bass Pro, Cabela's and Gander Mountain. I was able to resist the brunt of this sin for two reasons.

First, I'm old enough and stubborn enough not to be swayed by the "newest" and "latest" outdoor gear. I'll buy the same ol' reliables I've been using for decades, thank you.

The second reason is, uh, a bit more embarrassing. I'm too dumb to understand how 95 percent of this newfangled merchandise even works. There are reels on the market right now that require a degree from MIT before you make the first cast. And don't get me started on all the new lines; if you're not certified in polymers, forget it. Just take up checkers or crossword puzzles.

Lurid as they may be, however, the outdoor brochures are timid compared with the flower and vegetable catalogs. Talk about tools of the devil!

It's still winter. Bleak, drab winter, in fact, which can lash out at a moment's notice and freeze tender buds down to their stamens. Yet the likes of Park Seed and Burpee persist in rubbing my nose in this seasonal cesspool of squalor with lustful images of flowers and veggies.

Check out Pages 96-97 in the 2012 Park catalog, featuring row after tempting row of sweet corn. Except it's not just plain "sweet" corn any more. No! There's also "triple sweet" and "super sweet" and "sugar enhanced."

For Pete's sake, one photo even shows a steamy ear adrip with a pat of butter! I broke into a sweat and began breathing in fits and jerks the moment I saw it.

This is corn porn, and I am powerless to resist. They tell me I'll go blind if I continue looking at this perverted stuff. Could be.

Then again, maybe I'll just keep turning the pages until I need glasses.

DST and HAD

It's been 72 hours since HAD—the so-called "heart attack deadline"—passed. So if you're reading these words in the flesh, consider yourself alive, well and kicking.

Surely you've heard about HAD. It's been all over the news. It concerns a study by Dr. Amneet Sandhu of the University of Colorado, Denver.

According to what I read about Doc Sandhu's research, hospitals see nearly a 25 percent increase in heart attacks on the first Monday after Daylight Saving Time goes into effect in the spring.

I have nothing to judge the quality of Doc's study, but my gut reaction leans toward baloney.

Then again, my gut often leans toward baloney, especially if it's thick-sliced, tucked between two hunks of light bread and slathered with Duke's mayo. But that's not the heart attack-inducing baloney I'm referring to in this instance.

The reason I'm not wholly convinced is because any abrupt, one-day, 25 percent jump in heart attacks—or rickets, mumps, dandruff and ingrown toenails, for that matter—is huge. I'd have to see a lot more research before I started worrying about The Big One just because our clocks moved ahead 60 minutes.

Not that my body doesn't complain. It does take a day or three for me to adjust to DST, especially in the spring. But it's nothing more serious than an extra yawn. Not some sudden onset of—Aiiiiee! Thump!

Ha-ha. Just kidding. I'm still typing, so it's safe to say I beat the HAD rap one more time. Hope you did, too.

To DST or not to DST is a never-ending question for states to argue about. Arizona and Hawaii are the only two to reject it outright, although a couple of others in the West are threatening. Fine by me. I'm so sick of 24/7 standard news blather by talking heads, any change in the bickering cycle would be welcome.

Whether you're "fer it" or "agin it," though, the arrival of DST has been especially beneficial for snow-ravaged portions of the United States. I learned this nugget of knowledge from Sam Doughty, a longtime News Sentinel reader and this column's Resident Deep Thinker.

As Sam recently posted on my Facebook wall, "The extra hour of daylight sure has helped melt the snow and ice all across the country."

Sam didn't mention whether DST has changed the egg-laying habits of his chickens or the growth of his crops. No doubt more deep thinking is required.

I recommend Sam do it over a baloney sandwich. And I hope he chews carefully to avoid biting the tongue in his cheek.

Corrupting a foolish day

They don't make April Fool's Day hoaxes like they used to, and I know two reasons why.

1. TV reality shows.
2. Social media.

Back in that innocent era B.S.S. (Before Sheer Stupidity) in which many of us geezers grew up, it was easy to trick people with outlandish jokes.

One of my all-time favorites occurred on April 1, 1957, when the BBC reported Swiss farmers were on the verge of harvesting a bumper crop of spaghetti. According to the story, this was due to a mild winter and the elimination of the "dreaded spaghetti weevil."

The report included footage of peasants plucking long strands of pasta (otherwise known as string) from trees. There was even a suggestion for growing your own: "Place a sprig of spaghetti in a tin of tomato sauce and hope for the best."

Alas, this once-a-year holiday joy has been vanquished. In its place has come utter nonsense 24/7/365.

The aforementioned reality (insert laugh here) shows would have us believe all courtroom transactions unfold like they do on "Judge Judy," all Southern kids are a carbon copy of Honey Boo Boo and hunters everywhere mix businesses and pleasure like they do on "Duck Dynasty."

Which, of course, is a tractor-truck load of horse manure. Oops, correction. An entire convoy of manured-to-the-hilt trucks is more like it.

Social media may even be worse.

When otherwise sane people feel the need to describe the ham sandwich they just had for lunch to 2,000 of their closest and dearest friends—and these same 2,000 people read it and comment!—you know the end times are at hand.

Although I'd heard about the spaghetti harvest spoof for years, I was happily surprised to find it ranked No. 1 in the Top 100 best April Fool's Day tricks of all time, as rated by the "Museum of Hoaxes," a San Diego-based website.

There were some other doozies in the mix. Such as:

The German man who discovered how to power an airplane using his own breath (1934).

A floating iceberg in Sydney Harbor that had been purchased by an Australian millionaire and was going to be broken into 10-cent ice cubes for worldwide sale (1978).

A forest of orange-bearing pine trees in California (1950).

But you know what didn't make the Top 100?

The News Sentinel's famous 1974 April Fool's Day story about the signing of an 8-foot basketball player by the University of Tennessee, that's what. Thousands of Knoxvillians swallowed it hook, line, sinker, rod, reel and boat. It's still laughed about to this very day.

Clearly, the Museum of Hoaxes is incapable of recognizing true genius. And that's no foolin'.

Lucifer comes to dinner

Here on Memorial Day, I wish to discuss two old warriors who no longer walk among us. God rest them both.

It's how one of these characters went to his reward that makes the saga so special. The pair may have passed from our midst, but their story has reached legendary status at family gatherings and military reunions.

I'm talking about Bill Beckler's memories of "Lucifer," perhaps the only rooster to ever fly on three bombing missions during World War II.

I learned about Lucifer from Beckler's daughter, Lisa Gentry, one of my former News Sentinel colleagues. Her dad was a storyteller supreme. Months ago, she gave me a copy of one of her father's typed stories from the war. It's a scream.

Beckler, a former clerk in the Knoxville office of the FBI, served as a fighter pilot during WWII, flying 108 combat missions over France and

Italy. He died May, 24, 2010, age 89. Lucifer, alas, never made it out of the war zone alive.

As Beckler described him, Lucifer "was a rogue Italian who managed to escape death by the Germans who had executed most of his relatives. He was weak, lean and hungry. He was slight of build with thin facial features and small beady eyes that followed your every movement. It was his destiny to live up to his namesake."

Beckler found Lucifer, then a tiny yellow chick, in a deserted villa near his air base in Italy. He brought it back to the tent he shared with other Army Air Corps pilots.

"We figured if we raised this chicken, we could soon expect an egg every day," he wrote.

The lads may have been superb airmen, but they weren't poultry experts. This became apparent the day Lucifer began to crow.

And crow. And crow. And crow. And crow.

Wrote Beckler: "It became an obsession with Lucifer and a nightmare for the pilots who resented being awakened at dawn on days they didn't have to fly."

On three of Beckler's own missions, Lucifer stayed by his master's side—although when Beckler pulled out of one bomb run, he noticed the G-forces had mashed his bird "flat as a pancake."

On the ground, however, loudmouthed Lucifer was making enemies right and left. He simply had to go. Which he did with a flourish. Not to mention flour, seasoning and hot grease.

"I told the mess sergeant to prepare him Southern fried," Beckler wrote. "At the noon meal that day, my tent mates and I bade Lucifer a fond and delicious good bye."

Not your traditional July Fourth

What are your typical Fourth of July plans? Backyard cookout, perhaps? Ski trip to the lake? Company golf tournament? Maybe gather with family and friends for neighborhood fireworks at dark-thirty?

Lawrence M. "Laurie" Croft's agenda is a bit more modest. He just does some light reading. Only takes about 10 minutes. But what he reads—not to mention where and why—is the stuff of goose bumps.

At 5 p.m. every July 4th, Croft rises to his feet at Independence Hall in Philadelphia, Pennsylvania, and reads aloud the Declaration of Independence—a document signed by his many-generations-removed grandfather, William Hooper.

"You can run out of 'greats-' trying to recite the actual lineage," Croft told me with a laugh as he conversed via phone from his office in Richmond, Virginia. "He lived in North Carolina and, like all the signers, was not very popular with the British. His house was burned, and he stayed on the run for a year."

Croft, an attorney who specializes in insurance benefits, holds the volunteer office of "president-general" of a tiny association called DSDI. As in Descendants of the Signers of the Declaration of Independence.

Compared to the hundreds of thousands of members in larger historical groups—Daughters of the American Revolution, Sons of the Revolution and National Society of Colonial Dames to cite only three—the ranks of DSDI are sparse indeed. Currently a mere 1,350 are on roll. Despite this small number, they come from all 50 states and several foreign countries.

It's one thing to have a distant family member who inked his signature on parchment in 1776. But to be recognized by DSDI, applicants must have a direct lineal tie.

Of the 56 signers, 14 left no progeny. That makes for significant trimming of potential family trees.

"Yes, it does come as a disappointment for some applicants," Croft acknowledged. "Certainly, many people can claim a legitimate link through ancestors like a brother, uncle or cousin. But for our purposes, they must be directly descended."

Members gather at historic U.S. sites for spring and fall meetings, but their biggie always centers around July 4th in Philly.

"We're not a political group," said Croft—who, by the way, was a defensive end for the University of Virginia football team in the late 1960s. "In fact, our members represent political views from all across the spectrum."

But no matter who your forefathers were, and even if you don't belong to such an elite group as DSDI, be sure to celebrate the greatest country on this planet.

Happy birthday, America. May you have many, many, many more.

My kind of fraud

I'd love to celebrate National Grandparents Day on its traditional day in September, but that would be double-dipping.

I used all my Grandparents Day points on Friday, July 17, 2015. Coincidentally, that would have been the 101st birthday of my own father—a man who died, oh-so-young, before ever laying eyes on my children, let alone theirs.

Even more strange, I spent my G-Day equity in criminal fashion. I committed wholesale fraud. This occurred the week our tribe vacationed at Ocean Isle Beach, North Carolina.

The first day, grandson Max, 9, was actively probing the sand and surf with a small-mesh net. Among the minnows, coquinas, crabs, shells and other ocean detritus he captured was a tiny shark's tooth. This discovery sealed Max's fate for the rest of our trip.

He worked the net daily. No telling how many cubic yards of sand he displaced. Atlantic shipping lanes and tidal patterns surely were altered.

Alas, he never found another shark's tooth.

One night, daughter Megan and son-in-law Benny gathered all the grandkids and took 'em to a pirate show attraction. Six of us geezers drove to Southport for supper.

Strolling the sidewalks of that wonderful old town, we happened upon an antique-curio shop. Among the myriad items inside was a vast display of sharks' teeth. Black, serrated, menacing ones, some nearly two inches long.

I picked out a gem and forked over my lucre.

"Tomorrow," I announced, "Max is going to discover one hellacious shark's tooth."

Mary Ann was aghast.

"Don't you lie to that boy!" she admonished. "That's dishonest! Just give it to him."

"No way," I answered. "It'll mean more to Max if he 'finds' it himself."

Which, of course, he did early the next morning as he and I excavated yet another section of coastline.

Waiting until he turned away, I slipped my treasure into the mound of sand inside his net, then backed off. In a second or two, Max lugged the mesh into the surf to wash out sand and inspect the residue.

Max stared in disbelief momentarily. Then he shouted. He danced. We high-fived and hugged. I assured him a huge shark had died somewhere well offshore, that the tooth had taken years to wash in, and how lucky he was to find it.

He ran back to our rental house, the tooth clutched in his fist. Later that day, he spent his own money for a shell-studded jewelry case to display it.

"You'll burn for this," Mary Ann hissed.

Maybe. But when I exit this orb, if the last memory I have is seeing Max's eyes light up and hearing him joyously scream, "Dipsey! It's a giant shark's tooth!" over the roar of the surf, it'll be worth a few turns on the rotisserie.

Modern school 'daze'

Consider yourself a card-carrying geezer if you are stunned by back-to-school information long before the calendar flips to August.

Back in my day (another geezer clue, also a cue for non-geezers' eyes to glaze over), the words "August" and "school" were mutually exclusive. August had no more connection to education than June or July. Instead, it merely was the last of the vacation triumvirate.

Not anymore.

By mid-August—a time when we juvenile baby boomers had started to barely detect the first inkling that a new scholastic year loomed "somewhere" on the distant horizon—schools are going full bore all over the map. Some even earlier than that.

Driving home from the Grainger County Tomato Festival in late July 2014, I noticed the sign in front of Joppa Elementary School. It said classes were to begin in just a few days. I dang-near ran off Highway 11W in sympathetic shock.

Oh, well; at least it's refreshing to know some things in redneck academia never change. Specifically, the ol' hidden comic book trick. It is alive and well and still being practiced.

If you geeze, you know what I'm talking about. This was a ruse carried out in elementary and high school study halls (do they still have those things?) and libraries.

Pretending to be absorbed in the business at hand, the student would stash a comic book into the middle of his—it was almost always a he—textbook. Then he would stare into the volume as if entranced. With deft use of fingertips, the student could turn the pages of the comic book just the same as a textbook.

Thus, "The Adventures of Tom and Jerry" could be relished under the guise of "A Tale of Two Cities."

What if a teacher or librarian started making exploratory rounds? No problem.

The student would calmly close his book and begin "taking notes." Which, in reality, were little more than scribbles as Old Lady Jones paced the aisles. As soon as O.L. Jones returned to her seat at the front of the room, the "reading" resumed.

How does this relate to the present? At the aforementioned tomato festival, a teacher confessed her secret on how to survive boring in-service sessions at the start of every school year.

"For two or three weeks ahead of in-service, just clip the Jumble puzzle out of the newspaper," she said. "Paste them in your notebook and then work them during the program. That way, you'll always be the one 'taking the most notes'."

Dang. Sure wish I'd thought of that trick in O.L. Jones' class.

The blower brigade

The sounds of the season are upon us, and I ain't talkin' "Jingle Bells." I speak instead of leaf blowers.

Poke your head outside any waking hour during late autumn, and you'll hear the blower brigades blaring loudly.

Some folks object to this noise. They would prefer the more subtle, soothing sound of rake tines. A quarter-century ago, before leaf blowers evolved from casual trinkets to everyman lawn care necessities, I would receive occasional calls about them from angry homeowners.

"Those (expletive) things have ruined fall!" was the gist of this ire.

I always noted an important factor about these calls. In nearly every instance, they came from posh neighborhoods where leaf-gathering chores were assigned to the hired help.

No wonder Mr. and Mrs. Bigbucks were upset! They couldn't sit on the veranda and enjoy a fall afternoon while Booger, Joe Billy and Earl Gene did the "scritch-scritch-scritching."

T'was ever thus, I suppose.

I'm too young to remember when the only sound of recreational transportation on lakes, rivers and streams came from oars, paddles and sails flapping in the wind. There was no internal combustion interference back then. What's more, what began as the quiet "putt-putt" from six horses has escalated these days to the jet-roar of twin 250s in vast flotillas.

So yes, I do understand. On land or water, noise pollution is a problem.

But I also know it isn't going away anytime soon—even though newer leaf blowers and outboards are considerably more muffled than the originals.

If that makes me an industry apologist, so be it. When your house is plunked in the midst of a forest, as mine is, you jockey a leaf blower from September through New Year's. It's a decidedly more efficient way to round up millions of calling cards from maples, oaks, hickories, sourwoods, dogwoods and other deciduous trees after their autumnal beauty fades.

Much easier on the arms, elbows and shoulders, too. Especially, ahem, if you're dealing with rotator cuff issues.

Still, it never ceases to amaze me how some individual leaves flaunt the laws of aerodynamics. They stubbornly refuse to be lifted into flight, no matter the hurricane swirling inches away. All it takes is a bent stem in grass. Or a serrated edge clinging to vines. Or a spine caught just-so beneath an exposed root.

Nope. You can varoom to your heart's (or temper's) content. It won't budge.

For Pete's sake, I've even seen certain leaves virtually welded to pavement until the wind angle is slightly adjusted. Then they rocket off to parts unknown.

Booger, Joe Billy and Earl Gene didn't have those problems when they were "scritch-scritch-scritching."

Wood smoke signals a rite of fall

One of the finest birthday presents my wife ever gave me sits, rusted and a bit off-kilter, at the top of our driveway.

But be not fooled by appearances. By no means is this thing abandoned or neglected. Rusted is the condition it's supposed to be in. I wouldn't have it any other way.

The item in question is a metal, yet portable, fire pit. Mary Ann bought it for me half a decade ago. During the heat of summer it stays under cover in our cooking shed, aka "The Smoking Parlor."

But from the first hint of autumn crispness to the dead of winter and back again to spring's green-up, it sees regular duty. So much so that it has taken on a crooked stature, thanks to long and frequent exposure to glowing hardwood.

Mary Ann and I ate supper by this pit on three recent cool evenings. Food never tasted better.

Agreed, I am a fire freak. I haven't built one indoors just yet; probably won't until the weather turns permanently cold. Fine. The pit gives me a chance to jump-start the season on a whim. Just a few wads of paper, a couple of sticks of kindling and three or four crisscrossed pieces of dry oak and hickory. Add a match, and you've got instant relaxation.

I realize I'm preaching to the choir among hikers, campers, boaters, hunters, fishers and others who recreate in the outdoors, but there is something about this pyro-business that is deeply rooted in the human psyche. In 6000 B.C. or Modern Day A.D., immense enjoyment can be had from nothing more than a crackling blaze.

That's what is so odd. Unless necessary for heat or cooking, there's no sense even having a fire at all. Yet what is the first outdoor task? What image immediately comes to mind? Gathering fuel and laying the fire, of course.

Then, even better, comes the requirement to sit around it—sometimes talking, sometimes silent—as glowing embers build below and yellow flames lick into the darkness.

Pit fires have a sleep-inducing quality the strongest prescription medicines can't touch. Not deep slumber, necessarily; more of a checking-the-back-of-your-eyelids snooze. The kind of nod that permits awakening long enough to procure another log and set it carefully—no spark-showering tosses, for Pete's sake!—atop the coals, before nestling back into repose once more.

This is a sacred rite. The fire pit cracks and pops. The flames dance. Oft-told stories are retold once more.

For Cro-Magnon Man in his cave or Steve Suburbanite on his patio, here is utopia.

Evil mutants

We gather today to pay seasonal homage to sugar, corn syrup, titanium dioxide and food dyes Yellow 5 and 6, Red 3 and Blue 1, blended into a tooth-rotting, belt-expanding, artery-clogging delicacy known as candy corn.

I have written previously about this Halloween treat. I expect to write about it in the future. When something as heaven-sent as candy corn is concerned, overwriting isn't possible.

But there are storm clouds on the horizon. Evil mutants have been created, threatening to ruin this culinary experience.

I should have suspected chicanery was afoot. After all, confectioners have been messing with traditional Halloween candy corn for years. They started by adding chocolate. Bleech!

Not that there's anything wrong with chocolate—from Hershey to Ghirardelli and beyond. Chocolate is fine on peanut butter, as in Reese's cups. Also drizzled atop cherries, strawberries and apricots.

But chocolate-colored and chocolate-tasting candy corn is an affront to the eyes and taste buds alike. People of proper breeding and manners avoid it.

The people at Brach's further sinned by formulating a caustic purgative known as "caramel candy corn." Bleech II!

Caramel itself is divine. I recommend it straight or melted on apples or ice cream. But not cooked into candy corn.

Some combos are simply not meant to be. Guava paste on pork barbecue, for instance. Same with caramel and candy corn.

Indeed, the only mutated form of candy corn your obedient servant can recommend with a clear conscience is the round, orange candy corn pumpkin. True, these babies don't appeal to the eye like good ol' orange, yellow and white-tipped candy corn kernels.

But their generous size ensures you advance to the tooth-rotting, belt-expanding, artery-clogging stage that much faster.

Friday now has become Thursday

If the present trend continues, here's the start of a business story newspaper readers might see in the not-too-distant future:

NEW YORK, May 15—Based on the excellent results of Orange Friday last week, marking the start of the Halloween shopping season, analysts expect a better-than-average turnout for Black Friday on June 17, official beginning of the Christmas shopping season. If those two events post back-to-back profits, it is expected that Red Friday on July 18, kicking off the Valentine's Day shopping season, should break all records. At this early date, however, market watchers are hesitant to predict the outcome of Firecracker Friday on August 25, marking the official start of Independence Day sales.

Heaven help us. How did this happen? How did we let the holidays get so over-hyped and scheduled so far ahead of time? In particular, how did Thanksgiving become so butchered, so dissed? How did the one day of the year dedicated to family and friends, reflection and appreciation evolve into just another opportunity to turn a quick buck?

I suppose we should have seen it coming. Ever since Black Friday's opening hours crept backward from 8 a.m. to 6 a.m., then 5 a.m., then 4 a.m., then midnight, then 8 p.m. on Thanksgiving Day, it was only a matter of time before T-Day itself was wholly corrupted.

The result? No Thanksgiving respite whatsoever for store workers and their families. Instead, it is just another Thursday to clock in early and fire up the cash registers.

"Maybe the solution is to start Thanksgiving Day on Wednesday," Knoxvillian Charlie Thomas recently suggested to me.

Had to admit it was a decent idea. But you know what'll happen soon after that. Sure as Ben Franklin's mug graces the $100 bill, Black Friday will eventually creep into Wednesday, then Tuesday, then Monday, ad nauseam, until we're back at the third Thursday in November. Then the second. Then the first.

Thi$ i$ called progre$$.

Oh, well. Far be it from me to cast a pall on your Thanksgiving celebrations. May you and yours enjoy a quick turkey biscuit for breakfast before heading out to the malls. Along the way, here's a holiday hymn you might wish to sing:

Come, ye shopping people, come; no need to relax at home.

All our shelves are stocked within; let the Yuletide sales begin.

Latch a U-Haul to your ride; fill it high and deep and wide.

Come and help us make big bucks—all you frenzied, spending schmucks.

Hmm. Now that I'm in such a seasonal mood, here's another ode to the odious:

We gather together to ask Visa's blessings, that we—and not those jerks—will find the best deal.

We'll kick, shove and chop-block and make purchases non-stop. Sing praises to the bargain, and sing them with zeal!

Expensive songs of the season

How come "The Twelve Days of Christmas" always hogs the holiday economic limelight?

I speak, of course, of the cost of all those leaping lords, dancing ladies and drumming drummers. For more than three decades, a Pittsburgh-based bank has issued its "Christmas Price Index." This is a whimsical analysis of how much some dopey true love would have to fork over to supply 12 days' worth of piping pipers, milking maids, et al. At last tally, it was up to $34,131.

Big whoop. Anybody stupid enough to trash a house with calling birds, swimming swans, French hens and turtledoves would also have to spend a bundle to clean the joint up.

So why not subject some other Yule tunes to the same test? Such as:

"Deck the Halls." Holly boughs are cheap and readily available. But gay apparel could run into serious coin, even at a consignment shop.

"Go Tell It on the Mountain." Checked the price of Gatlinburg real estate these days? Despite the recession, we're talkin' mucho moolah.

"Jingle Bell Rock." Leasing Jingle Bell Square for you and your friends could blow the gift budget.

"Chestnuts Roasting on an Open Fire." Chinese chestnuts don't cost much, but locking down an open-fire permit could be dicey if the weather is unseasonably dry and windy.

"Santa Claus Is Comin' to Town." Tin horns and toy drums may be little, but they carry a huge price tag at high-end stores.

"Little Drummer Boy." See previous entry.

"Frosty the Snowman." Given the plummeting coal market, this could be a bargain. Just be wary of legal fees; you might get dragged into court for exposing kiddies to smoking pipes, corncob or otherwise.

"Away in a Manger." My neighbor recently sank a bundle into a new horse stable. Money well spent, for sure, but I'll bet he'd tell you renting the Ritz-Carlton's penthouse suite would be decidedly less expensive.

"Do You Hear What I Hear?" The price of hearing aids is astronomical. Medicare and private insurance won't cover it, either.

"Dashing Through the Snow." You could buy a decent used 4WD for the cost of a sleigh and bob-tailed horse, not to mention access fee for some farmer's open fields. And the 4WD will serve you during spring, summer and fall as well as a few days of snow in winter.

"I Saw Three Ships Come Sailing In." Whoa! If those vessels belong to Royal Caribbean, Norwegian Cruise Lines or Holland America, your Visa better have a $100 million line of credit, minimum.

"We Three Kings." Forget this one. Donald Trump won't let 'em enter the U.S., no matter how many gifts they bear.

Let me be brief

Oh, what a boring life I've led! I thought giving a man underwear for Christmas was unimaginative at best, crude at worst. You know, like a frying pan for the missus and zit medicine for your kids.

Perhaps that's because I've always worn the same-old, same-old white briefs.

Little did I know there's a wild world of skivvies available for Yuletide gifting. Thankfully, I have colleagues and friends who (1) wish to broaden my sartorial horizons and (2) know I'll jump on any cheap holiday column idea.

First up for your consideration are bacon-scented undies. News Sentinel food writer Mary Constantine called them to my attention.

According to an accompanying news release by the manufacturer, J&D Foods, this product "represents the gold standard of meat-scented luxury undergarments. Each pair is handcrafted in the USA to offer the support of briefs, the freedom of boxers and the smell of breakfast cooking in your pants."

When I read that line, the first thought that flashed through my mind was, "Whoa! Stinky drawers are a no-no up and down the line. But anybody who has bacon cooking in his pants has a more serious problem than odor. Aaaiiieee! His privates are turning crispy!"

Apparently not. The company claims it is using "scent-emission technology stolen from NASA" to embed the aroma of bacon into the fabric. Further, it says the scent will remain through repeated washings for up to six months or even a year. In addition, it advises potential wearers to avoid "dogs with razor-sharp teeth" and "hiking in the woods where bears are known to roam." Consider yourself warned.

The second product comes via Knoxville travel writer Katy Koontz. For lack of a better term, it's "non-underwear underwear."

Its name is "Birddogs—the Yoga Pants for Men."

"Why should women be the only ones who get to revel in the joys and solace of such wonders?" said a company info sheet. "We have concocted a pair of gym shorts that free men from the tyranny of underwear. Birddogs are made with a silky-soft liner that gives just a hint of support, only during times when you need it. All the support of underwear, without the discomfort."

Translation: These things are supposed to be worn commando.

Sigh. I have never viewed underwear as a tyrannical garment. Nor do I wish mine to smell like a slab of bacon. What's next? Sushi slacks? Hot dog hankies? Hamburger hats?

The more I think about it, the more I believe a six-pack of 100-percent cotton, plain white briefs would be perfect for me this Christmas.

Who says the tree must be green?

When it comes to Christmas trees, the Venables have pretty much been there, done that.

Through the years, our home has seen artificial trees, freshly cut trees, trees in a ball of soil to be planted in the New Year. We've had hemlocks, firs, cedars, pines. Tall ones that had to be tied to the loft railing. Short ones that could've stood in a coffee can. Fat. Skinny. You name it.

But until 2015, we'd never had a leafless, bare-limbed Charlie Brown tree. Or, I should more accurately say, a Charlie Brown tree on steroids. Therein lies a story.

I was coming in from deer hunting one afternoon and happened to notice the barren crown of a large tree in the woods. It was a perfect triangle. And it got me to thinking, "Hmmm."

The next morning I was back, this time with a hand saw instead of a rifle. I prowled around in a nearby overgrown field, looking for saplings that weren't surrounded by competition. That way, they were less likely to be one-sided.

I located and sawed three eight-foot specimens—hackberry, yellow poplar and Bradford pear.

The hackberry turned out to be too bushy. The poplar was too thin, not enough decent limbs for ornaments. But the Bradford pear, after a bit of surgery, was perfect.

Please understand. I'm talking a tree without one leaf whatsoever. Nothing but trunk and branches. I put it into the stand, screwed everything down tight and positioned it in the "Christmas tree corner" of our log house.

Mary Ann and I prefer tiny white lights for our Yule tree, so we set about circling it with cord. The job was going OK-ish when M.A., ever the artist, stepped back, studied a moment and said, "Wait. Let's wrap the wires around each limb, up and down."

So done. Then out came boxes of decorations.

Holy holidays! You'd be amazed how easily they went on! No poking fingertips with needles. No needles to shed, either. No sticky sap.

The heavier ornaments were ideal for weighing down the larger, more vertical limbs. Lighter ones filled in the gaps on horizontal branches. Yet something was missing.

Of course! A pear Christmas tree needs a partridge. And I knew the perfect candidate.

Decades ago, my Aunt Eva had a large mimosa removed from her yard. A woodworker friend of hers took it. In exchange, he carved her a pair of quail. Eva gave them to me long before her death in 1986.

With hidden tape and a bright red ribbon, we mounted one "pot'tidge" on a limb and declared this was our prettiest, if not most unusual, Christmas tree ever.

Now, if I could just get those dancing ladies, leaping lords, milking maids and golden rings out of my head.

Occasionally a serious thought overcomes even the most committed of humorists. My pat, flippant remedy for situations like this is, "Take a cold shower and hope the mood passes quickly."

But sometimes you can't. There are too many subjects that need addressing with tongue planted firmly outside of cheek.

As each year goes by, I find myself writing more and more obituary columns. Comes with the territory in my age demographic. I just hope a super-duper, extra-long time passes before I wind up the subject of a few lines in someone else's obit essay.

With the passing of each year, I also understand ever more clearly the stark reality that life is fleeting. Tomorrow is never guaranteed.

Not of all my serious pieces involve death, however. I much prefer to speak of the living, especially "the least of these." Here in the 21st century, legislators find it quite easy to apologize for slavery and the ethnic cleansing of native people. It takes a lot more guts to stand up for the rights—in the here and now—of same-sex couples.

Through these and other issues, I've discovered an abiding truth that transcends the ages: There is unquenchable optimism in the human spirit. May this forever be the case.

Chapter Eight
REMEMBRANCES AND REFLECTIONS

Life can be gone in an instant

In Rodney Kuhn's horse pasture, directly across the road from my driveway, is a memorial cross and a small willow tree. They've been there since Shaniah Mitchell, 15, a student at Hardin Valley Academy, died as the result of a horrific one-vehicle, three-person crash.

I was on my way home that day when I heard a radio news bulletin about the wreck and the traffic snarl it created. I tried to telephone my wife to see how close to our house it occurred and what alternate route I might consider.

Mary Ann didn't answer.

One reason is because two utility poles had been snapped and lines were now snaking up and down the metal-and-glass-covered roadway.

Yet the more abiding reason is because she was at the scene, along with our neighbor Dennis Smelcer, cradling the two conscious survivors in their arms.

Even inside our house, more than 500 feet up the ridge, Mary Ann had heard a boom that occurred when the car careened off our rural road and began tumbling end-over-end through Rodney's fence, coming to rest on its top in his pasture.

She rushed outside, heard frantic screaming, ran downhill and waded through the ruins to offer whatever help she could render to the hysterical teens. She, Dennis and other neighbors and passers-by stayed until emergency workers arrived and transported all three victims to the hospital by helicopter and ambulance.

Here was every parent's worst nightmare. During the Christmas-New Year's holidays, of all times—as if there's any good moment for such an awful turn of events to occur.

You talk to your kids about safety. About speed. About paying continual attention to the business at hand. About how quickly accidents can happen.

Beyond that, all you can do is hope and pray.

In a set of coincidences too bizarre for explanation, this wreck occurred only three hours after a freak accident in the south end of the county claimed the life of a 30-year-old Knoxville woman. Tiffany Nichole Raley was driving along Colonial Road when a 60-foot-tall white oak fell across her car, crushing her in an instant.

This giant tree was perhaps 70 years old. Eighty? Ninety? More? Yet it dropped at that precise moment. Three eye-blinks either way would have meant the difference between a scare and unspeakable tragedy.

Life is precious. Life is fleeting. There are no guarantees about the future—10 seconds or 10 years hence. Live and love like there's no tomorrow.

That's something we all need to remember. Constantly. Not just at the start of a new year.

You gotta be famous for something

Anyone who ever visited Nancy Tanner's home in South Knox County immediately realized she had an interest in birds. Not just any bird, even though she was quite knowledgeable about the feathered tufts gathered 'round her feeder. Rather, she identified with a much larger creature. Much rarer, too. The central theme among numerous porcelains and paintings in her living room was the ivory-billed woodpecker.

"Nancy never actively collected those things," said her longtime friend Stephen Lyn Bales, author and senior naturalist at Ijams Nature Center. "Instead, people were always sending them to her because they knew of her link with the ivory-bill."

This delightful lady died of complications from leukemia. Her passing marked the final chapter of a fascinating life story.

Nancy Burnham Sheedy Tanner—96 years young, Harvard-educated, world-traveled, a university professor, homemaker, great-grandmother, tennis buff and lover of life—was the last person on Earth to claim a "universally accepted" sighting of the aforementioned woodpecker, an extinct species that has gained almost mythical status among environmentalists, amateur and professional alike.

"'Universally accepted' is the key phrase," said Bales. "There have been occasional reports of ivory-bills over the years, but Nancy was the last living person who unquestionably saw the bird."

This occurred in December 1941 when Nancy accompanied her husband, Dr. James Tanner, on a research trip into Louisiana's desolate, swampy Singer Tract. He found a nest of the then-vanishing birds and photographed one of their young. The 14 black-and-white shots he took that day are the last proof ever recorded of the ivory-bills' existence.

"Everybody has to be famous for something," she once quipped to me about her "last-person" honor.

"That was typical of Nancy," said Bales. "Even when she wasn't feeling well, she never lost her sense of humor."

In 2010, the University of Tennessee Press published Bales' acclaimed Ghost Birds, the story of Jim Tanner's legendary research. The ornithologist, who taught at UT for many years, died in 1991.

"During three years of book research, when I saw Nancy almost weekly, I always left in a better mood than when I arrived," Bales noted. "Her good humor was that contagious. I will miss her dearly. Even though she was frail, she had an intense determination to live.

"I visited with her shortly before her death. She signed one last book that a friend had asked me to take to her. As I stood to leave, she took my hand in hers, looked deeply into my eyes and said, 'Goodbye, love.' I cried all the way out."

Missing the overall message

To paraphrase Pogo, we have met the Grinch, and he is us. That's the way I feel about the fuss over what kind of Christmas greetings to exchange.

Oops, I've goofed already—at least in the minds of people who wear their religion and traditions on their sleeve. I used the word "greetings" (as in season's) instead of pointedly shouting, "MERRY CHRISTMAS!"

Only in 21st-century America could such a joyous season be tainted by some who insist there is only one expression of tidings. Reminds me of the grumpy cook we had at Camp Pellissippi in the Pleistocene era of my Boy Scout days. Anytime you'd offer a "g'morning," he'd angrily bark, "What's good about it?!"

I always suspected Cookie's gruff demeanor was more for show than anything. But I don't detect that same underlying spirit in the way some people issue a defiant "MERRY CHRISTMAS!" You can almost hear them daring you to challenge their right to speak those words above all others.

If so, methinks they've missed the overall message.

I call your attention to a spiteful letter to the editor that appeared in the News Sentinel on Friday, December 11, 2015. The writer concluded his I'm-right-and-you're-wrong rant with, "If all you've got is 'Happy Holidays,' spare me."

Huh? Someone conveys happiness and the guy takes offense? May he get lumps of coal in his stocking.

I just tickled a few computer keys and found 14 Christian holidays late in the year. Everything from Advent (fourth Sunday preceding December 25) to Krampusnacht (eve of the feast of Saint Nicholas in parts of Europe on December 6) to Saint Lucia's Day (December 13) to Christmas Day (December 25) to the Twelve Days of Christmas (December 25-January 6) and more. What better way for Christians to celebrate than with an all-inclusive "Happy Holidays!"?

What's more—and I realize this may be unnerving to good and faithful people who believe Christianity is the only religion stamped with God's seal of approval—the world brims with bazillions of other folks, just as good and faithful, who follow different customs and religious traditions. Yes, (gasp!) including Muslims.

One Christmas long ago, my late father, an Army infantry major, was stationed in Europe. He was among tens of thousands of troops mustering for the invasion of Japan. An invasion, thankfully, that wasn't necessary. Surely he and his men weren't worried about details for sharing their joy.

There was never a more devout, practicing follower of Jesus Christ than Big Sam. His favorite holiday expression was "Season's Greetings!" And he meant it from the bottom of his warm, wonderful heart.

Go thee and speak likewise.

A few cheers for the graduates

I'm about to violate two cardinal rules of geezerdom.

First, I'm not going to rail about how the lazy, ignorant youth of America are leading this great nation to hell, in a handbasket or otherwise. Second, I'm not going to chew my gums about how much better things were in the good ol' days.

As each day passes, my generation gets closer to the moment we will pass down the reins. This is going to occur whether we like it or not. It happened to our parents' generation and the one before. And before and before and before. We might as well accept the reality of this situation.

So I'll say it loud and proud: I am quite optimistic about the future, thank you very much. And I realize this sentiment just amounted to full-blown geezer heresy.

Aged croaks like me are supposed to sigh at the very thought of tomorrow's leaders. We are expected to list their many shortcomings and their utter lack of real-world experience. Duty requires that we shudder and wring our hands.

But I'll have none of it.

Freshly minted high school and college grads may drive me batty with their constant texting and earbud listening habits. But they've forgotten more technical skills than I could learn in three lifetimes.

They will use these skills as the world grows more complex around them—and then wince when it dawns on them that another generation has come along, one that knows even more than they do. Life has a habit of sucker-punching humans that way.

As a group, today's young people are more accepting, more diverse and less set in their ways than my alleged cool, hip clan.

True, they can be nutty, sometimes common-sense dense, perhaps a bit reckless.

Guess what? So were we.

But we figured things out. They will too. Probably a lot faster and more effectively than what occurred on our watch.

Several times in recent years it has been my privilege to serve on committees selecting recipients for scholarships and non-academic awards. On every occasion, I have been stunned by the energy, passion, creativity and hard work of today's young people.

The vast majority are everyday Janes and Joes. They're neither at the top of their class, nor are they the dregs.

Instead, they're cut from the same cloth that keeps producing doctors, teachers, sales clerks, cops, mechanics, lawyers, engineers, designers, farmers, insurance agents, contractors and 10,001 other skilled workers.

They'll do just fine. Better than we deserve.

It's never too late—or too early

It took Tennessee more than 180 years to get on the right side of history. We're making progress. But we're not there yet.

In March 2014, the State House passed a resolution expressing regret for the Indian Removal Act of 1830 and the Trail of Tears that followed. It was sponsored by Republican Caucus chairman Glen Casada of Franklin and adopted 90-0.

True, this was merely a symbol. A gesture. A nod to the past, replete with flowery "whereases" and "therefores" adding up to an official "sorry."

Despite its rather benign name, the removal act amounted to genocide via ethnic cleansing. It authorized the forced evacuation of Native Americans from their ancestral homes in the Southeast. Back in the day, this was considered the correct step to take against "savages." It was deemed necessary to make room for growing populations of "peaceful" settlers, farmers and business interests.

Among those forced out were more than 16,000 members of the Cherokee nation, plus others from Chickasaw, Yuchi, Creek, Choctaw and Shawnee tribes. They were marched to reservations in present-day Oklahoma. Untold thousands perished along the way from disease, starvation, exposure and murder at the hands of their oppressors.

Does the House resolution bring these dead back to life? Does it absolve the guilty? Does it rewrite history?

Of course not. In many respects, this effort can be boiled down into four words: too little, too late. But at least it's an official acknowledgment that a shameful, heinous wrong was carried out by the government.

Recognition of yet another grave political and societal injustice apparently is on its way. Casada says he is preparing a resolution to apologize for Tennessee's support of slavery. I have no doubt this measure also will pass without a dissenting vote.

To repeat: Rewriting history is impossible. Nonetheless, events can be changed before they become "historical." Just don't bank on that happening anytime soon.

No sooner did the U.S. Supreme strike down laws against same-sex marriage, many states, including Tennessee, proposed legislative end-arounds. A Tennessee attorney general's ruling said the Supreme Court decision "frustrates the will of the people."

Translation: Prejudice and persecution are still alive and well. Just in a different form.

I'm quite certain if you had polled Tennesseans in 1830, and again in 1860, "the will of the people" would have been four-square in favor of evicting Indians and owning slaves.

The soul of Pittman Center

Over the past eight decades, much has changed in the Sevier County hamlet of Pittman Center, tucked deep into the verdant woodlands of Emert's Cove, just north of Greenbrier.

For one thing, it's no longer an unincorporated community but a full-fledged city (population 502), replete with its own mayor and town hall.

Acres of river bottom fields, at one time lush with corn, hay and patchworks of tobacco, have yielded to developed communities and a golf course.

Gone also are many of the barns and country stores once wedged into crevices off State Highway 416 as it twists, rises and falls along Middle Prong of the Pigeon River. In their place are pricey rustic mansions, gated entrances, security cameras and stark "No Trespassing" signs.

You see more khaki slacks and L.L. Bean loafers these days, fewer faded overalls and high-topped brogans.

But despite governmental, vocational, economic and social changes, one thing always remained constant. Until August 10, 2014, that is. When Rev. Melvin David Carr, 89, broke his earthly chains, the soul of Pittman Center died too. If mountains and trees and rocks could cry, they did so that sad day.

Yet I'm just as certain there was a joyous heavenly reunion with his only son Dannie, killed in Vietnam in 1969, and his beloved Eunice, wife of 68 years who crossed to the other side two months before her husband.

Melvin and I met in the early 1960s through mutual friends and the medium of outdoors. He was an extraordinary grouse hunter and trout fisherman, never hesitant to share his skills with unschooled hooligans.

Here was one of the kindest, most humble people I've ever known. He stood a good 6-3, straight as a poplar, narrow at the waist, hickory-bark tanned, Hollywood handsome, with eyes that twinkled, silver hair that curled around his ears and a warm smile welded to his lips. When Melvin spoke, it was always softly, with genuine concern.

Many a warrior has found salvation during the heat of battle. Often the condition is temporary. Not so in this case. Still a teenager, Melvin fought in some of the fiercest naval campaigns of World War II. One particular day, as Japanese aircraft zeroed in on the USS Pennsylvania, he pledged his life to the Lord—"if You'll let me see my family and the mountains again."

Done. And done.

Throughout his Baptist ministry, Melvin pastored 10 churches— preaching, marrying, burying and caring, living every minute as a witness to The Word.

You've heard the term "a true man of God"? I have, and I don't use it often or lightly.

Here was one.

No stopping her will to succeed

A message for stressed-out, unappreciated and underpaid teachers at the end of every school year: Students like Loretta Ann Starnes are the reason you chose this profession.

They're the ones who send you back to the classroom each fall with renewed dedication, a fresh sense of purpose and restored confidence you can make a positive difference in someone's life.

Starnes was one of more than 1,000 students who received diplomas during spring 2012 graduation ceremonies at Roane State Community College. Not only did she earn an associates of applied sciences degree in occupational therapy, she also was named winner of the President's Award.

At 26, Starnes was a bit older than her classmates. Heaven knows she overcame more challenges along the path than most of the others.

Her journey began in 2001 in Arcadia, Florida. She was a high-school dropout. Freshman. Pregnant. No hope of a decent future for herself or the child in her womb.

"I hated school," Starnes recalled. "Anytime I could skip out of class, I did. When I left DeSoto High, I never planned to set foot in school again."

She married, bore a son and assumed "all I could do was have another baby." Which she did.

About that time, Hurricane Charley intervened, ripping apart her home and extended family. "We all sorta trickled up to Tennessee," she says with a sweet smile.

They wound up in Sunbright. Husband James found work as a guard at Morgan County Regional Prison.

Starnes began glancing at the textbooks her young sons brought home from school. A renewed interest in education suddenly flickered. She went to the Morgan County Career Center, her mind set on earning a GED. In 2007, she made it.

Then she aimed her sights higher.

"Learning doesn't come easy for me," she said. "When I got to Roane State, I had tons of developmental courses to take. But I had encouraging professors all along the way. I remember making 100 on a math test one time. The teacher (Jeff Sexton) told me, 'Good job, Loretta.' I can still see the look on his face and remember how proud I felt."

She lit into other courses with a passion, boosting her grade-point average to 3.84 by graduation.

Starnes and her family are about to move to Dandridge. She has accepted a job as occupational therapist at a nursing home, helping patients with physical, mental and emotional disabilities. James has been hired at the juvenile detention center there.

"When I was growing up, I believed college wasn't for people like us," she said. "We were raised to think we'd never succeed. I refuse to believe that now."

An abrupt change in attitude

What a difference one hour can make.

"Everything went from jovial to somber," Harry Moskos remembers. "Boom. Just like that."

It was November 23, 1963. Moskos, then 27, was bureau chief for the Associated Press in Honolulu, Hawaii. His assignment that sleepy day was to drive to nearby Hickam Air Force Base and knock out a few paragraphs about some Washington bigwigs who were flying to Japan.

"I don't recall everyone who was on the flight," said Moskos, retired News Sentinel editor who lives in the Fox Den community, several miles west of Knoxville. "But I distinctly remember two of them: Pierre Salinger, the White House press secretary, and Robert McNamara, secretary of defense. They were going to a conference in Tokyo and stopped at Hickam to refuel.

"I can't even remember what we talked about. Everything was light. They were having a great time."

Little did anybody realize what was taking place that very moment in faraway Texas.

Moskos and Malcolm Barr, another AP reporter, left the airfield and drove back to their office. Just as they walked through the door, reporter Jim Lagier barked, "The president has been shot!"

"We learned the plane was headed back to Hickam," said Moskos. "I don't know why; surely it wasn't to take on more fuel. Maybe they were supposed to get orders on what to do in the emergency. Anyway, we quickly drove back to the airbase."

When the plane landed, its occupants were in a state of complete shock.

"All I can remember is how crestfallen everybody was," said Moskos. "It was the most vivid change in tone you can imagine."

From the perspective of half a century, it's easy to see what was transpiring. But minute-by-minute events back then were different.

"Everyone was in the dark about what had happened in Dallas," he said. "Nobody knew what was going on. I remember filing a story about the mood at the air base, but I couldn't tell you now what it said. One thing does stand out, though, now that I look back on it. It's the fact that Salinger's assistant was doing all the talking in Dallas because he (Salinger) was in Hawaii."

Moskos left AP in 1969 and went to the Albuquerque (New Mexico) Tribune. He eventually moved to the El Paso (Texas) Herald-Post before being named News Sentinel editor in 1984. He retired in 2001.

"The biggest story I ever covered in Hawaii had nothing to do with JFK," he told me. "Instead, it was on Christmas Eve 1968, when the crew of the USS Pueblo (held captive for 11 months by North Korea) reached American soil. I was the only print journalist there. The Navy called and said there was room for one reporter.

"We flipped a coin with United Press International. I won."

Deliver us from pandering

As far as toothless legislation is concerned, a new Tennessee law is about as ho-hum as it gets. It's no different from nonsensical resolutions honoring Dandruff Awareness Day, Strawberry Pancake Syrup Week, Prevent Ingrown Toenails Month or any other baloney on which lawmakers waste their time and our money every time a gavel falls in Nashville.

It's a voluntary law, at best, meaning you're free to abide by it or ignore it. It's unenforceable. There are no penalties, no fines, no nothing. So there's no sense losing sleep over it.

Except ...

This is yet another attempt by Christian evangelicals to influence everyone else with their notion of religion. Unlike many similar bills, this one was a cupcake. It generated less interest than a $2 savings account. It was overwhelmingly approved by both chambers and almost immediately signed into law by Governor Bill Haslam. I never heard a word about it until I noticed brief mention in my old colleague Tom Humphrey's blog post.

The law calls for a "weekend of prayer over students" at the first of August each year. During this time, "Tennesseans are encouraged to pray for protection, guidance and peace, and for opportunities and blessings on the students of Tennessee."

I agree with the general theme.

But I disagree that it's any business of the Tennessee General Assembly to set something like this in stone, especially when the genesis came from a far-right Christian group seeking to "extend youth ministries into public middle and high schools."

That last quote comes from a Republican Senate Caucus news release. It is credited to First Priority Blue Ridge of Johnson City, the aforementioned evangelical association.

Pop quiz: How quickly would this bill have died had it been proposed by a non-Christian religious organization? You know the answer as well as I.

Let's be clear on this. I'm not against prayer. Quite the contrary. I encourage it. As the Bible says, we should "pray without ceasing."

But it needs to come from within. Not by edict.

Heaven knows there are millions of Tennesseans who need praying over in addition to students and teachers. Police officers and firefighters, for example. Parents. Nurses. Truckers. Musicians. Newspaper columnists. Workers of all stripes. The washed. The unwashed. And on and on.

While we're at it, perhaps it wouldn't hurt to also pray for relief from pandering politicians.

No fear, no worry, no brain

ITBOM just flew past my house. Again.

It prompted me to say a silent prayer. Again.

This is a routine I've been following for well over a year.

ITBOM is my acronym for Idiot Teenaged Boy On Motorcycle.

Before you ask, the answer on both counts is no; I don't know the age or gender of this cyclist. But having once been an idiot teenaged boy myself, I'd lay serious coin on the odds.

ITBOM always announces himself well in advance. I can hear him revving up, louder and faster, as he rounds the turn onto our rural road and heads west.

We're not talking a throaty Harley roar. This kid's bike is much smaller. The sound it makes is more like a mosquito on steroids: eeeeeEEEEE!

But speed is speed, no matter what size vehicle. When ITBOM passes my driveway, I would conservatively guess he's doing 60, maybe 70 mph. There are times he can't be far off 80. I'm serious.

eeeeeEEEE! *Zzzzzzzz*ip!

Gone in an eye-blink.

Not only is our road little more than a country lane, it undulates like a shaken rope. On many stretches, visibility is as little as 75 yards. All it would take is a split-second miscue and ITBOM would be launched halfway to Dixie Lee Junction.

Thus my continued silent prayer—for ITBOM, his family and especially any potential victims in his path. It's only been by extraordinarily good fortune that someone hasn't pulled out in front of him. Or, God forbid, walked across the road to their mailbox at the worst possible moment.

According to the Tennessee Department of Safety and Homeland Security, more than 100 motorcyclists on average are killed every year on Tennessee roadways. My gut tells me a fairly substantial number of them are ITBOMs.

My gut tells me something else: If ITBOM's parents had any remote idea he was racing along at these speeds, his ride would be parked in the front yard with a "For Sale" sign across the handlebars. And ITBOM would be walking, not to mention grounded during non-school hours, for forever and a day.

At least I hope that's the case. But you never know. When Little Precious can do no wrong in mama and daddy's eyes, speeding is just another offense to ignore, aka condone, along with doping, drinking, shoplifting, unprotected sex, you name it.

To reiterate. I've been an idiot teenaged boy myself, albeit without a motorcycle. But I know all too well how easily the accelerator of a car can be stomped when you're young and bulletproof. Hopefully, ITBOM will safely outgrow his lunacy.

The sad reality is, a new ITBOM will be ready to take his place.

He lit the flame

The next time you see a snappy newspaper lead, a clever play on words or a declarative sentence that leaps off the page, thank Kelly Leiter. Odds are he had a direct hand in training the hands that wrote them.

For 24 years, Kelly taught journalism at the University of Tennessee. He started as an instructor in 1966, back in the manual typewriter-paste pot

Dark Ages when J-school was an afterthought in the College of Business Administration. He, the curriculum and technology advanced together. By the time of his retirement in 1990, Kelly was dean of the College of Communications and Information. Hundreds of appreciative students learned their craft on his watch.

You're looking at one of them.

In 1967, I was foundering in forestry at UT—thanks in no small part to a full year of chemistry requirements—and took Journalism 111 on not much more than a whim. Kelly was my teacher.

Maybe it was the coursework that won me over. Maybe it was Kelly's enthusiasm—ever bubbling, always challenging. Maybe both. Whatever, the tree geek who could barely hunt and peck on a Royal typewriter soon switched majors and never looked back.

Kelly died in his sleep November 15, 2014. One year shy of 90, he was the youngest-at-heart geezer in the history of aging. Who else would leave his own obituary describing an "unimpressive trek through life"?

In my mind's eye, I can see Kelly chuckling as he typed those words. He laughed often and loudly. The only time a smile left his lips was when his self-described "Irish temper" got the best of him. Then it was wise to duck for cover as the cursing intensified.

Speaking of which, I daresay the ol' prof would've exploded at the obituary use of his formal name, Dr. Barnard Kelly Leiter.

"I've always hated Barnard," he once groused to me. "It's despicable. Parents should be required to simply number their kids and let 'em choose their own name when they get to be adults."

Already an accomplished, street-smart reporter by the time he entered academia, Kelly infused his lectures with vivid illustrations of life in the trenches. He knew this crazy business from all angles—reporter's notes to rough draft to spit-and-polished article.

Foremost, he was a stickler for descriptive verse. He once scribbled these words atop one of my stories: "Jesus, Sam! Put some zip in it! You've taken the most interesting person in America and made him seem like a dog food salesman from Bulls Gap."

You gotta love a guy who can scold like that.

Kelly's last letter to me arrived in August. In it, he reflected: "Like most old farts, I wake at 3 a.m. and have to go pee and then can't get back to sleep. I stare at the ceiling and wonder if I made even a modest contribution as a teacher."

Have mercy. You better believe he did.

Big changes rarely come quickly

"Cigarets Called 'Guilty' in Cancer."

So read a banner headline across the front page of The Knoxville News-Sentinel on Sunday, January 12, 1964.

Oops, hold on a sec. Before we get to the point of this trip down memory lane, I must point out several editorial changes since the 1960s. "Cigarets" was how the word was spelled back in the day. Also, "The" was an official part of the newspaper's name back then, thus was capitalized. Furthermore, there was a hyphen between "News" and "Sentinel," as Gawd Hisself intended, before some meddlesome mortal decided we needed to be "modernized." Those of us in the College of Codgerly Curmudgeon Columnists are slow to accept change.

So too is society at large.

If you doubt it, scroll through some microfilm and see what happened in the wake of the U.S. Surgeon General's blockbuster report on smoking.

Even though doctors and scientists had long suspected tobacco was the root cause of many diseases—lung cancer chiefly among them—it wasn't until 1964 that the full weight of the "guvmit" entered the fray.

Naturally, this news was met with skepticism from smokers, not to mention the tobacco industry. In the months and years that followed, many disbelievers laughed off the findings and bragged they'd never quit. The vast majority of these folks have either changed their ways or have long-since been pushing up posies.

I bring up this nugget of nostalgia because of a legal event that occurred in 2013 in New York City. This was an attempt to ban the sale of supersized sugary drinks.

Before I'm accused of comparing Big Apples with oranges, I readily concede there are worlds of differences—legal, medical, dietary, cultural, you name it—between court cases involving Camels and Cokes. I further concede that trying to force people out of bad health habits rarely works in the long run.

These things take time. They take tweaking. They take education and changes in thinking. There are fits and starts, wrongheaded or otherwise, all along the way.

It's laughable to think outlawing "big gulps" is going to trim waistlines in New York or anywhere else. The obesity crisis in America is multifaceted. This curse is not due simply to excess food and drink (aided and abetted by slick ad campaigns, fast food's version of the Marlboro Man), but also to a nationwide epidemic of "couch potatoitis."

Still, everything begins somewhere. In 1964, could you possibly have imagined smoke-free restaurants, offices, stores, homes and airplanes?

You have to live through it

All three of my grandchildren are in elementary school. I'm stunned by their scholastic abilities.

Max, Lucy and Ella Kate read at a much higher level than I did at their age. Back in the day, I was struggling to recite "See Dick run. Jump Spot jump." When the grandkids come over to spend the night, they often read complete children's volumes—"chapter books," they call 'em—to me.

Their math skills are off the chart, especially compared to mine at the same grade level. (Then again, numbers never were, nor will ever be, my strong suit—even when barefoot, the better to cipher beyond 10.)

And don't even mention savvy with electronics. Despite their tender ages, their comfort with a computer keyboard far exceeds mine when, as a 29-year-old adult, these strange contraptions entered my life.

But there's one educational facet in which I'm leagues ahead of my grandchildren. And everyone in their generation. I'll never need to take an American History class to know the horror of 9/11.

Max and Ella Kate were born five years after the attacks by al-Qaida, Lucy two years later than that. Their "memories" of that awful day will forever be limited to photos of smoke billowing from the Twin Towers and videos of terrified New Yorkers fleeing as buildings collapse.

T'was ever thus.

An early-round baby boomer, I didn't arrive until six years after the assault on Pearl Harbor. Thus, my perspective on the "date which will live in infamy" is the same Max, Ella Kate and Lucy have of 9/11.

It doesn't matter that I studied World War II in high school and college. Or that I've read hundreds of news dispatches by legendary war correspondents Ernie Pyle and Don Whitehead. Or that I've analyzed battle plans resulting in victory and disaster on all sides.

I still have no intimate involvement. I will never know this war on a personal basis. I'm constrained by fate of birth. I'm linked only by black and white images of the USS Arizona listing to one side amid angry clouds of smoke and grainy D-Day newsreels of Allied troops staggering ashore under German machine gun fire.

So what else is new?

My mother's 90 years spanned two global wars in which her father and husband, respectively, were involved. Plus Korea and Vietnam, the latter of which sent her second son to Southeast Asia. Be assured she felt these events to the core of her soul.

Yet her personal connection to the Spanish-American War came only from textbook assignments and paintings of the Rough Riders charging San Juan Hill.

And again: Both of my grandmothers were raised among soldiers from the Civil War. But they tasted its visceral reality only from tintypes of uniformed teenagers and the nightmarish memories of one-legged veterans.

That, literally, is the hell of it. The more we learn about conflicts from the past, the less we seem to know.

Maybe we aren't worth the effort

Any time I gaze into the night sky, the same age-old question comes to mind: Is anything or anybody Out There?

The thought kicked into higher gear recently when scientists proposed there could be billions more potential stars in our galaxy alone, some that are Earth-sized and feature hospitable climates. This report was published in the professional journal Proceedings of the National Academy of Scientists. It suggested there are 8.8 billion such stars in the Milky Way.

"For perspective," an Associated Press article noted, "that's more Earthlike planets than there are people on Earth."

If your mind isn't spinning already, now consider there are billions of other galaxies. Or, in redneck terminology, Earth is a single grain of sand along the entire beach at Panama City. Teeny-tiny, indeed.

The journal's report raised a conundrum posed by one of its authors, Geoff Marcy of the University of California at Berkeley: "If we aren't alone, why is there a deafening silence in our galaxy from advanced civilizations?"

Good question. It's one humans have debated since the dawn of our creation. But I take perfect comfort in either of two possible answers.

1. We simply haven't been "discovered" yet.

Even though Earth is estimated to be 4.54 billion years old, that's a split-second in infinity. It might take another 4.54 billion years, or 454 billion, before we hear, "Hello out there!"

2. "Somebody" has already viewed us from afar and decided we weren't worth messing with.

Given war, disease, pollution, human rights violations and a host of other earthly woes, can't say I blame 'em for moving on to some other place that offers more promise.

As Mark Twain so famously and accurately observed, "We have the best government money can buy."

Newspapers have long been the watchdogs over this official misconduct. I'd like to think our sacred role will never fade. Yet I can't ignore the fact that ever-tightening corporate media budgets could ultimately allow political chicanery to flourish unchecked. Time will tell.

I've never been much of a pulpit-pounding columnist myself. Real pros are much better suited for this role. I find it more enjoyable to poke fun at antics like Tennessee's "jock tax," "whiskey wars" and other nonsense.

In recent years, I've also discovered government isn't the only entity that needs watching over. Big Business Brother is everywhere, and I'm not so sure his snoops aren't more invasive than Uncle Sam's.

In April 2010, during coverage of a phone-hacking trail in U.S. District Court, I listened as the chief of security for Facebook testified that emails, cell calls, tweets and other social media interactions never go away, even if you purge, delete, de-frag, re-program and re-install. Still, hardly a day goes by that some high-profile politician, athlete or entertainer isn't bitten in the butt by a "private" exchange. The same goes for average Joes and Janes.

"The man" may or may not wear a badge. But you can bet he's taking notes.

Chapter Nine
I WOULDN'T RUN FOR
DOG CATCHER!

A shameful showing for our state

Third?! A survey of the most corrupt states in the union comes out, and Tennessee ranks third?

How embarrassing. I thought we would've at least placed second.

Tennessee has a long, proud tradition of producing crooked politicians and business people, which is redundant. And the best we have to show for this effort is a paltry third? Sigh. I hang my head in homeboy shame.

According to Fortune magazine, we can't hold a flame to the big guys. The magazine cited a study conducted by the University of Hong Kong and Indiana University—a diverse educational consortium in and of itself—that looked at more than 25,000 public corruption convictions between 1976 and 2008. Researchers then correlated the data with state spending.

When all the numbers were crunched—or cooked, in proper parlance—turned out the most fertile fields for official fleecing existed in Mississippi (first place) and Louisiana (second).

OK, I'll give 'em Louisiana. Having once worked Down There, I know certain libertie$ are part of the $tate'$ birthright, if not it$ con$titution. The Kingfish himself, Huey Long, set high standards. Still, to get drubbed by Miss'sip is degrading to hillbillies and Cajuns alike.

At least we largely kept this honor in the South. With the exception of Illinois (fourth), Pennsylvania (fifth), Alaska (seventh) and South Dakota (eighth), Dixie sparkled like a handful of stolen diamonds. In addition to the Mississippi-Louisiana-Tennessee trifecta, the Top 10 list included Alabama (sixth), Kentucky (ninth) and Florida (tenth). Yee-haw.

What's more, the study said this costs each person in the 10 states an average of $1,308 per year.

Three things immediately leapt out as I perused the results.

One, we don't refer to these transactions as "corruption." That sounds nasty, evil, sinister. It's how those secular communists behave in Russia. We take the high road, preferring to think of this as "conducting business."

Whether it's a "civic donation for effective legislation," criminal pardons for sale, inflated salaries and benefits for public officials or any of 10,001 other examples of "friendly governance," we continually marvel at how efficiently this greased machine putters along. Thus, we happily re-elect the operators.

Two, considering how many millions of dollars in under-the-table donations are made by the bigwigs, $1,308 per head makes each of us feel like we have our own little stake in the aforementioned "friendly governance."

Third, you will note that many of these high-ranking corrupt states also are the scene of campaigns to have "In God We Trust" posted on public buildings.

Duh. Of course we trust in God. Everybody else pays strictly in cash.

A law in need of sharp tweaking

For once, members of the Tennessee General Assembly used their heads for something besides a hat rack. They got downright innovative with a revenue enhancement plan.

Our wise solons came up with an ideal way to raise money with a minimum of billfold discomfort to John and Jane Public. It was perfect. Uh, almost.

Turns out our legislators weren't innovative enough. As a result, their brilliant "jock tax" program runs the risk of being eliminated.

Here's a bit of background for those scratching their heads, if not their jock itch: Even though Tennessee doesn't have a state income tax, per se, a "privilege tax" is levied on certain professionals. Dentists, lawyers, stock brokers and others of their ilk must fork over $400 annually.

A few years ago, the Legislature extended this fee to a different type of professional—players from the National Basketball Association (Memphis Grizzlies) and National Hockey League (Nashville Predators) who compete in lavish, new, publicly funded arenas.

To the tune of $2,500 each. Per game.

That may be pocket change for super stars who earn more per free throw than you and I will in 20 lifetimes. But for players on the lower end of the curve, it quickly adds up to real money.

At a recent hearing in Nashville, reps from the NBA and NHL argued the "jock tax" is an unreasonable burden on players making their leagues' $500,000 minimum. If every state and Canadian province charged a similar fee, the lesser-known players would pay more in taxes than they even earn.

Point well taken. That's why I say legislators didn't think far enough outside the box when they came up with this gem.

First, they should have extended it to football, professional and collegiate alike.

Second (and far more important), instead of a "jock tax," they should have based their plan on "jock tacks." Yes, tacks. Those sharp, pointy things deployed on bulletin boards.

Make it a law that opponent football teams competing in Tennessee have to wear tacks inside their athletic supporters. Lord knows both the Tennessee Titans and Tennessee Volunteers could use this assistance. Neither has set the athletic world on fire of late. So perhaps a "jock tacks" law for the visiting team might help bring back the glorious days of old.

Who knows? Jubilant Titan and Vol fans might even pay $2,500 per game to see it happen.

Ping-pong games of government

Welcome to the exciting sport that's always sweeping Tennessee: "Legislative Ping-Pong." This game is played by members of the Tennessee General Assembly.

First, these goofs trip all over themselves to pass pandering, broad-brush, special-interest laws. This action, in sports terminology, is called the "serve" (aka ping).

Soon thereafter comes the "return" (aka pong).

It occurs when these half-baked regulations take effect and—Aiiee! What have we done?!—lawmakers realize what one royal mell of a hess they created. Thus the pinging and ponging continue to the delight and dismay of everyone else.

Delight when we watch this comedy of errors unfold. Dismay when we realize what dolts we keep sending to the Capitol.

A fer'instance is the whiskey barrel controversy.

In 2013, legislators created a law specifying what constitutes "Tennessee whiskey." Among the requirements, hooch must be aged in new oak barrels, then charcoal-mellowed.

Ping! And if that sounds strangely similar to the recipe for Jack Daniel's, consider yourself well-versed in "likkerology."

In 2014 came a group of other Tennessee-based whiskey makers, including George Dickel, who maintained that Tennessee whiskey can also be aged in reused barrels—even though Dickel isn't. Furthermore, they said, being forced to closely mimic the Daniel's recipe stifles smaller, micro-distillers.

Phil Prichard, owner of Prichard's Distillery in Kelso, Tennessee, had a gem of a quote in the Nashville Tennessean: "If I wanted my whiskey to taste like Jack Daniel's, I'd make it like Jack Daniel's."

Pong!

Then the game heated up in the form of bills that would make "rejuvenated" barrels OK, after all.

Ping! And it never ends.

This occurs on other legislative fronts, too. Such as how to "Christianize" the "student free religious expression" measure that recently cleared the House 90-2.

"Under the proposal," said an Associated Press dispatch from Nashville, "a student could express belief about religion in homework, artwork and other written and oral assignments, free from discrimination based on the religious content."

Ping!

You know, I know and the Rev. Fire N. Brimstone knows if a student uses this directive to express religious belief outside the bounds of Christianity, the ponging, not to mention Bible-thumping, in both chambers will be deafening.

Wonder what kind of whiskey they'll serve at halftime of the match?

The latest way to create confusion

Even though I can tie my own shoes, write with a No. 2 pencil and operate a two-floor elevator, I don't claim to be the sharpest knife in the drawer, the baddest dog on the porch or the fastest fish in the pond.

Which is why, after opening an envelope from the state of Tennessee and perusing its contents, I said, "Whot'nhell are they talkin' about?"

The envelope contained my new driver's license.

My old one had been about to expire. So when the re-up notice arrived a few weeks ago, I wrote a check and mailed it to Nashville.

Correction. I, personally, handled neither duty. My wife did them for me. I guess Mary Ann was worried I might fill out the check with a No. 2 pencil instead of a pen. Or else trip on my shoelaces walking to the mailbox. In any event, she processed the paperwork well ahead of the deadline.

The finished product arrived back at our house well ahead of schedule, too—even before my old license expired. I scissored the old one into itty-bitty pieces and replaced it with the new one. I'm good to go for five more years.

But that's not what had me scratching my head. Rather, it was paperwork that came with the new license. It was a voter registration form, complete with instructions to "cut along the dotted line and submit bottom portion to local election commission."

Below were eight blocks where I was supposed to include my stats: name, address, sex, birthdate, phone number, Social Security number, blah-blah. Then there was a "voter declaration" block for me to confirm I'm a U.S. citizen, a resident of Tennessee, at least 18 years old, never convicted of a felony, that sort of stuff.

On the reverse were more instructions: what color INK to use, be sure to PRINT (their capital letters, not mine.) Then mail the whole she-bang to my local election commission. "You are not registered to vote until you receive a voter registration card," it warned.

"But I am registered to vote," I thought to myself, "and have been for decades. Is this something new, a part of that wacky voter ID law that recently went into effect?"

No, as it turns out; after a call to the Knox County Election Commission, I was assured I was indeed registered. And had been. This merely was for people who aren't registered in the first place.

"But since this thing arrived with my new driver's license," I said, "it looked like a new requirement."

The staffer agreed. In fact, she said the election commission has fielded many calls just like mine.

Same ol' song. Once you start monkeying with established practice, it creates more confusion than ever. No doubt the Legislature will clear up this perplexing mess next time around.

You may begin holding your breath now.

Hizzoner's fist-bumping precedent

Instead of being remembered as the first black president, author of the Affordable Care Act, ending the war in Iraq, turning around the U.S. auto industry and offing Osama bin Laden, what if Barack Obama primarily goes down in history for popularizing the fist-bump instead of the handshake?

Stranger things have happened. Those of us who came of age during the Kennedy era still chuckle that one of JFK's "major accomplishments" was removing fedoras from the heads of American men.

At least Mister Prez has health and science on his side this time. As more and more research is proving, fist-bumping spreads far fewer germs than the traditional grip.

The latest test came from the University of Wales. None other than the American Journal of Infection Control and the Association for Professionals in Infection Control and Epidemiology weighed in positively on the study.

Makes sense, of course. Tapping knuckles exposes much less skin surface to potential germ transfer. But will it catch on as a popular form of greeting in American culture?

Hmm. When I think back to some of the more famous moments of handshaking in American history, I can't help wondering what if?

• What if Ulysses S. Grant and Robert E. Lee had fist-bumped at Appomattox Court House on April 9, 1865?

Grant: "All right, Bob! Let's just click paws and end this thing once and for all. Four years is a long time to be at war."

Lee: "I agree, suh. But I also notice you fist-bump with greater force—indeed, with brute and barbaric braggadocio—than a true gentleman would. I can only take this to mean you wish to further continue the conflict. Orderly! Return mah sword, please!"

• What if President William McKinley had extended a fist-bump to the bandaged hand of Leon Czolgosz on September 6, 1901?

Instead of being mortally wounded by the pistol hidden in the assassin's bandage, perhaps McKinley might not have suffered anything worse than bloody knuckles.

• What if Egypt's Anwar Sadat, U.S. President Jimmy Carter and Israel's Menachem Begin had participated in a triple fist-bump—ménage à tap, perhaps?—on March 26, 1979, instead of that awkward laying-on-of-hands, like they were picking batters for the White House baseball tournament?

Carter (blushing with obvious glee): "Don't tell Rosalynn or mah mother, but this is the furst time I've ever been involved in a three-way! Always before, I only thought about it in mah heart."

The quiet type of money

There's a big money battle going on in Congress these days. But it isn't your typical Washington fight over budgets, taxes and other fiscal matters. Instead, this concerns the money you might soon be carrying in your pocket.

Repeat, pocket. Not wallet.

You see, there's yet another effort afoot to replace the one-dollar bill with a one-dollar coin. Oddly enough, it's a bipartisan measure. In a recent interview with National Public Radio, one of the sponsors noted, "It's way more efficient than a paper dollar. Canada has a coin that's worth $2. Switzerland has one worth about $5. And yet, what have we got? We've got a 25-cent piece."

So? One thing that's All-American, Yankee Doodle Dandy, apple pie and motherhood is our aversion to this switch.

Yes, metal money lasts longer than paper.

Yes, many other developed countries have made the switch.

Yes, metal money works much better in vending machines.

But time after time—from Susan B. Anthony dollar coins to Sacagawea dollar coins to presidential dollar coins—Americans have demonstrated they prefer quiet money over the noisy variety.

I remain steadfastly among them. As much as I enjoy the sensation of carrying filthy lucre in my jeans, I want it to be folded in a money clip, not bulging and jangling like a double handful of lock washers.

This reminds me of the government's huge push for conversion to metric measurements back in the 1970s.

Yes, metric makes great mathematical sense.

Yes, metric is the official language of science.

Yes, many other developed countries operate on the metric system.

But no—indeed, hell no!—metric did not fly, and will not fly, in America. We want our inches, ounces, pounds, quarts, gallons and miles, as Gawd Hisself and the Founding Fathers intended.

The crazy thing is, this whole metal-versus-paper brouhaha is likely to burn itself out in a few more years because most young folks don't carry real money at all. They use debit and credit cards. I can't tell you the number of times I've watched some kid go through the card-swiping process just to pay for a hamburger or a can of Mellow Yellow.

For my money, these folks have neither cents nor sense.

A strange switch in reputations

I'm going to toss two unrelated national news events into a bowl and turn on the beaters. In so doing, I shall mix apples with oranges—or lemons, as the case may be. I shall mix politics with sports. I shall mix history with the here-and-now. You have been warned.

Nonetheless, I simply cannot get over the 180-degree irony that occurred within days of each other in early 2012, when Joe Paterno died and Newt Gingrich won the Republican presidential primary in South Carolina.

Talk about a last-minute switch in reputations!

On one hand, there was Paterno—the beloved "Joe Pa" to generations of Penn State athletes, students, faculty, alumni and fans—whose golden legacy will forever carry the asterisk of a sex scandal.

On the other hand, there was Gingrich—the bed-hopping, wife-dropping hot rod with enough personal baggage to fill the cargo hold of a 747—who got the nod from a political party purportedly built around "family values."

Amazing.

Paterno spent his lifetime as a role model for the wholesome side of sports. He won big time. Forty-six seasons with the Nittany Lions, best-in-the-nation 409 total victories, 37 bowl games, two national championships, three Big Ten titles, more than 250 players progressing to the NFL.

He won with dignity and honor, as well. No hint of classroom scandals that plague many top-ranked programs, a consistently high rate of player graduation, 49 academic All-Americans.

Paterno was an ever-present figure on the Penn State campus, as well. He lived modestly at the edge of school property, his own number listed in the phone book like everyone else's. He donated millions of dollars to the university.

Yet at the 11th hour of his illustrious career, he was felled by the unspeakable acts of one of his assistants. In his dying days, Paterno tearfully lamented he "wished he had done more" to pursue sexual-predator accusations against Jerry Sandusky.

Compare that to Gingrich, who wrapped himself in a cloak of purity during President Bill Clinton's sex scandal with intern Monica Lewinsky.

With every breath, Gingrich called for Clinton's impeachment, while he himself was having an extramarital affair with a U.S. House staff member. What's more, he eventually resigned the House enshrouded in a breach of professional ethics.

Let's be clear. Gingrich's personal life is just that. It's personal. I don't care what he does between the sheets. Or with whom.

But the sheer hypocrisy of it all! This guy became the standard-bearer for morality and family values?

Wow. I take back the word "amazing" I used earlier. This was more than amazing. It was astounding, flabbergasting, mindboggling.

He wasn't no poet and sho' did show it

Today's sermon has no direct link to Knoxville. The whole thing played out in North Carolina. I call it to your attention, however, as a classic example of how political and bureaucratic ham-handedness can quickly escalate into embarrassment all around.

This subject dominated Tar Heel news for more than a week. There were Page 1 stories, stinging editorials and angry letters to the editor. One newspaper asked readers to contribute poems about the kerfuffle. Some were positively hilarious.

TO RETIRE? OR NOT TO RETIRE?

It all started when Gov. Pat McCrory selected a new N.C. poet laureate.

By long-held tradition, Hizzoner is supposed to seek input from the state's arts council. Nominees are then vetted on a variety of factors, including their education, writing skills, teaching qualifications, number of publications, previous literary awards—in other words, a true professional review.

I don't know if McCrory didn't care about protocol. Or if he had no feel for poetry. Or if he was busy with his golf game. Or if he was checking birth certificates in bathroom stalls. Whatever the case, he came up with Valerie Macon, an employee of the North Carolina Department Health and Human Services who likes to write poems. Then he all but casually announced, "Meh, she'll do."

Wowzers. Within days of the appointment, poop plastered the propellers, splattering everything and everybody from Murphy to Manteo.

Turned out Macon's entire track record consisted of two small volumes, both self-published. What's more, she was a student in a distinguished poet program, not a winner as the governor had announced.

Immediately, both sides went on the attack.

Literary groups accused McCrory of being an unlettered dolt who wouldn't know iambic pentameter from a hole in the ground. The governor charged they were elitists unwilling to consider someone not of their ivory tower ilk.

Poor Valerie Macon was caught in the middle. By week's end, she resigned the position.

My opinion? The governor flubbed, big time. He put a novice in an impossible position. Sorta like grabbing an eighth-grade quarterback and throwing him into the SEC championship game.

Macon may well develop into a poet who makes significant contributions to her craft. I dearly hope so. This mess wasn't her fault. Instead:

Roses were red.
Violets were blue.
The guv'nor stepped into
The deepest of doo.

If the shoe fits, fling it

I'm tempted to say the face of politics is changing. But that's not wholly accurate because faces change frequently in political circles.

What's really changing, though, is feet. Specifically, what goes on them. That would be shoes.

Once upon a time, shoes didn't play a role in campaigns, except as an indication of how much leather a candidate had worn thin on the trail.

Turn your American history textbooks back to the presidential race of 1952, and you'll find a famous news photo snapped of the "holey" shoe sole worn by Democratic candidate Adlai Stevenson. At first blush, this might have been considered a sartorial gaffe by the wealthy Illinois governor. But his handlers quickly turned it to an advantage, portraying their guy as an everyday Joe. They even had the image copied onto lapel pins and posters.

That was then.

Political shoe news in the 21st century is totally different. It is not a statement of fashion. Rather, it involves shoes thrown at politicians in protest.

These outbursts may occur on a regular basis in foreign cultures—Arab and Asian come immediately to mind—but they're rather new to Americans.

Hillary Clinton was a target in 2014. Shortly before she was to address a convention in Las Vegas, she had to duck an orange-and-black athletic shoe from a woman who had walked toward the VIP seating area and let fly.

Surely you remember what happened in December 2008 to President George W. Bush. He had to dodge not one, but two, shoes flung by an Iraqi journalist during a news conference in Baghdad.

I suspect these incidents are going to factor into homegrown campaigns more and more often. Thus, we should expect wholesale changes as everybody gears up for them.

No doubt the shoe industry will develop a full line of brogans, sandals, slippers, boots, flip-flops and tennis shoes that are ergonomically and aerodynamically designed for accurate delivery.

At the same time, sports medicine experts will need to come up with the latest bandages and exercises for the prevention and treatment of muscle strain, carpal tunnel syndrome and hand-arm-elbow tendinitis brought on by excessive shoe-tossing.

The media also needs to hop on board, pronto. This will require special correspondents trained in the nuances of shoe-throwing: right arm versus left, shoe color, size, lace-up versus slip-on, that kind of detail.

Don't laugh. Before the televised debates between Richard Nixon and John F. Kennedy in 1960, what candidate would ever have worried about 5 o'clock shadow?

He tells it like it is—or isn't

Just in time for Election Day, I discovered the last fence-straddling voter in the entire United States. After months on end of heated primary arguments, debates, emails, snail mails, multimillions in PAC ads, live TV coverage, radio talk shows and barbershop politics ad nauseam, there remains only one person in the country still vacillating between candidates.

The guy's name is U.N. DeCided. I caught up with him at a local eatery, where he was kind enough to spare me a few minutes and speak his mind.

Here's our conversation, word for word.

Sam Venable: Please tell me where you were born.

U.N. DeCided: That's always been a subject of family controversy. My dad says Los Angeles. My mom says Miami. I've been meaning to dig out my birth certificate, but frankly, I don't know whether to believe it or not.

SV: Your age?

UNDeC: You're as young or old as you feel at any given moment.

SV: What sort of occupation do you have?

UNDeC: I'm what you might call a jack of all trades. No job too big or too small.

SV: Would you mind revealing your income?

UNDeC: It varies. Some years I qualify for food stamps. Others I manage to squirrel away a few million bucks in offshore banking accounts.

SV: Any recreational pursuits?

UNDeC: Football, basketball, baseball, tennis, hockey, gymnastics, curling, water skiing, snowboarding. In fact, I enjoy so many activities I occasionally give them all up and take on a completely different slate of new ones.

SV: Impressive! Do you actually participate in that many sports or simply follow them as a fan of the professional leagues?

UNDeC: Both.

SV: How would you define your political leanings?

UNDeC: Depends. Probably the best description is a left-leaning Republican with right-leaning Democrat tendencies. Some people say I'm a conservative liberal; others describe me as a liberal conservative.

SV: What was your reaction to the presidential debates?

UNDeC: A 50-50 tie, right down the middle.

SV: Well, at least you are going to cast a ballot today, aren't you?

UNDeC: That would be a definite maybe.

SV: Have you picked a candidate yet?

UNDeC: Yes and no.

SV: You mean that after all this time, you still don't know who gets your vote?

UNDeC: Certainly I do! It's just that the secrecy of my strong political convictions prevents me from discussing them with myself, let alone other people. Good day, sir. Or good night, whatever it is.

If you doubt America's obsession with food, do three things.

Walk the tiled canyons of your favorite shopping mall, visit any of the 45,293,589,472 fast-food joints lining the streets of every city in the land, and check out the New York Times' bestseller book list.

At the mall, you'll see the most amazing public display of human flesh this side of a nudist camp. I know this for a fact because I occasionally mall-walk for exercise.

You won't see nearly as much flesh on display at all those fast-food joints. That's because the vast majority of customers remain in their cars, slowly snaking along—one vehicle-length at a time—in the drive-through. The drive-through might stretch for half a mile, but rest assured you'll get prompt service at the counter inside because there's never a crowd.

As for the Times' bestseller list? That's what makes this entire episode so hilarious. Almost every week, there's a brand new entry for diet books. Makes me wonder if people eat these publications instead of read them.

This comes as no surprise, of course. When you consider Americans spend fewer hours sleeping and more hours ingesting food, it's no wonder we show the effects.

Hey, far be it from me to judge. You're looking at the original Sir Lunchalot, in the flesh and at your service.

You gonna finish those fries? I'll be happy to take 'em off your hands.

Chapter Ten
OUR PLATES
RUNNETH OVER

If it isn't fried, it isn't food

As a native Southerner, I bear witness to a culinary truism. With sinfully few exceptions, any item of food can be improved by frying, preferably deep-fat.

You'd be hard-pressed to find a better public display of this craft than at the Grainger County Tomato Festival in Rutledge, Tennessee. Trust your Uncle Lipids in this regard. The only sound louder than antique tractor engines and bluegrass-gospel music was the roar of thousands of arteries collectively expanding and contracting with every bite.

Doing their best to contribute to this gluttony were members of the Grainger County Ridgerunners car club. As they have for 23 festivals, these folks washed, sliced and fried green tomatoes until the last customer cried "No mas!"

"Actually, we were down a little bit this year," said club president Jamie McDaniel. "We only fried about 15 bushels."

Over at Wendy and Ray Burton's food stand, green tomatoes weren't the only veggie being dunked into scalding oil. Their menu also included fried mushrooms, fried green beans and fried pickle slices.

It's the crunch we crave, of course. It's in our DNA as well as our waistlines—and not only in Grainger County.

Chocolatier and retired home economics teacher Rita Key of Talbott has been invited to submit entries for the inaugural "Deep Fried Tennessee" contest at the Tennessee State Fair. Sponsored by the Tennessee FFA Foundation, this competition is the official search for the most unique fried eats from throughout the Volunteer State. There are only two requirements. The food items must be raised in Tennessee, and they must meet their fate in a sea of molten fat. I trust teams of EMTs will be on standby.

Just the mention of frying had folks talking recipes.

Union County historian Bonnie Peters told me about a yellow squash and onion favorite of hers: "Just chop up the squash and onions, stir with flour, salt and pepper, drop them into a skillet and fry 'em like potato cakes."

Walter Lambert, WVLT-TV's on-air chef and cookbook author, has had great success with thick, peeled cucumber slices (seeds cored out) stuffed with a mixture of lean, ground pork, soy sauce and chopped onions, then fried four to five minutes per side.

Ah, yes; cucumbers. You know what I said earlier about "sinfully few exceptions" in the opening paragraph? As an experiment, some of the car club women tried thin-slicing several cukes and frying them like green tomatoes.

And?

"We all agreed," said president McDaniel, "it's an idea whose time has not yet arrived."

Some hybrid foods to consider

You'd think anybody who has eaten rattlesnake, groundhog, alligator, coon, coot, mountain oysters, starling, pigeon, haggis, boudin, blood pudding and turducken would know what a pluot tastes like.

You would be wrong.

For that matter, you would be wrong if you thought I, the aforementioned eater, even knew what a pluot was. Verily, I was clueless until recently when I saw a display of pluots (or should that be pluoti?) in the produce section of a grocery store.

Come to find out this is the cross between a plum and an apricot. It was created by Floyd Zaiger, a California fruit breeder.

I bought a pluot, along with a regular black plum, and took them home for comparative sampling. Both were quite good, quite sweet. But I liked the plum better. It was juicier and had better texture. Perhaps I purchased a poor pluot and pitted it against a perfect plum. Further research is necessary.

Prompted by the experience, however, I poked around and discovered there are many hybrid fruits and veggies I never knew existed. Apparently I don't get out much. Or else my taste buds have remained bound by tradition lo' these many years.

According to the website mentalfloss.com, such combinations as the tayberry (blackberry-raspberry), the rabbage (radish-cabbage) and the jostaberry (gooseberry-black currant) have been around for decades.

But why stop there? Mix away, I say. I'd like to sink my choppers into delectable combos like these:

- Okrato. Stewed okra with tomatoes has long been a Southern dish. Tasty, yes, but slimier than a bowl of garden slugs. If someone could figure out how to blend a tender okra pod with a green tomato, coat the creation in seasoned cornmeal and fry it to a golden brown, that person would be in line for the Nobel Prize.

- Bappie. Bass and crappie are two popular and delicious freshwater fish. Widespread, easy to catch. Bass have better texture, crappies better flavor. But combining them would result in fillets so positively scrumptious, I've gained three pounds just typing these words.

- Coconut pake. Take a dense coconut cream pie, cross it with a light, fluffy coconut cake and to hell with calories or cholesterol.

- Chardisky. Chilled, refreshing chardonnay blended with Tennessee whiskey would—Aaak! Pa-tuii! Gag! Barf! Strike that from the record!

Some combinations are so disgusting, the mere suggestion should be purged and the hybridizer flogged.

Food for thought about vittles

Two food memories to chew upon as we sling today's hash.

- Several years ago, I was seated solo near the breakfast bar at a Knoxville restaurant. Because of my location, I couldn't help but overhear the conversations of numerous patrons as they moved through the line.

A particular threesome really caught my attention. One after another, they marveled at a new item on the buffet. Pork chops.

"Whoever heard of eating pork for breakfast?" they continually remarked.

As casually and unobtrusively as possible, I slowly glanced toward the line and noticed each plate of these astonished diners was heavy laden with bacon and sausage.

The smart-ass in me sorely wanted to suggest they take a quick course in Animal Identification 101. But I decided the best course of action for my mouth was to keep it shut and chewing.

• At the Tennessee Valley Fair decades ago—I couldn't have been more than 10 or 11 years old at the time—samples of grilled horse burgers were being dispensed at a booth along the lakeside "corn dog and candy apple row."

I don't know if the sponsor was a food industry trade group or state farm organization. All I can recall is saying, "Huh? Horse meat? Yuck!"

At the insistence of my mother, who not only was an adventuresome diner but also a woman open to different cultures, I nibbled a bite.

Not bad, I remember admitting. Frankly, I doubt I could have distinguished it from the hamburgers being served up at adjacent booths.

I ask you chew on those two morsels as the Tennessee General Assembly makes its annual flirtation with the notion of permitting horse-slaughtering facilities. Don't expect action anytime soon. This always generates more passionate arguments than baggy pants, guns, public employee unions and evolution. Emotions and political maneuvering being what they are, the issue likely will tied up for years.

Will people who regularly consume chickens, turkeys, hogs, cows, sheep and fish recoil at the thought of sticking a fork into horse flesh?

Will these same consumers—who quite likely have never ventured closer to a slaughterhouse than the sanitized meat department of their supermarket—think killing a horse for food is uncivilized and inhumane?

You tell me. I learned long ago that human sensitivities make strange bedfellows.

Strange diners, too.

Peace comes to the Cornbread War

I have seen the light, children. And its name is Linney's.

This has been an epiphany for me, a life-changing event. As a result, the gentle spirit of marital bliss has settled across the Venob household like sweet dew on a June morning.

The Cornbread War is over.

No more shall epithets and threats be shouted. No longer will arms be taken up. Verily, the sword has been beaten—not into a plowshare, but something more serviceable: a spoon to stir Linney's cornmeal mix into succulent repast.

As with the study of any prolonged conflict, historical perspective is necessary. So we shall cease chewing long enough to set this two-pronged stage.

First was my 2008 admission that I preferred sweet—dare I say Yankeefied?—cornbread over the more traditional Southern (aka dry, bland, coarse, stick-in-your throat) variety.

I might just as well have renounced my religion.

Readers dismissed me as a fraud, a faux son of Dixie. I was even summoned to a Knoxville radio station to defend what was deemed by the host as "contemptuous, blasphemous heresy."

Defend I did. When you come out of the closet on an important matter like cornbread, you don't back down. If other persons—including a certain Mary Ann Venable—elected to continue eating bland, dry, cardboard cornbread, that was fine by me. But I would stick with sweet.

Then came the blockbuster announcement in 2009 that the jelly heads at J.M. Smucker Company, owner of the Three Rivers brand of cornmeal mix, were ceasing production.

Again, the outpouring of wrath was palpable. The University of Tennessee might just as well have abandoned orange and white and renamed itself "Gator Nation."

But you can bet your mama's cast iron skillet that peace has prevailed in the form of cornmeal from Linney's Mill, Union Grove, North Carolina.

I was alerted to this ambrosia several months ago by a longtime reader. Here is his direct quote: "Linney's makes the very best cornbread I've ever tasted. As a matter of fact, it made me wish Three Rivers had left this area years earlier."

Like a dolt, I ignored the advice. And a certain Mrs. Venable and I continued to feud over cornbread. But recently I bought a bag of Linney's, and hostilities abruptly ceased. This magic stuff pleases all cornbread tastes, guaranteed.

So praise th'Lawd and pass the butter! Ain't gonna study war no mo'!

Nothing will ever beat homegrown

It's a common question that is frequently discussed from late May through early September when geezers get together: "Before air conditioning, did we get as hot in the summer as we do now?"

The short answer is yes. Definitely.

We suffered, sweated, fussed, fumed and swam ourselves to sleep atop drenched sheets because 90 degrees in the humid South is pure-T misery and always has been. Period.

But having come of age in an era when AC was a luxury of the exceedingly wealthy and not available to us unwashed masses of the hoi polloi, I will acknowledge this: We didn't know there was anything different.

We suffered and sweated because that's the way our part of the world was created. Our parents suffered and sweated. As did their parents. And theirs and theirs as far back as you wish to go. Not until AC became a societal given did we realize cool air was available at the push of a button.

I bring up this climatological history lesson because of another geezerly question that surfaces every summer: "Isn't it wonderful that we have fresh fruits and veggies in stores all 12 months and don't have to wait for certain items to 'come in'?"

This time, the short answer is no. Definitely not.

Agreed, vast strides have been made in certain vegetative corners. Tomatoes, for one.

It used to be that a "winter tomato" was another term for "red baseball." Except a red baseball had decidedly better flavor. Much more tender, too.

There is still a chasm between store-bought 'maters in June and homegrown 'maters in July and August. But it is narrowing rapidly, and I shout hosannas for this agricultural progress.

Alas, the same simply cannot be said for certain other foods. Sweet corn, for instance. Also green beans, blueberries, strawberries, cantaloupe and watermelon.

I don't care how carefully they are farmed somewhere far away, nor how quickly they are transported to market. Nothing can compare to the taste of a suppertime meal that was still on the vine that morning.

Against my better judgment, I once bought a delectable-looking watermelon in May. It was big—as in mistake.

It did not crack open when I creased it with a knife. Indeed, it did not "crack" at all. I had to pry the halves apart after sawing them asunder.

There was no watermelon perfume. No watermelon texture. No watermelon taste. Nothing but red mush. The raccoons and 'possums barely nibbled this glop during their nightly visits to my compost pile.

Ah, but the divine local produce season isn't far off. And thanks to AC, I do believe I can hold out for it.

Hot dog dogma

I wish to lay an important baseball statistic on you. This number is much more significant than runs, hits, errors, ERA, RBI and other boring fluff that clutters the sports pages between April and the World Series.

It's 21,357,316.

That's the estimated number of stadium hot dogs fans munch during a typical major league season, according to the Washington, D.C.-based National Hot Dog and Sausage Council.

I'm intrigued by the word "estimated" in the previous paragraph. If the hot dog council had tossed out rough figures like "21.3 million" or "between 21 and 22 million" in its report, I wouldn't have blinked an eye. But to specifically cite 21,357,316 and then call it an "estimate" makes me think these people are chasing their dawgs with high-octane colas.

I know the food industry uses high-tech monitoring techniques to chart consumption of its products. But what happens if, say, a fan at Yankee Stadium orders a concession stand hot dog, then abruptly changes his mind and requests a hamburger instead? Does this mean someone deep inside the hog dog council's research bunker suddenly starts cursing and banging his desk because the "estimate" has now been reduced to 21,357,315?

But let us not quibble over details. Quite the contrary. I wish to lavish praise on the National Hot Dog and Sausage Council for its tips on dog-dining etiquette.

High time, if you ask me. In a perfect world, infants would emerge from the womb with certain knowledge wound into their DNA: how to build a snowman, how to pick their noses, how to eat a hot dog, important stuff like that.

But no. We have heathens in our midst who never were taught the art of doing dogs, and society has suffered tremendously.

You can find the entire condiment list at www.hot-dog.org. But one entry is of such importance, I must bring it to your attention: "Don't use ketchup on your hot dog after the age of 18."

Amen, brothers and sisters. Preach on. This advice should be adopted as federal law and printed on all hot dog packages.

I speak with personal shame in this regard. My dear wife of 50 years has many sterling qualities, but there is one flaw in her character. She puts the red stuff on her hot dog. Yes, I would welcome any prayers you might offer up for her salvation.

Alas, an alleged expert does the same. There's a new cookbook on the market: "Haute Dogs," by native Texan Russell Van Kraayenburg. It features 47 recipes for dogs, 15 of which include ketchup as an acceptable condiment. Blasphemy!

If Davy Crockett had known such heresy would emerge from Texas, he never would've gone to the Alamo.

Pork by any other name is still hog

I guess pork isn't "the other white meat" anymore.

Not that it ever was that color, except possibly for lean pork loin after it's been overcooked. If somebody offered me a "white ham" sandwich, I'd ask for peanut butter and jelly instead. Nonetheless, ever since a slick marketing campaign from 1987 deemed hog meat the same color as fish and chicken—and, in theory, healthier—that's what consumers have been led to believe.

Now it's time for a redo.

The National Pork Board and Beef Checkoff Program recently announced a new naming system for their respective products. No colors need apply.

Instead, similar cuts of meat from the two different animals will be labeled with the same wording. No longer will, say, "rib-eye" apply only to parts from dead cows; there will be "rib-eye chops" from dead pigs as well.

According to the Akron Beacon Journal, this step is being taken "to make cuts of meat more easily identifiable so that customers know what they are getting. But beef and pork producers are hoping that the changes also will take away some of the mystery of the meat case, so shoppers aren't afraid to try a larger variety of cuts."

So? What else is new?

The names of food products change all the time. If you don't believe it, take a stroll down several aisles of your local supermarket.

What used to be called "prunes" are now "dried plums." The old "high fructose corn syrup" is now "corn sugar"—which, I suppose, sounds more palatable than its introductory trade name: "glucose." And, of course, there's everybody's favorite frying medium—"low erucic acid rapeseed oil." Except you know it these days as "canola."

It's even weirder in the seafood section.

"Chilean sea bass" certainly whets the appetite better than the original, "Patagonian toothfish." Not to mention "orange roughy," which previously went under the nauseating handle of "slimehead."

This marketing alchemy applies to nonfood products as well. Prior to 1924, for example, businessmen in trademark blue suits worked for "Computing Tabulating Recording Corp." It's known today as IBM.

So fire up the ol' grill, I say, and heap on the meat—white, red, rib-eye or otherwise.

All tastes like hickory smoke and barbecue sauce anyway.

Speaking up for plants' rights

One year for my birthday, my sister and brother-in-law took Mary Ann and me to Brasstown Valley Resort, a fancy outfit in the mountains of North Georgia. It was a delightful weekend, mostly devoted to eating.

Imagine a landlocked cruise ship where each day's agenda goes something like this: You finish the deluxe breakfast buffet just in time to loosen your belt one notch and prepare for the deluxe lunch buffet, leaving barely enough opportunity to grab a nap before the deluxe supper buffet opens.

Our hosts had visited Brasstown before and were well-acquainted with the menu. It leans heavily to meat—beef, pork, fowl and fish predominating—and is presented in a delicious array guaranteed to ratchet cholesterol levels double digits per bite.

"You and I aren't going to worry about that this weekend," Tony announced at the start. "For the next two days, we are going to be plants rights' activists. Nothing that grows from the soil shall pass our lips. No vegetables, no fruits. Only meat."

Pardon the bragging, but I did an excellent job of following his courageous lead.

Ever since, Tony and I have frequently discussed the theory of plants' rights. We even have toyed with the notion of launching PETV: People for the Ethical Treatment of Veggies.

Perhaps now is the time. According to a recent story in The Week news magazine, researchers believe plants actively communicate with each other—some with distinct sounds, others via chemical release.

Monica Gagliano, lead author on the project, said this doesn't necessarily prove plants are conscious in human terms, but "it opens up a new debate on the perception and action of people toward plants as living beings in their own right."

Please understand that your friendly local columnist is a confirmed carnivore. Also a hunter. Quite often, he invests more honest sweat equity acquiring meat than scanning plastic-wrapped packages through the supermarket's self-check aisle.

Nonetheless, this is going to give me pause next time I twist a tomato off the vine in our garden. Or pluck a green pepper by its stem. Or move through the okra rows, slicing pods into a basket with deft use of a kitchen knife.

In fact, I'm starting to grow so concerned about this revelation, I may swear off terrorizing the blades of grass in my lawn for the rest of the summer. Poor little things. Just when they've recovered from the drought and are happily chit-chatting in mass profusion, why should I harass them with a mower?

Far better to mix a gin and tonic—foregoing lime butchery, of course—and grill a deer steak.

Another Christmas miracle?

I can't believe I did what I just did.

I just ate a brussels sprout. And survived.

This was not the result of an alcohol-induced dare. There was neither pistol at my head not knife at my throat. No familial hostages were being held.

Quite the contrary. I performed this gastronomic feat of my own volition.

To grasp the significance of this culinary moment, you must understand my six-decades-and-counting loathing of these horrid veggies.

I am founder, president and CEO of I Hate Brussels Sprouts, the Whole Brussels Sprouts and Nothing But the Brussels Sprouts, Inc. I have written about my visceral disdain many times through the years. I has become somewhat of a standing joke among my older (which is redundant) fellow writers. That Venob would even consider ingesting one of these vile little cabbages requires a leap of faith and trust in humanity not visited upon our planet since thawing of the Cold War.

It happened at the News Sentinel editorial department's annual Christmas gorge-a-thon, to which retired old croaks are still invited— provided they bring a dish of goodies, of course. As the conference room table was filling with homemade dishes and platters abubble in cheese-smothered lipids, cholesterol, sugar and preservatives, Christina Southern casually walked in and plunked down a bowl of the dreaded b.s.

I nearly reflux-hurled.

But then I forced myself to take another look. Blame the charitable spirit of the holidays.

Christina's brussels sprouts were kelly-green orbs, not olive-drab mush. Their scent bore no taint of mildewed gym socks. Perhaps due to dementia or an odd alignment of the stars, I placed one, ever-so-hesitantly, upon my plate.

Repeat: one. It was the smallest b.s. in the bowl. Immediately, I camouflaged it with other, more traditional holiday fare.

Hidden in a vacant cubicle, I popped it into my mouth, prepared for the worst. I chewed and swallowed. Amazingly, it wasn't bad at all.

No, my taste buds weren't exactly singing praises. Yet the fact I didn't immediately and forcefully regurgitate was impressive.

It gets weirder. I went back for seconds.

Poof! They were all gone. Even the bowl itself had been removed from the buffet—leading me to believe other people had tried them or else the entire brussels sprouts episode was a cruel joke at my expense. I'm still not sure which.

But I solemnly swear on my mother's grave: If somebody brings beets to next year's Christmas gorge-a-thon, I ain't trying them. No way, no how. Some things never were meant to be.

Spraying our way to Thin City

There's a new way to eat more and weigh less. No more counting calories. No more exercising. No more apologizing for your fifth helping of chocolate cake.

I'm so happy I may chug-a-lug a pint of brown gravy.

It's all because of a product that just hit the market. It's called "Spray Thin Appetite Suppressant." Here, straight from a company news release, is how it's supposed to work:

"Spray Thin is a specially designed and produced scent (sweet or savory) that stimulates the brain during eating and helps you stop eating sooner. This suppressant is designed to be sprayed on food during meals. Spray Thin does not create weight loss by changing the taste of food. The scent is believed to activate nasal sense receptors that trigger patterns of electrical activity in the region of the brain that affects appetite. During each meal or snack—"

Wha-huh? Hang on just a dang minute.

Nasal receptors? Brains? Electrical activity? Wow. I've been eating food all these years, and I just learned I've been putting it in all the wrong places!

I thought vittles were supposed to go down your swallow pipe, aka goozle. Who would've ever thunk otherwise? Oh, well. Far be it from me to tell these weight-loss experts how to chew the fat. Indeed, let them sell skinniness (at $30 per tube) until Americans are so shriveled they must carry anvils, lest a strong breeze waft them into the adjacent county. In fact, I'm starting to think this makes the New Age cycle complete.

Consider the old Thanksgiving-Christmas traditions of feasting.

In days of yore, people gathered around a table and inhaled vast amounts of roasted turkey, oyster dressing, yeast rolls, cranberry salad and endless varieties of desserts. Then they would slowly and laboriously rise from their chairs—or be pulled by group effort, if necessary—and waddle into the den to smoke half a pack of post-gluttony Marlboros.

These days, all they gotta do is coat a package of Ramen noodles with Spray Thin, consume their feast, and repair to the den for a round of vaping electronic cigarettes.

You reckon these new smokes come in turkey and pecan pie flavors, just to make the holiday experience complete?

Anybody in the mood for McKudzu?

Amid the glory of spring, when daffodils, dogwoods, redbuds, irises, roses and tulips send forth new life, something much more sinister also defies the grave.

Kudzu, scourge of the South.

This suffocating plant has been leafing every spring since the late 1880s, when humanity committed environmental high crime and introduced kudzu from the Orient. But this year, instead of reaching for herbicide, perhaps you should consider cookware.

I have it on good authority that young, tender kudzu leaves—emphasis on young and tender—aren't bad on a plate or in salad.

"Just don't wait too long and let 'em get tough and hairy," Ila Hatter says. "At that stage, there's no way anything but a goat can eat them. Once, I tried mature kudzu leaves that had been tempura-battered and deep-fried. Not so good."

If anyone should know about these things, it's Ila. A resident of Bryson City, North Carolina, she's my go-to source for information about wild edibles. Her expertise has been featured in venues as diverse as the Smithsonian Folklife Festival, CNN, NBC, the Great Smoky Mountains Association and the University of Tennessee's Smoky Mountain Field School.

"Kudzu is a lot like spinach," she said. "I've used it in pesto and pasta. A friend of mine has tried it in quiche."

Just be advised a little goes a long way.

"Once I was at a kudzu festival and ran into some students from the University of Georgia who had experimented with a lot of ways to cook it," she said with a laugh. "They even compiled a cookbook with 101 different recipes. Several of those students told me they couldn't wait to graduate and move up north so they'd never have to look at kudzu again!"

The reason I contacted Ila is because of a letter I recently received from Knoxvillian Cassie Sexton. It contained a recipe for kudzu blossom jelly. Soon as the j-word rolled off my tongue, Ila's kudzu mood improved immediately.

"Oh, now that's a different thing," she noted. "I've eaten kudzu jelly several times before. A woman who lives near me makes it. It's quite good. Tastes a lot like grape jelly."

Just one problem. Acquiring enough raw materials is a monumental task.

"I've never been able to pick enough blossoms to make even one batch," Ila told me. "Apparently it's just the older vines that bloom. The blossoms always seem to be too high, way out of my reach."

Figures. This is one more reason why kudzu is a major pain in the neck.

Only one kind of C-sauce

Like any couple closing in on a half century of matrimony, my wife and I have marked differences.

Mary Ann suffers from "throwawayitis." I am plagued by "packratium."

She enjoys high-quality British drama on Netflix and PBS. I follow the football Vols on high-def cable.

She is an organizer of everything, from clothes to garden tools. I adhere to the "make a new pile" method.

When someone asks us to mail a letter, she sits down at the computer. I reach for an envelope and postage stamp.

She likes to hike in the woods. So do I, but prefer to be carrying a shotgun.

If we both come home tired and tuckered at the end of the day, she would rather whip something up in the kitchen. I can whip up a dozen good reasons why we should dine at a restaurant.

And so it goes.

But there is one area of agreement—on the fourth Thursday in November or the Fourth of July. Mary Ann Hill Venable and Samuel Anderson Venable Jr. dearly love our jellied cranberry sauce.

Yes, that gelatinous, dark-red, cylindrical blob of tart sweetness that disgorges—ker-plop!—from the can intact, complete with "Ocean Spray rings," and then is whack-sliceable with anything from a dull butter knife to a fillet blade so sharp it can split atoms.

I defy you to check our pantry any day of the year and not find at least one can of jellied C-sauce. We're just as liable to eat it with burgers in August as turkey on Thanksgiving.

To reiterate: jellied. Not whole-berry. There is only one exception to this rule. We have a dear West Tennessee friend, Roberta Richardson, who cooks a cranberry wine sauce to die for when ladled, hot, onto rare, smoked duck, goose, pork or venison.

Yes, I have the recipe. No, you may not have it. I gave a blood oath to Roberta when, after years of begging, she passed it to me.

As a faithful listener of NPR's "Morning Edition," I always tune in for Susan Stamberg's annual Thanksgiving tribute to "Mama Stamberg's Cranberry Relish." Wouldn't miss it for the world, even though the thought of a cranberry dish that (1) includes horseradish, (2) must be frozen and (3) is Pepto-Bismol pink makes me want to hurl. If you must have the recipe, go online and create to your heart's and belly's content.

Mary Ann and I shall reach for a can opener (it helps to pierce the bottom with an old-time church key for easy removal) and enjoy our jellied cranberry sauce, thank you very much.

If this is what successfully binds our marriage, so be it.

Taking a bite out of bankruptcy

I just did something positive and proactive to bolster both the American work force and the American waistline. I bought a two-pack of Twinkies and savored every bite of their preservative-packed, cream-filled sponginess.

As you may have heard, Hostess Brands, Inc., maker of Twinkies and Wonder Bread, has filed for bankruptcy protection. According to an

Associated Press dispatch, which I clutch in my sticky fingers as we speak, Hostess "listed its estimated assets between $500 million and $1 billion."

Wow. Even for a wise, seasoned and tubby financier like me, those are some pretty liberal parameters.

It's sorta like dialing the weather forecast when you climb out of bed and hearing that the afternoon high temperature will be "somewhere between 37 and 128 degrees."

Or having your golf partner tell you his score on No. 11 was "somewhere between a hole-in-one and a triple bogey."

This is how the system works. Companies are permitted to play loosey-goosey with one set of numbers, yet are held to strict accountability with others.

Maybe Hostess can "estimate" a canyon of $500 million-$1 billion in its financial assets. But on every pack of Twinkies, it clearly states this 300-calorie colossus contains exactly 9 grams of fat, 35 milligrams of cholesterol, 420 milligrams of sodium, 54 grams of total carbs and 2 grams of protein.

That's what I call delicious precision.

Still, this is a sad commentary on the sorry state of our sovereign nation. I grieve at the very notion of Twinkies, the twin pillars of wholesomeness supporting the basic food groups, going under.

What's next, pray tell? Ding Dongs and Ho Hos?

Oh my. Those are Hostess products, too. Pray for our country.

As the title of this chapter suggests, it deals primarily with football subjects. There's a nod to swimming, the Winter Olympics and basketball, but the vast majority of this verbiage relates strictly to matters of the oblong.

Football is the one organized sport I know a wee bit about. Emphasis on "wee." I was a member of the varsity—consistently competing miserably, softly and ineptly, I hasten to point out—during the seasons of 1962, 1963 and 1964 at Knoxville's Young High School. I still limp, and the creaking in my neck bones sometimes is audible at 25 paces. But at least I understand and appreciate the game. From the first collegiate kickoff in August through the Super Bowl in February, I often have a football game on the TV or radio at home, if only for pleasant background noise.

Not so for basketball, hockey, golf and all the rest. With the exception of the World Series, I don't follow baseball enough to know which teams are in first place or last—or even what divisions they're in.

Regardless of the sport, though, I'm always intrigued by oddball stories. As I was preparing material for this book, I ran into my source for the column titled "Vols were jinxed from the start." As soon as I brought it up, he immediately grimaced and hollered, "Those were my brother's ashes! Why couldn't he have reached up and tripped that Alabama player?"

To learn the embarrassing details, check inside. And as one of my old coaches used to implore, "Quickly! Quickly! Show a little hustle!"

Chapter Eleven
FOOTBALL AND
A FEW OTHER SPORTS

Vols were jinxed from the start

The place: Neyland Stadium, Alabama versus Tennessee.

The date: Saturday, October 15, 1994.

The outcome: A last-gasp, utterly demoralizing (to the home crowd) Bama victory, 17-13.

I defer to the wonderfully crafted opening of News Sentinel sports writer Mike Strange's report of the sad affair: "Tennessee remains under Alabama's big Crimson thumb for at least another year, maybe forever. Once again, the Vols inched up to the brink of their most agonizing threshold, only to fall back for the ninth year in a row."

Late in the game, the Vols were in command, 13-10. But with a mere 3 minutes, 4 seconds to play, the Tide capped an 80-yard scoring drive to go ahead. UT refused to give up. Guided by a freshman quarterback—his name escapes me right now; it was Manging, Maiming, Peyton Place, something like that—the Vols drove to the Bama 7, only to run out of downs with 1:01 on the clock. End of story.

Uh, not quite —

You see, Tennessee may have been cursed from the get-go because of an illegal event that occurred 24 hours earlier. I've been in correspondence with two members of a Tennessee family who know precisely what I'm talking. I shan't name names because one of the direct participants requested anonymity, rightly worrying that some Vol partisans might seek a pound of flesh in revenge.

That's because once-living flesh—as in cremated human ashes—is the key to this story.

Official UT policy forbids the practice of scattering ashes on the field. But on Friday, October 14, 1994, someone did it anyhow. The remains in question were those of a Nashville man described by his widow as "the most rabid Big Orange fan to ever walk planet Earth."

He wanted his ashes scattered on Shields-Watkins Field, and the family went through official circles to gain permission. No dice.

So, the afternoon before the game, another family member and an old fraternity brother filled their pockets with ashes and idly wandered onto the field, making casual conversation with workers and "scooping out" when they got the chance.

"We didn't sprinkle a lot," the family member said. "Just enough to comply with his wishes."

Family and friends went to the game the following night, content their mission was accomplished. But, horror of horrors, where had those ashes been placed?

"Right where Alabama scored to win the game!" the guy moaned.

Now, do you see why he's in the witness protection program?

A call for the ol' ball coach

Thirty minutes before kickoff of every Oak Ridge High School football game, a call rings out across the public address system at Blankenship Field: "Your attention, please. Will Nick Orlando—Nick Orlando—please report to the press box."

That will be Guy Hamrick's voice at the microphone. He's been issuing the same statement before home games for more than 30 years. But it's highly unlikely Nick Orlando will respond.

You see, he's been dead since 1997. And therein lies an Anderson County sports tradition dating back to the late 1960s.

The diminutive (5-foot, 2-inch) Coach Orlando was an institution in Oak Ridge athletics and recreation for eons, almost from the time Uncle Sam's bulldozers began moving dirt to build the Secret City. A New Jersey native and son of Sicilian emigrants, he landed at Jefferson Junior High and stayed 31 years. He coached football, tennis, track, cross-country, soccer and golf—in addition to teaching physical education classes. No telling how many thousands of students honed their physical skills under his tutelage.

"He was gruff on the outside but a teddy bear at heart," said Hamrick. "He was a real cut-up. Everybody in town knew him, and he knew them."

In 1968, Hamrick's father, Tom, was the PA announcer at Oak Ridge games. One Friday night, the press box phone rang. The caller asked to speak to Coach Orlando. Thus, Tom Hamrick pitched his now-famous words to the crowd for the first time.

"Coach Orlando was sitting a few rows away, but he didn't want to talk to anybody on the phone," said the younger Hamrick, who took over PA duties from his father in 1981. "As it turned out, Oak Ridge scored a touchdown right after the announcement."

Moments later, the caller dialed the press box again. Once more, the PA summons for Orlando went out. Once more, Orlando didn't respond. Once more, the Wildcats scored.

"If I remember correctly, my dad made that announcement four times, and Oak Ridge scored after every one of them," Hamrick told me. "Dad started saying the same thing before every game as a sign of good luck."

When the ol' coach died, many wondered if the tradition would continue. Would it be in bad taste? Perish the thought!

"I called the Orlando family to see if it was OK," Hamrick said. "They were delighted. It was a great tribute to his memory."

And something tells me at that stadium in the great beyond, Coach O's toothy smile is as wide as ever.

Paying proper Big Orange respect

Tricia Roskop told me this story shortly after the start of the University of Tennessee's 2013 football campaign. She swears it's true. Given societal customs of the Southland, I don't doubt her one iota.

Roskop works for the U.S. Census Bureau. She and husband Fred have lived in Knoxville for more than two decades. Hopping about is second nature. She was born in Ohio, lived briefly in the South during childhood, then took up residence in a variety of distant locations including Illinois, Colorado and New York—with her high school years in England, to boot.

"My father worked for International Harvester," Tricia told me. "He always taught us that wherever we lived we should adapt to the customs of that area.

"For instance, in England we didn't behave like ugly Americans and demand more ice in our drinks. We just drank it the way the locals did. Also, wherever we were living, my mom would collect local sayings and write them down. That way we could always keep up."

Tricia followed the same advice when she and Fred came here from upstate New York.

"My parents were raised in Stuttgart, Arkansas, so they knew something about the South," she recalled. "When my dad found out we were coming to Tennessee, he said one thing I should always do is pay attention to funeral processions.

"He told me it was rude not to honor cars going to a funeral. He said don't pass them. Don't weave in and out. Instead, pull to the side of the road and show respect."

And wouldn't you know it! Her very first day on Tennessee soil provided an opportunity to practice what had been preached.

"I flew into Nashville because the airfare was cheaper," she said. "I rented a car and started driving toward Knoxville. I hadn't been traveling on the interstate very long when I ran into a funeral procession. In fact, I was immediately inside of one.

"I pulled over to one side of the highway and slowed down, but then I realized the procession was taking both lanes. I couldn't get away from it. I distinctly remember thinking, 'Wow! Somebody really important must have died! I wonder who? And I wonder where the cemetery is?'

"I was positive it was a funeral because all the cars were flying the same flag. It was from a funeral home that began with the letter 'T.'"

Yes, brothers and sisters—a 'T' as in the University of Tennessee. It was game day in Big Orange Country.

"Oh, I know all about UT car flags now," she said with a laugh. "But back then, I was convinced somebody had died."

Do tell. After Tennessee's back-to-back 59-14 drubbing by Oregon and 31-17 loss at Florida in 2013, perhaps Tricia's first impression wasn't too far off the mark.

Not your average lap swimmer

Joyce Kickels swims half a mile, twice a day, in a very large pool. So large, in fact, it's not practical to measure its size in the conventional units of feet or yards.

How about 193 miles up and down both sides and 5,470 surface acres?

Such is the case when you take your morning and afternoon dips in the main channel of Melton Hill Lake.

If you've ever boated in the first big bend above Melton Hill Dam, you've likely see Joyce stroking along, often in company with "Tuney," her Weimaraner. Sometimes Joyce's husband Wayne joins her during the afternoon session.

This regimen started in 2001, shortly after Joyce and Wayne moved to East Tennessee from Plainfield, Illinois.

"We've always been boaters and skiers, so we had to have water," she said. "Soon as we got settled, I started swimming."

This isn't a year 'round exercise program—although Joyce and Wayne have been known to swim in wetsuits when it's too chilly, even for their seasoned Yankee blood.

"I usually start in April and go through October," she said. "It all depends on the weather—and how much water TVA is bringing in upstream from Norris Dam. Some years the water stays cold well into spring, and I can't get started until late May."

Joyce isn't talking "skin estimates" about temperature. She takes precise readings every day and has been amazed how quickly conditions can change. The day she and I talked, the surface temperature was 84 degrees F. when she set out. By the time she finished her morning run, it had dropped to 79.

"It didn't look like it, but obviously TVA was pulling a lot of water off the bottom of Norris, and it was coming right down the channel of Melton Hill."

Hers is a three-part exercise routine. The Kickels' house sits 167 steps above their dock, where a flotilla of ski boats, kayaks and floats is moored. There's also one very old rowboat, complete with oars. That's her ride across the lake.

"I row over, tie up, get out and swim, then row back across and climb the steps to the house. Well, sometimes I cheat and take our electric tram back up!"

She swims near the bank, so there's never been a close call with a powerboat. In fact, the only real scare she's had in decades came from a water snake.

"Normally snakes don't bother me," she said, "but I didn't see this one until it was about 10 feet away. Apparently it didn't see me, either. All of a sudden our eyes met. I screamed out loud.

"I know snakes can't scream, but if they could this one certainly would have. I've never seen a snake so surprised in my life! It immediately dove, which, of course, made me think, 'Oh goodness! Where is it now?'"

Probably still swimming frantically, miles and miles away.

Learning new jock words

I'm desperately trying to understand jockspeak, particularly as practiced by Tennessee head football coach Butch Jones.

You'd think I would have learned this odd language long ago. After all, I was raised by a father who coached and taught physical education. I played football throughout high school. The first 15 years of my employment at the News Sentinel were in the sports department. Surely I should've mastered the mother tongue by now.

Alas, no. This glaring deficiency has revealed itself repeatedly in recent days as I attempted to read the latest news about Big Orange practice sessions.

First, I stumbled across "PBU."

(Is that a new tailgating sandwich?)

On its heels came "FBI."

(Are federal agents involved?)

And then there's Coach Jones' frequent reference to "the power of one."

(What happened to the other 10 players? I knew UT's ranks were seriously depleted, but had no idea the situation was that bad.)

Thanks to a quick tutorial from sports writers Mike Strange and John Adams, however, my fluency in jockspeak and Butchspeak has increased exponentially.

Turns out "PBU" means "pass break up."

"FBI" means "football intelligence." An oxymoron, mayhaps?

And "the power of one" means—well, nobody's absolutely certain. But as John recently opined in his column, it has something to do with "one moment, one play, one practice, one game, one mindset and one team."

Hmm. All those ones add up to six. In the name of mathematical correctness, should His Coachness change this mantra to "the power of half a dozen?" Just wondering.

Now that we have broached the subject of athletic multilingualism, what about some acronyms and buzzwords from the fans' perspective? Don't we deserve a special language, too?

Of course we do. Here, then, are a few to consider as the season approaches and progresses:

TS: "tickets scalped."

HDE: "hot dogs eaten."

LHIJP: "likker hidden in jeans pocket."

LBBRFJP: "likker bottles broken removing from jeans pocket."

TSIRRL: "time spent in rest room line."

SCBVWTS: "still can't believe Vandy won two straight."

FTC: "fire the coach."

SPBBMINS: "stop playing boom box music in Neyland Stadium."

WIWIOTV: "wish I'd watched it on TV."

Gave 'em all a chance to stretch facts

The University of Tennessee's 2014 home football opener against Utah State gave players on both teams a bragging point for future conversations.

It was a minor bragging point, for sure. A misleading one, as well. Still, it was the truth, the whole truth and nothing but the truth. Someday way down the pike, pot-gutted, out-of-shape has-beens can casually and accurately allude to the NFL by saying, "Oh, yeah. I used to play on Sunday myself."

This, of course, was because the Vols' traditional Saturday game was bumped 24 hours later to accommodate the Boomsday fireworks show. Keep this in mind the next time you're playing Vol trivia.

You know you're a card-carrying geezer jock when you remember football anecdotes like that and the first thought that crosses your mind is, "It sure wasn't like that when I was playing." Which was precisely the case when yours truly thumbed through the newest edition of the News Sentinel's Prep Extra magazine.

What's different from now and the mid-1960s?

Just about everything—from flashy uniforms to staffs of specialty coaches to customized training camps these talented young men began attending approximately seven months after they learned to walk.

But the Number One shocker? High school players with beards, that's what. Holy hair! As I gazed at pictures of high school players, I saw enough facial foliage to make Bigfoot proud.

During my years at Young High, only one teammate shaved regularly. That was hulking lineman and future trucking company executive Bill Reed, whose 5 o'clock shadow earned him the nickname he carries to this day: "Fred Flintstone."

The envious rest of us could barely squeeze out a tuft of peach fuzz.

On the other hand, if you think today's high-impact, ultra-protective gear is a modern phenomenon, think again.

Knoxvillian Bill Alexander called my attention to this little-known fact after reading the late Russ Bebb's book, The Big Orange: A Story of Tennessee Football.

Seems that during the 1901 season, legendary Vol Nash Buckingham sewed aluminum pads into his pants "and nearly disjointed a Clemson player early in the game," Bebb wrote. "Buckingham's uniform was subsequently examined, and the referee prevailed upon him to dispose of the metal pads before the game could continue."

Buckingham later became an author with a huge national following. But he might have made more money if he'd gone into athletic gear R&D.

Going for the gold a different way

I'm sorry. I failed again. I tried—as I do every four years—to become absorbed in the magic of the Winter Olympics. But it just isn't meant to be.

This isn't a slam on the athletes who compete in these rigorous events. Quite the contrary. I greatly admire their dedication and derring-do.

It's just that I'm so ready for winter to be over by the opening of the Winter Olympics, the words "recreation" and "snow" are mutually exclusive.

Oops, wait. I did watch one recorded Winter Olympic "event." Several times, in fact, and howled in delight throughout. I received it in an email from my daughter Megan, who inherited her father's warped sense of humor.

This is a figure-skating routine that has been overdubbed with a variety of flatulent sounds. Every time the skater twists, leaps and lands gracefully on the ice, a different blast occurs. That's what I call a gold-medal performance.

Maybe these games would appeal to me if they involved winter activities to which I can relate. Such as:

- Indoor bug hunting.

Is there a homeowner anywhere in the South who's not up to his or her thorax in ladybugs and stinkbugs by late winter? Aaakk! Where do these awful things come from?!

Every day, my wife and I compete to see who can capture the most.

I prefer the masking tape approach. My personal best is eight ladybugs collected in a single length of tape. Each was plucked, one at a time, from the window in our living room.

Mary Ann is a devotee of the Dust Buster. She's the fastest draw in the South. A few days ago, she even nailed a ladybug on the wing in midair.

- Curling.

No, not that stupid game involving brooms and stones on ice. I'm talking real curling, testing the flexibility of coach potatoes universally.

In this event, contestants vie to see who can curl up fastest on a sofa, in a recliner or in bed. First to snore wins.

- Skeleton.

Again, this has nothing to do with that insane Winter Olympic sport wherein competitors, lying prone on a Popsicle stick, hit speeds of 130 mph. This one is safer, not to mention yummy.

Each entrant is given a whole, baked chicken. First to reduce it to a pile of bare bones gets the gold.

- Ice walking.

I thought of this event a few days ago while attempting to traverse the frozen tundra of a downtown parking lot. The object is to see who can perform the most hilarious contortions while fighting to remain upright.

Every joint in my body still aches. And thinking back, I may have emitted some of the same noises that are on the email Megan sent me.

Who needs the game itself?

No wonder the Roman Empire deep-sixed. (Oops. I mean deep-VIed.) Can you imagine the hassle of hanging around the Forum all day, discussing something like the Super Bowl?

"Those idiots had it IInd and III inches at the XXV late in the game, yet in II tries, they couldn't make it!" Tiberius might exclaim. "Dammit! Why didn't they kick a field goal on IVth down, for Zeus' sake? They could easily have made it and gone up by I. As it was, they lost by II! Jerks! We oughta throw 'em to the lions!"

To which Claudius might deadpan: "What good would that do? If you will recall, the Lions went IV-XII last year."

OK, perhaps that's lame, numerically or otherwise. But even after XLVIII-plus years, I have trouble telling Super Bowl XXVII from Super Bowl XXXIV, let alone Super Bowl XLVII. In 2016, the NFL did us all a huge favor by simply calling the 50th anniversary game Super Bowl 50. But now, these idiots insist on returning to Roman numerals. Go figure.

At least there's one saving grace about this annual nuttiness. We don't have to wait until game time to see the commercials.

Such wasn't the case a few years ago. Back then, TV viewers—many of whom couldn't care less which team won, or even played—had to sit through excruciating sessions of blocking, tackling, passing and penalties just to see the newest line of funny, innovative commercial messages. These days, you can watch 'em well in advance, without having to bother with actual football.

In 2013, for instance, I was able to enjoy more than a dozen Super Bowl ads four full days ahead of kickoff. All I had to do was tickle a few computer keys. That's what I call technological progress.

Some were the full deal, start to finish—like a rib-tickling VW spot where an office worker from Minnesota spoke with a perky Jamaican accent. Plus a steamy Mercedes-Benz clip—hmm, I think it was Mercedes-Benz; could have been Ford or Chevy, but who cares?—featuring swimsuit model Kate Upton.

Others offered only teasers. Such as a Skechers pitch for running shoes showing a man chasing a cheetah across the African plains. Based on the grunts and screams that followed, we're led to believe the guy actually caught and subdued the big cat.

(Maybe he does in today's world of Photoshop fiction. In real life, of course, those shoes would serve as an excellent source of fiber for the cheetah as it devoured a tasty meal of warm, bloody flesh. But I digress.)

Too bad we had to wait until the game was over to learn the final score (Baltimore Ravens 34-San Francisco 49ers 31.)

Yawn! That was sooo XXth century.

Heads? Tails? Where?

In more than 40 years of officiating high school football, Benny Blackstock has pretty much seen it all.

Horribly busted plays that go for a long touchdown. Cupcake passes inexplicably dropped. Missed blocks. Muffed tackles. Wrong-way punt returns. Wildly caroming pigskins graphically illustrating the term "that's the way the ol' ball bounces."

But Blackstock says the Number One entry in his list of bizarre on-the-field experiences occurred before an opening kickoff.

"Craziest coin toss in the history of the game," he said with a broad grin.

You may know the event of which I speak. You may even have seen it on YouTube. If not, Google "Jerry Rice coin toss" and prepare to laugh.

This occurred August 27, 2011, at the much-heralded Alcoa-Maryville game. Maryville prevailed 26-19, breaking Alcoa's 44-game winning streak.

The buildup to this contest was huge. The aforementioned Rice—pro Hall of Fame receiver with perhaps the greatest set of hands the modern game has ever witnessed—was selected to flip the coin.

"He did more than flip it," Blackstock recalled. "He launched it."

The 50-cent piece went so high, it got lost in the bright sunshine. Thus ensued a spirited search by everyone, not the least of which was Ref Blackstock.

"We couldn't find it!" he said. "It flat-out disappeared. Finally, one of the Maryville players said, 'I think it went down my shirt'."

As you can see by watching YouTube, the vanishing act catches everybody off guard. Rice nearly falls over from laughter as Blackstock digs furiously, albeit fruitlessly, in the back of the player's jersey.

"That was the only coin I had," Blackstock said. "There wasn't anything to do but ask if anybody else had one. The TV camera man reached in his pocket and dug one out. Just as Jerry was about to flip again, the kid said, 'I think it just fell out'."

Indeed, it had. Somehow the coin dislodged from hiding and came tumbling to the turf at the player's feet. Blackstock quickly waved everyone aside and peered into the grass.

"Maryville had called tails, and that's what it was. I hollered, 'Tails!' Maryville wanted to receive the ball, and so we were able to start the game. I sure didn't want to go through another coin toss like that. Ever."

Blackstock lives in Friendsville. He works in the tax enforcement office for the city of Knoxville. He was a 145-pound blocking back under John Clabo at Knoxville's Young High School, 1960-62. Reminiscing, he wonders if the 2011 fluke wasn't simply par for the course.

"I often called the toss for Young during my senior season," he said. "We went 4-6 that year."

Skip and Big Sam

My dad fell dead of a heart attack on Saturday, June 17, 1972—one day before the first official national observance of Father's Day, as signed into law by President Richard Nixon. Yet even after all these years in the grave, he still speaks to me.

Not literally, of course. But every time I hear a "Big Sam" story from one of his former colleagues or students, my father springs back to life.

Not long ago, I heard one from Skip Plotnicki.

Skip has lived in Texas for decades. He's vice president of engineering for Hamilton Form, a precast concrete company in Fort Worth. But anyone familiar with vintage Knoxville sports history will immediately recognize his name.

Skip was a basketball superstar at Catholic High School. During his senior year, he was among the leading scorers in the old Knoxville Interscholastic League. He went to the University of Tennessee on scholarship and played varsity for the Volunteers during the seasons of 1962-63, 1963-64 and 1964-65. He graduated with a degree in civil engineering, followed by a master's in engineering mechanics.

To say the Plotnickis and the Venables "knew each other" is 14-karat understatement. The lives of both families have been intertwined since shortly after World War II, when professors Ben A. Plotnicki Sr. and Sam A. Venable Sr. joined the faculty of the old UT department of Health, Physical Education and Recreation.

"Coach P." and "Coach V." occupied adjoining offices in the Alumni Memorial Gym, passing their shared telephone back and forth through a cut-out in the wall.

Whistles around their necks and clipboards in their hands, they timed wind sprints, counted sit-ups and mentored legions of future coaches.

They officiated high school and college events, primarily basketball and track, alongside each other.

They raised their families with each respective set of kids knowing "Mr. and Mrs. Venable" and "Mr. and Mrs. Plotnicki" as all but surrogate parents.

That kind of close.

Skip and I still stay in contact with each other. Recently, our families and basketball Vols of yore got together for a picnic lunch at the old Plotnicki home place on Fort Loudoun Lake. That's when he told me the story I'm sharing today.

It began during Skip's sophomore season as a Vol. (Freshmen didn't play varsity back then.) Coach Ray Mears sent him into a game at the old Armory Fieldhouse.

Skip did what was required of all subs. He approached the officials' table, ID'd his number (34) to the scorer, then knelt so as not to block the view. When the buzzer sounded, that was his signal to enter the fray.

At all Vol home games, the scorer happened to be Big Sam.

"This was really an awkward moment for me," Skip recalled. "He wasn't just 'the scorer.' He was 'Mr. Venable,' a man I'd been around all my life. I didn't know what to say."

No problem. Big Sam played the moment cool, as always. He was forever a stickler for the rules. In black-and-whites on the hardwood or a business suit at the scorer's table, he showed no favoritism to anyone, anytime. Thus, he didn't acknowledge Skip more than any other player.

"It was like he'd never known me," Skip recalled with a laugh.

That same pattern continued throughout Skip's collegiate career. Before or after a game, Big Sam was always down-home friendly with him. At the tip-off, however, he became Mr. Cold Shoulders.

And then —

"It was the final game of my senior season," Skip said. "We were playing Tulane. Coach Mears sent me in for my very last time in a Tennessee uniform. I checked in and knelt at Mr. Venable's table, just like always."

The buzzer sounded shortly thereafter. Skip rose to his feet and was about to trot onto the floor. Just then, Big Sam spoke quietly in his wake: "Good luck, Skip."

Skip turned and glanced back. For the briefest of a split-second, the scorer winked, nodded and smiled—an acknowledgement of love across all those years.

Then it was back to the serious business of basketball.

One of the advantages of befriending a country doctor who enjoys hunting is that everybody in the region owes him money. Thus, all those "No Trespassing" signs translate to "Welcome Doc and friends!"

Which explains why Dr. R.B. "Sonny" Baird and I were rattling along a gravel road in rural Hawkins County one autumn afternoon back in the mid-1980s. Grouse and quail were the menu.

Doc eased his truck alongside a fellow who was clearing brush in a roadside ditch. After a few moments of polite ice-breaking, the conversation turned the same direction it had countless times before: Why, yes, he knew where a few coveys were located. Oh, and don't worry about those signs. You know you're always welcome around here, Doc.

"Who is that guy, Doc?" I casually inquired after we had parked, put on vests, uncased shotguns and liberated the anxious dogs.

"Can't remember his name, and it sure does bug me," he replied. "He's been a patient of mine for years. I know his name like I know my own. I did a hemorrhoid job on him one time, and I never forget a face."

Hoo-boy. You can't script that kind of comedy. It's built-in.

The folks you're about to meet in this chapter cover the landscape. Some are humorous. Some have poignant stories to tell. One or two are gone from our midst. But up and down the line, they're my kind of people. They don't come any finer.

Chapter Twelve
MY KIND OF PEOPLE

'I've got to remember who I am'

Take it from my old friend and "Appalachian Hippie Poet" Bill Alexander: If a day is going extremely well for you and you hate to see it end, no problem. Just repeat everything tomorrow.

Bill's been following this advice since 2013, when he discovered he was born on two different days. Ever since, he's been enjoying twin birthdays, twin Christmases, twin everything.

"All my life, I've listed October 10, 1946, as my birthday," he told me. "That's what my mama and daddy always said. So that's what I always wrote down any time I was filling out paperwork."

"Paperwork" in Alexander's situation is a bit more complicated than that of your average Joe. You see, he holds degrees from two universities and spent 26 years with Oak Ridge National Laboratory—with Q-level security clearance, to boot.

"Not once in all those years was I ever asked for a birth certificate," he said. "I know that for a fact because I've never seen my birth certificate. I just always went by what mama and daddy said.

"In fact, I didn't need one until a few years ago when I applied for a passport. So I sent a request to the vital records department with the state of Tennessee."

When the document arrived, it showed Bill's birthdate as one day earlier: October 9, 1946.

"It listed my arrival time as 3:16 a.m.," he said. "This is just a theory on my part, but having worked night shifts myself, I'll bet it was 3:16 on the morning of the 10th, but the nurse on duty probably forgot the date had changed at midnight and wrote down the 9th."

No big deal, right? Considering Bill has spent all those years on Earth without hassle, what's one day either way?

Plenty, as far as medical records are concerned.

"Somehow between my Social Security paperwork and my Medicare paperwork, I got shifted back to the 9th," he said. "So when I went to my doctor's office for a procedure, they couldn't find me. I told 'em to try the 10th, and it went right through.

"I've got to remember who I am for whatever piece of paperwork I'm dealing with at any given time," he laughed. "On my driver's license, I was born October 10. But on my passport, I was born October 9."

The only fly in this ointment is that all these double dates mean double trouble every spring. Poor ol' Bill now faces back-to-back April 15 deadlines for filing his income tax return. All things considered, he's just thankful a Friday the 13th isn't mentioned somewhere along the line.

Almost late for his own funeral

If you search the News Sentinel's obituary archives from September 16, 2001, you will find the name of Cecil Edgar Wells, 76. It lists facts about Mr. Wells' life, his survivors and plans for graveside services at Tennessee Veterans Cemetery.

What this obituary does not reveal, however, are details of how Mr. Wells got to the cemetery. And therein lies a story that has taken on legendary status in the family's history.

"Everybody agrees he would have gotten a big laugh out of it," is how one daughter-in-law, Holly D. Wells, puts it.

A Knoxville native, Cecil Wells worked in the insurance business. He had moved to Lafayette, Louisiana, in the 1980s. In early September 2001, he suffered a massive stroke. It would take his life on September 12.

As you surely remember, this was one day after one of the most tragic events in U.S. history.

"My brothers-in-law drove to Louisiana as soon as we heard about the stroke," explained Holly, who works in human resources at the University of Tennessee. "The rest decided to wait and see how he was doing, then go ourselves."

Alas, all travel plans went out the window when hijacked jetliners turned New York City, Washington, D.C., and Shanksville, Pennsylvania, into war zones.

"They had a funeral for him in Lafayette," Holly recalled, "but he had wanted to be buried in Knoxville. Any other time, this wouldn't have been a problem. But after 9/11, all the planes were grounded."

The family checked into having Mr. Wells' casket shipped via a commercial trucking company. It was too costly and would take too much time.

So they did what any resourceful East Tennesseans would do.

"They rented a regular-sized U-Haul trailer, hooked it to the pickup and brought him here themselves," said Holly. "Soon as the funeral was over, they loaded him up and came to Tennessee."

This took a bit of planning, she remembers. First, permits had to be obtained to transport the body across state lines. While that was being done Holly, still in Knoxville, contacted Rose Mortuary so the casket could be taken directly there.

"They drove almost nonstop," she said. "Just pulled in long enough to get gas and go to the restroom. They got here the same night, and we had his graveside services the next day."

Nobody in the clan makes merry of either Cecil Wells' death or the tragedy of 9/11. Still, the irony isn't lost on them.

"Everybody keeps saying how much of a kick he would've gotten out of this," Holly noted. "We all said he would agree his funeral wouldn't be typical. I guess if your casket arrives in a U-Haul trailer, it's a pretty redneck event."

She's really on a roll

Katrina Chalifoux does more than squeeze the Charmin.

She also cuts it. Sews it. Curls it. Twists it. Glues it. Tapes it. Irons it. And in so doing, turns it into a beautiful wedding gown.

So beautiful that the Knoxville resident placed second in the 2012 annual Cheap Chic Toilet Paper Wedding Dress Contest. This national event is sponsored by Procter & Gamble, maker of the TP "Mr. Whipple" always warned his customers about mishandling. It attracted 710 entries.

This wasn't Chalifoux's first trip down the aisle, either. She won the contest in 2008 and placed second in 2007.

"The first time I heard about it, I thought it was a stupid thing to do," laughed Chalifoux, who moved to Knoxville with husband Ray from Rockford, Illinois, in 2009.

"That was in 2007. If you remember, lots of couples were getting married on '7/7/7'. I read about the contest in our local newspaper in Rockford. I do a lot of sewing, so I thought, 'Why not give this a try?'

"I found out it's a lot like working with cloth. You fold it and drape it and sew it the same way."

Working with her hands is nothing new for Chalifoux. She's a certified automobile mechanic. Before that, she worked as a maintenance technician, repairing two-way radios for Motorola.

"I never have minded getting my hands dirty," she said, "although they sure have to be clean before I start working with toilet paper!"

Her 2012 entry was a sweeping affair, heavily bedecked with intricate flowers—roses, lilies and pansies—as well as feathers as elaborate as the egret plumes favored by milliners in the early 20th century. And every square inch of it was made of TP. Twenty-eight double rolls, in fact.

This isn't something you put together on the spur of the moment. Chalifoux estimates she invested 200 hours from design to finished product.

"These contests have been fun," she said. "Some of my family came down from Illinois to visit while I was making the dress. My niece, Frances Maravich, modeled it for me. But I don't know if I'll enter again. It takes so much time."

Chalifoux earned $1,000 for her efforts. The winner pocketed $2,012— for year 2012, get it? Third place received $500.

"They take the winning gown each year and put it in a Ripley's Believe It or Not museum somewhere around the world."

Do the others get, uh, "recycled" in more traditional fashion?

"No," Chalifoux replied. "There's so much glue and tape in them, I doubt it would be a pleasant experience."

A name to remember

I don't care what nonsense you've heard to the contrary, but Buddy Holley was not killed in an Iowa plane crash in 1959.

He is alive and well, thank you very much. Retired after a long career at Oak Ridge National Laboratory, he serves on the city council in Harriman. I just finished an enjoyable telephone conversation with him. So forget all that "day the music died" malarkey.

Well, OK; if you insist on pesky details, the guy I spoke with isn't the Buddy Holley of rock and roll fame. In fact, you shouldn't ask him to sing so much as a single note.

"Not unless you want to clear the room," he said with a laugh.

Still, the coincidental links between musician Buddy Holley and mechanical engineer Buddy Holley are striking.

The Buddy who was killed February 3, 1959—along with fellow pop stars Ritchie Valens and J.P. "The Big Bopper" Richardson—was officially named Charles. As in Charles Hardin Holley. He was called "Buddy" by his family from childhood. His meteoric musical career began as a teenager. His real surname was Holley (with an "e") but he changed it to Holly (no "e") after it was misspelled by Decca records. His widow's name is Maria. His black-framed glasses are icons of the era in which he lived.

Harriman's Buddy also is officially named Charles. As in Charles McGhee Holley II. He was called "Buddy" from childhood because his sister had a tough time saying "brother." He played drums in a high school dance band—but since there was no stampede among recording companies to sign his group to a contract, he has retained the "e" in his surname. His wife's name is Mary. He wears glasses, but not black-framed ones.

What? No Peggy Sue anywhere in the mix?

"That's an interesting story," he replied. "Once when I was working on a project at K-25, they set me up with 'Peggy Sue' as my computer password. I said, 'No way that'll ever pass security! It would be too easy for somebody to figure out.' So they changed it."

Harriman's Holley is a native of West Virginia. His family moved to Oak Ridge when he was in high school. He graduated in 1960 and went on to the University of Tennessee, earning his engineering degree in 1965.

"Yeah, I get a lot of good-natured teasing about my name," he said. "But as I tell people, at least they're going to remember it.

"One time when I was working at the lab, they made up business cards for us. Mine said 'Charles McGhee Holley II.' Everybody I came in contact with said, 'Who the heck is that?' So I had 'em make me a second batch that read 'C.M. "Buddy" Holley.' Then everybody said, 'Oh, yeah, that's the guy we know'."

Nothing like a 'little' road trip

Jim Atkins has a relativity short commute to work—14 easy miles from his home in Morristown, Tennessee, to his place of employment in White Pine.

After that, though, the drive becomes a bit lengthier.

Try 257 miles. One way. Then he turns around and drives back. Atkins travels this route Monday through Friday, which translates to 2,570 miles every week.

Just another session behind the wheel for a trucker.

Atkins, who drives for Old Dominion Freight Line, has been on the White-Pine-to-Greensboro route for six months. Prior to that, his daily voyage was White Pine to Hamburg, Indiana, a round-trip of 552 miles.

He sums up his job in three short words: "I love it."

He pulls out at 10 p.m. and usually is back home by 9:30 the next morning.

"The sun is coming up by the time I get to Hickory (North Carolina)," he said. "With patches of fog down in the valley, it's absolutely beautiful. And then I get to enjoy the gorge on the Carolina-Tennessee border.

"I don't make quite as much money on this route as I did going to Indiana, but the scenery more than makes up for it. Also, there's a lot less traffic.

"When I was going to Hamburg, I always hit Louisville (Kentucky) right during the 8 o'clock rush hour. The way my route is now, I'm going over during the night when traffic is light. The main thing I have to watch out for is deer."

Atkins acknowledges that some motorists might not enjoy weaving through the gorge, especially flatlanders unaccustomed to mountain terrain.

"There's a long stretch where 18-wheelers can't pass," he said. "If we happen to wind up behind someone who's intimidated by the curves and is going 35, well, that means you're in for a slow, scenic drive."

As you might expect, inclement weather is the bane of his existence.

"A lot of people don't realize how fast they're driving in the rain," he said. "They really need to slow down. It doesn't take much to hydroplane."

Born in Jellico, Atkins has lived in Morristown since early childhood. He's a 1981 graduate of Morristown East High School and spent 10 years in the Army before entering the trucking business.

His wife Paula works at Sam's Meat Cleaver, a butcher shop in Morristown. Their work schedules mesh—in a manner of speaking.

"She goes to work about the time I go to bed," Atkins said. "But then I'm up when she gets home. We have some time together before I head out."

How do they spend their weekends? On the road, of course.

"We've got a Yamaha motorcycle and a Jeep Wrangler," he told me. "We love to take off and drive to the mountains."

A math quiz, By Ned

Math teachers, I have a problem you can pose to your students. See if they can come up with a plausible answer. It involves fractions.

This numeric conundrum has been floating around a certain East Tennessee farm for decades. I came across it a few days ago during casual conversation with Toby and Scott James, part of a three-generation agricultural family.

They learned about it from "By Ned."

"His real name was Perry Smith," Toby told me. "He worked for Daddy for years. All us young'ins called him 'By Ned' because that's what he said with nearly every breath. He'd always start or end every sentence with 'By Ned.' It'd go something like this:

"'By Ned, we need to get that hay hauled in. I'll go fetch the wagon, By Ned. Mr. James, By Ned, it shore is gonna be hot out there today.' Stuff like that. That's the way he talked all the time."

Anyhow, it came a good, damp day in the late fall one year, the perfect opportunity to "hand-off" tobacco. That's the old-time process of stripping leaves from stalks that had been hanging in the barn to air-cure, in preparation for auction. The leaves get stacked by grade, arranged into bundled "hands" and secured together by a wrapper leaf.

"This was back when everybody had a certain-sized plot they could raise," added Scott. "It's not like today where tobacco is grown in large fields under contract.

"How you got the profit was all on shares. It depended on a lot of things. Who owned the land, who supplied the seed and equipment, who did the labor. You might be in for a one-quarter share or a one-third share or a half-share or a two-thirds share, whatever you worked out ahead of time."

That morning the James gang—father, brothers, sisters, whoever was available, along with By Ned—was handing-off up a storm. Talk turned to shares and how the various breakdowns were "this" third and "that" third.

By Ned listened intently as the banter grew. Finally, he turned to Toby's and Scott's father and spoke decisively: "Mr. James, I'm gonna start growin' my own 'bakker next year. And I'm puttin' in for four-thirds."

Toby says By Ned has long-since gone to that big farm in the sky. Alas, he never got around to raising that four-thirds crop.

"But with his kind of mathematical genius, By Ned sure missed his calling," Toby mused. "He should've worked for the government."

Safe Driving 101

I've just learned some excellent advice for wet-weather driving emergencies. It works for rain or snow.

This tip comes from Campbell Countian Ray Penn. Years ago, he made a discovery that not only involves safe motoring, but also spiffy dressing. If that's not the epitome of multitasking, I'll eat a dipstick along with my hat.

It occurred during the days of Ray's doctoral studies at Northwestern University. (At this point he broke into the NWU fight song, gleefully chanted during athletic events whenever "the other" school scores: "Hey, hey, that's OK; you will work for us some day!" How weird. You never hear anything like that during games at Tenniss, uh, Taness, aw, you know, Big Ornj Country. But I digress.)

On weekends, Ray would pilot his Chevette from the NWU campus in Evanston, Illinois, to his tiny (population 450) hometown in central Illinois. After visiting his folks and doing laundry, he'd head back to school.

"I always took the toll road around Chicago," he said. "It's a multiple-lane road, and I usually drove in the middle lane."

Ray continued as only a novelist would appreciate: "It was a dark and stormy night, rain pelting my windshield like a sandblaster. Suddenly, to my panic, both wiper blades fell off at the same time!"

This is bad enough when it happens to a single blade. To have it occur in stereo is off-the-charts bizarre.

Ray's vision instantly was reduced to zero. Nonetheless, he knew he had to get off the road to assess the situation. He turned on his right blinker and inched over.

"Still hyperventilating, I tried to figure out how to replace those blades," he said. "Somehow, my eyes fell to my laundry basket. On top were two pairs of black, knee-length socks. Braving the deluge, I put one on top of the other on each wiper arm. To my surprise and relief, they did the trick until I was able to find a service station.

"Ever since, my travel motto has been 'Long black dress socks. Never leave home without them.'"

(Hint to fellow UT alums: A 12-pack of Walmart white crews oughta work just as well on our pickup trucks.)

Custom conditions on demand

If teaching and writing ever play out, Gordon Sisk and I have a fallback. We can open a weather planning service.

In certain outdoor circles, gray-bearded Gordon, who teaches social studies at Karns High School, is known as "Grizzly." He is a member of, and chief meteorologist for, a group of backpackers called Team Rainmaker.

It is a most deserving name.

All Gordon has to do is lace up his hiking boots and a perfectly cloudless day will turn gray. Soon as he hits the dirt—urban footpath to Appalachian Trail—a monsoon is certain to follow. This is an ironclad fact, proven through decades of soggy experience.

I, on the other hand, am Doctor Drought.

This talent came nearly one year ago with the purchase of a Frogg Toggs rain suit. It has yet to see action.

This lightweight outfit has accompanied me to the summit of Mount LeConte in the Great Smokies. To the Alps in Switzerland, Austria and Germany. On numerous fishing trips. As long as it remains within easy reach, rain will stay away. Leave it at home, though, and it's Soaked City.

One brilliant day summer day in Innsbruck, Austria, I forgot to stick it into Mary Ann's backpack. (It's always best, harrumph, to travel with a strong wife who will shoulder your load as well as hers.) The result? An impromptu downpour, that's what. I had to pay tourist prices for a gift-shop umbrella.

Later that fall, at Halloween, fierce storms were predicted for trick-or-treaters. I'd already made plans to accompany my son Clay and his tykes, Max and Lucy, on candy patrols of their neighborhood that evening. Fearing the worst, I even took waterproof boots along with the Frogg Toggs.

Not necessary.

Truth be told, I did wear the jacket part of the rain suit that brisk evening, but only as a windbreaker atop my shirt. When Max and Lucy retreated to their house to ceremoniously dump the contents of their plastic pumpkins onto the carpet, we were drier than a two-hour sermon. Later that night, long after the Frogg Toggs and I were safely back home, the skies opened up like Bald River Falls. I rest my case.

Gordon and I may launch our campaign under a banner on the order of "Wet 'n Dry" or "No Precip? No Problem!"

If your lawn or garden could use a steady, extensive soaking, Gordon's your man. On the other hand, if your outdoor plans call for a wedding, political rally, barbecue, bar mitzvah or football tailgate and you need clear skies, give me a ring.

Satisfaction guaranteed either way.

Hicks is down but never out

The poster boy for grit-against-all-odds sits in a wheelchair on the fourth floor of a North Knoxville hospital. I'm confident this condition will only be temporary.

His name is Bill Hicks. He is 65 and lives in Sweetwater. He is learning how to walk. For the third time.

Hicks' first experience in upright mobility occurred the old-fashioned way, around the age of 12 months. He grew up like many East Tennessee country boys—running and roaming, wherever and whenever, with a fishing rod or shotgun in tow.

All that changed in 1969.

Hicks was roughhousing with friends. Nothing serious, just horseplay. He fell. His head struck a rock.

"Nothing really hurt," I quoted him in a 1984 outdoor page column. "Matter of fact, I sat up in the truck while they took me to the hospital. That may have done a lot of the damage."

His neck was broken. Vertebrae at the base of his skull were crushed. He was paralyzed. Doctors told him he'd never stand again, let alone walk.

Those doctors didn't know Bill Hicks.

After countless months of physically and emotionally painful rehabilitation at a facility in Warm Springs, Georgia, he managed to stand unassisted. Then move about on crutches. Then a walking stick, his constant companion ever since. All these decades, Bill and that stick have enjoyed the hills, hollows and waterways of this state. Slow and ungainly, perhaps, but steady.

Until recently.

"I started getting this tingly feeling in my feet," he told me. "The next day it spread up my legs. By the time it got to my waist, I told my wife something was bad wrong and to get me to the emergency room. I'd had more operations on my neck several years ago, plus a bone graft, and I figured one of those screws had come loose."

Nope. Something worse. He had contracted Guillain-Barré syndrome, a rare disease in which the body's immune system attacks the nervous system.

He got medical help in the nick of time. "They told me another day or two, and it would have gotten into my chest and stopped my lungs."

After massive rounds of immunoglobulin treatment, his symptoms appear to be reversing. Ever-so-slowly, Hicks is getting some feeling back in his legs. His feet tingle to the point of driving him bonkers. Twice a day, he undergoes intense physical therapy, hoping once more to breathe life into unresponsive limbs.

"My daughter and her husband just bought 60 acres up near Bulls Gap," Hicks drawled, his blue eye sparkling, his crooked smile big as ever. "They tell me it's eat-up with deer and turkeys. I plan to find out soon as I can move around again."

There is absolutely no doubt in my mind that he will.

The 'other' Roger Tory Peterson

On July 30, 1945, America lost the most famous wildlife artist you never heard of.

Earl O. Henry was a Knoxville dentist. His office was in the Medical Arts Building. At the start of World War II, he was a member of the Naval Reserve. By 1942, he was on active duty, ultimately serving as dental officer on the USS Indianapolis.

On that ill-fated July day, shortly after the Indianapolis dropped off key components for the atomic bomb at Guam, it was torpedoed by a Japanese submarine. The ship went down in 12 minutes. Of 1,199 on board, only 317 survived.

This tragedy still holds the dubious honor of being the single greatest loss of life at sea in U.S. Navy history. Among the hundreds of casualties was Lt. Commander Henry, whose skills as a dentist were surpassed only by his ability to paint.

As a youngster in Knoxville, Henry's love of birds was sparked by drawings that came in packages of baking soda. He immersed himself in taxidermy and painting, both largely self-taught. He joined the Tennessee Ornithological Society, rising to president. He trekked all over the then-new Great Smoky Mountains National Park, viewing birds and memorizing more than 60 of their calls. Simply stated, here was a walking, whistling, brush-wielding genius who happened to fill teeth Monday through Friday.

One of his many outdoor friends, the late Bob Burch of the old Tennessee Game and Fish Commission, once relayed this high praise to me: "If Earl had survived the war, his name would have been as familiar to bird and art lovers all over the world as Roger Tory Peterson's."

His only child, Earl O. Henry Jr., a retired banker in Nashville, never laid eyes on his father. He was born six weeks before the Indianapolis was sunk.

But thanks to his father's reputation in dental and wildlife circles, the younger Henry may well "know" his dad better than the children of surviving veterans.

"I'm blessed to have learned so much about him," he told me via telephone.

During his short life, Henry created approximately 45 bird paintings, mostly as gifts to family and friends.

Yet his legacy lives on and is available to the general public through prints and note cards. His collection of more than 80 mounted birds has been donated to Ijams Nature Center. Every year, his professional life is recalled at the Earl Henry Memorial Dental Clinic.

Not bad work for a kid from Knoxville who died at sea, 33 years young.

These were the good ol' days

When demolition crews tore down G&R Automotive Company, they did more than make room for a new entryway into Fort Dickerson Park. They also drove the last nail into the coffin of an iconic South Knoxville business location.

Let's hop into the Way Back Machine. Before G&R. Indeed, we'll reverse all the way to 1947, when a former Marine Corps sergeant and Tennessee Highway Patrolman returned to civilian life. That's the year Charles B. "Red" Simpson bought a tiny service station on Chapman Highway, at the intersection of Woodlawn Pike.

Simpson's operation eventually expanded into a full-service automotive repair shop, complete with a custom upholstery and trim division. But first and foremost, it dispensed Shell gasoline. Its large, yellow, revolving "Shell" logo became the official welcome sign to SoKno.

"Daddy always told his employees the last thing they were supposed to do before closing at night was to make sure the Shell sign was lined up so drivers could see it from either direction," recalled his daughter, Betty Lou Simpson, retired after 32 years in elementary education. "That was important to him."

Verily, details mattered to Red Simpson, who died in 1977. He learned that in the Marines. Where else besides his station would employees be instructed to take down florescent lights periodically and dust behind the tubes?

Want more?

"We used to have a display case with cans of oil and other Shell products," recalled former employee Barry Mitchell, now assistant director of facilities services at the University of Tennessee. "The label was stamped on the metal. Those cans were cleaned so many times, the graphics would almost get wiped away."

As for service when a customer pulled to a stop at one of the pumps?

"It would terrify people these days," Mitchell said. "One person would be pumping gas. Another would be checking under the hood. Another would be filling your tires with air. Somebody else would be sweeping your floor mats."

"That was a job I got to do," recalled another daughter, Olivia Corum, retired after a career with First Tennessee Bank. "I thought it was great to clean the mats with a whisk broom."

If the term "family business" comes to mind, you're on the right track. Betty Lou Simpson remembers the time her brother Chuck (who became a Mercedes-Benz dealer in Atlanta before his untimely death in 2004), was pictured in a newspaper article at age 6.

"Chuck had his own tiny Shell uniform," she said. "In the picture, he's smiling. You can see that one of his front teeth is out."

And you thought Mayberry only existed in grainy B&W reruns on TV.

Sweeping out the trash

Ben Ream and his wife, Heather Burchfield Ream, have a different—some might say "dirty"—way of celebrating any occasion.

They pick up roadside trash.

Alas, there's never a shortage of raw materials. If the Reams had the time, they could fill a dump truck with garbage cast aside by the (bleeping) idiots determined to foul their—and our—nest.

Heather and Ben do more than simply bag garbage. They have formed a volunteer organization "committed to hearing the opinions and concerns of the residents of South Knoxville to make our community safer, cleaner and more prosperous."

Its name?

"SKODoubleB."

Which stands for South Knoxville Old Brooms Brigade.

The Reams and other volunteers take their mission to heart—or bent back, as the case may more accurately be. You name the trash, and they've picked it up.

"What is it with these knuckleheads who have lost all control of their actions and senses?" she exclaimed. "Why would they throw out a dirty diaper, a completely sealed TV dinner or an old pillow onto a public street? And yes, unfortunately, we have collected all of those things, and more."

What makes some people think of streets, ditches and sidewalks as open trash pits?

"Maybe it's a symptom of a larger problem," she answered. "Maybe it's lack of self-esteem.

"Or maybe it's simply because they're lazy jerks!"

Worth his salt

Wherever Jim Bordwine goes, he carries a few gallons of clear liquid—a solution that dates back centuries in Southern Appalachian history.

But it's not what you're thinking. Hillbilly jokes notwithstanding, you couldn't drink his stuff even if every pistol in town was cocked and pointed at your head.

Bordwine hauls brine, not 'shine. He's a salt maker from (where else?) Saltville, Virginia. Retired after a career in construction, Bordwine now travels the Southeast, conducting 20-30 demonstrations annually at folk festivals, schools and Civil War re-enactments. I happened to run into him one autumn morning at the Mountain Makin's craft show in Morristown.

"I've been making salt for over 10 years, and I'm still amazed," he told me as we sat around his fire outside the Rose Center. "It's not only the process, but also how much salt a gallon of brine will produce. It's so simple, so easy. You just heat the brine until it evaporates."

Bordwine nodded toward a nearby apple butter demonstration and grinned: "They gotta keep stirring to keep their product from scorching. All I gotta do is keep the fire hot and this kettle filled with brine."

Bordwine should have been born in the 19th century. With his gray whiskers and buckskin clothing, he looks very much the part of someone from that era. His interest in the history of our region dates to his childhood.

"I used to love to sit around with my grandfather and listen to him and his friends talk about the old days and old ways," he said. "I'd lots rather do that than play with kids my own age."

The old folks' conversation often turned to salt making because Saltville sits atop a huge reservoir of brine thousands of feet below the surface. Long before Europeans began probing these mountains, natives were drawn to the many natural saline seeps and the wild game they attracted.

"Salt is necessary for humans to exist," he explained. "It was a valuable commodity in pioneer days. One of its biggest uses was for food preservation. But it was also needed for medicine and leather tanning, then later for industrial applications. You can go to the store today and buy a box of salt for next to nothing. But way back when, it was a real money maker for communities like Saltville."

Brine is inordinately saltier than seawater, he said. Just one gallon will produce 2½ pounds of usable salt.

"They tell me at one time, there was something like 3,000 kettles, 100 gallons each, in the Saltville area. I've heard there's still enough brine under Saltville to supply the world for a thousand years."

So what kind of water comes out of the tap? Is it salty?

"Not in the least," Bordwine answered. "Our town also sits on artesian well. We've got the purest, best drinking water you ever tasted."

That's what you call the best of both worlds.

On January 17, 2014, I answered a telephone message that launched the most important project of my newspaper career.

Charles Moulden's deep voice was on the other end. "I understand you're looking for me," he said quietly.

Was I ever. The story of Moulden's ambush shooting in 1968 had haunted me for decades. I'd heard bits and pieces of it during my stints at three Tennessee daily newspapers. But with no names or archived background material, I never was able to tie any of the details together.

Charlie's call changed everything.

What resulted was a six-part series that ran for three consecutive days during Black History Month. I've included the entire series here, just as each installment appeared. The chapter concludes with two columns that were published in the wake of the series.

This project, titled "Fragments of Hate," resulted in the Sigma Delta Chi national feature-writing award by the Society of Professional Journalists and the Investigative Reporting Award by the Tennessee Press Association. It was nominated for a Pulitzer Prize—ultimately not a winner, but it was gratifying enough just to be invited to the dance.

All those accolades were nice. I was humbled by them and sincerely appreciated the gestures. But knowing Charlie Moulden's tragic saga of injustice finally got told was the greatest award I could ever hope to receive.

Chapter Thirteen
THE CHARLIE CHRONICLES

A shooting that history ignored

TELLICO PLAINS, Tennessee—Charles Moulden didn't hear the sound at first. That comes later, he explained; it takes a second or two for your subconscious to process what just happened.

For the moment, all he knew was (1) he was face-first in the gravel of a narrow road alongside Tellico River and (2) his left thigh was stinging intensely.

"It was like a mad hornet on steroids," Moulden related a few days ago as he strode the same roadway, now paved with asphalt.

"I thought I must have gotten into some bees. I pushed myself back up on my feet and looked down at my leg. I thought I'd find some kind of huge stinger poking out."

All Moulden saw was a hole in his pants. He squeezed the flesh beneath it. Instead of a stinger, out came a trickle of blood. Immediately, excruciating pain erupted in the back of his leg.

"That's when I looked up and saw him again," Moulden continues, gesturing toward a small rise in the bend of the road up ahead.

"He had stepped out from behind the bush. His arms were straight down by his side. Then he raised one arm, and I saw the pistol."

Moulden makes a circle with his fingertips.

"Man, the end of that thing looked like it was three inches wide. He aimed directly at me. I shut my eyes and grimaced."

This time, Moulden heard the gun's report. Forty-six years after the fact, he considers that a good omen: "If you hear the 'pow,' it means you didn't get hit. By the time the sound gets there, the bullet is long gone."

IT WAS WEDNESDAY, April 10, 1968, and the news was riveting.

One day earlier in Atlanta, 150,000 marchers followed a mule-drawn wagon carrying the casket of Martin Luther King Jr. to a service at Morehouse College, shortly after his funeral at Ebenezer Baptist Church.

TO RETIRE? OR NOT TO RETIRE?

In Memphis and throughout the U.S., teams of investigators were sorting through tips—some intentionally misleading, as it turned out—in their frantic search for the gunman who had assassinated the civil-rights leader six days earlier.

In Chattanooga, a curfew was in effect after looting broke out following an MLK memorial service.

In the highlands of East Tennessee, however, the mood was a bit more festive, despite gray skies and sporadic showers. It was the long-awaited opening day of trout season.

Moulden, a 24-year-old brick mason from Sevierville, was among the army of anglers who turned out.

A few of these sportsmen deployed fly rods and tiny, hand-tied insect imitations in hopes of catching rainbow, brown and brook trout. The vast majority, like Moulden, used spinning equipment and an array of "live bait"—everything from nightcrawlers to doughballs to the ever-popular yellow kernels of canned corn.

Yet there was one major difference between Moulden and the other fishermen. A difference that transcended equipment and tactics. A societal difference that mattered greatly in those not-so-good old days.

His skin was black.

"I'D BEEN FISHING all my life," says Moulden, now 70, an Oak Ridge resident and site superintendent for Summit Contractors in Knoxville. "Douglas Lake, Cherokee Lake, I was all over them. But I never had fished for trout."

He pauses to chuckle and shake his head. "When they told me you could catch trout on corn, I was like, 'Aw, c'mon!' But Bill, 'Arvilee' and Leroy insisted it worked. They invited me to come along with them that morning."

That would be Bill Williams, Arvil Lee Parton and his son Leroy.

Arvil ran a masonry and concrete-finishing business in Sevier County and often sought Moulden's skills. Williams and the Partons were white but saw nothing unusual about including a black friend on the trip. Particularly if that friend was Charles Moulden—born, raised and widely known by folks of all races throughout Sevier County.

By the standards of that era, of course, such mingling ceased at the schoolhouse door.

Moulden and his five siblings attended the all-black Pleasant View Elementary School in Sevierville. At the ninth grade, their only educational option—and that of most black students throughout the region—was to be driven into Knoxville to the all-black Vine Junior and Austin High schools.

That changed for Moulden in the fall of 1963, aided and abetted by the fact he was a gifted athlete.

In his senior year, he was in the first group of black students to enroll in Sevier County High School. As a quick, muscular Smoky Bears running back, he also was the first black athlete to play football in the old Knoxville Interscholastic League. Moulden was popular with classmates, graduating in 1964 along with a blond bouffant country music singer—another Parton, this one named Dolly.

"I never really thought anything about going fishing with white guys," he says.

"I already had a fishing license, but I went to Carl Owenby's hardware store in Sevierville to buy a trout stamp. On the way down to Tellico, we stopped somewhere to buy a daily permit. I remember it cost one dollar."

Moulden doesn't recall much else about his inaugural trip into the rugged Monroe County mountains. Not because of mental erosion during the intervening years. He simply never had a chance to see the landscape: "Me and one of the other boys rode in the bed of Arvilee's pickup truck. He had a camper shell on it. It didn't have any windows, except one in the very back. Arvilee had busted up a couple of bales of straw in there, so me and whoever else it was slept most of the way.

"It wasn't until 2010, when I rode with some friends to Tellico Plains on our motorcycles, that I even knew how to get there. I had to look it up on a map."

THE FOURSOME attracted some unwanted attention from the start.

"It was still early, and me and Charlie were walkin' down the road, goin' from one pool to another," says Leroy Parton, now 66, who still lives in Sevierville.

"This old white man walked up to us. I'll never forget the look on his face. He had a long, white beard that must have gone to his waist. He looked at us and said, 'You're gonna have to git outta these mountains!'

"He glanced over at me and said: 'Not you! Him!' He pointed to Charlie, and then he stomped off.

"I said, 'Charlie, what are you gonna do?' He shrugged, 'Why, I'm goin' fishin'.'"

Even today, the mood of that unsettling moment is fresh on Leroy Parton's mind: "I remember thinking, 'Wow, these people down here must even hate their own mothers!'"

It took Moulden a while to get the hang of drifting his bait through moving water instead of casting into the placid environs of a reservoir. Soon enough, though, everything clicked.

"I caught a couple of little 'cigar' trout and threw 'em back," he says. "Then I realized I'd do better if I fished in the slow, deep holes instead of the rapids. I caught four good trout real quick.

"I had just come up out of the river and was walking down the road to find another place to fish. That's when he drove up."

The car that approached was a black, early-1950s model Chevrolet, Moulden recalls. It may have had some green paint on the fender or hood. But he has vivid recall of what transpired between him and the driver.

"He came all the way across the road and brushed my leg with his fender. He revved the engine real loud. Then he started cussing me. It was 'nigger this' and 'nigger that'."

Moulden felt an immediate flush of rage. Instinctively, his fists began to clench. In another place, he might have punched the driver senseless through the car's open window. But he had the presence of mind to know he was in foreign territory.

"I could smell alcohol on him, but he wasn't what you'd call drunk. He knew exactly what he was saying and doing. Finally, he said, 'Didn't you see the sign?'

"I said, 'What sign is that, sir?'

"He said, 'The sign in town that says: 'Nigger, read and run. Don't let the sun set with you in this town'.'"

Moulden was all-too familiar with warnings of "the sign," real or fictive. He'd heard them all his life. Thus, he adopted a ploy that had often worked in similarly tense situations.

He played Stepin Fetchit dumb.

"I SAID: 'No, sir; I didn't see no sign. I was ridin' in the back of this here truck when we came through town. Besides, it wouldn't have done me no good to see it 'cause I can't read or write'."

"That figures!" spat the angry driver, who then issued an ominous warning before speeding away: "You get outta here! Next time I see you, you're a dead nigger!"

Moulden's friends quickly gathered. Leroy asked again, "What are you gonna do, Charlie?"

"I'm tellin' you, I'm goin' fishin'!" Moulden reiterated, now more determined than ever.

"I said, 'Leroy, if I paid attention every time a white man called me a nigger or threatened me, I'd be too scared to come out of my house.' Oh, I was sensitive to the N-word, all right. I didn't like it. I knew how to fight. But it's like my dad had always said to me: 'Son, you can't fight 'em all.'

"I told Leroy: 'All I can do is hope the Good Lord is riding with me today. That's the only protection I got. That's the only protection I need.' So I went on fishing."

After a few hours, the party moved several miles upriver to a spot just above the old Tellico Lodge. They found a promising stretch of water. Arvil pulled his truck to the side of the road. Everyone got out.

At virtually the same moment, the black Chevrolet flew by.

"One of the boys said, 'Charlie, there goes your buddy'," Moulden recalls. "He drove on around the bend, and I figured he hadn't seen me. I saw a nice eddy in the river and started walking up the road to reach it."

That's when one of his friends uttered four words Moulden will never forget:

"Charlie, there he is."

"I looked up and sure enough, there he stood. He was on a little bit of an incline, trying to hide behind a bush. I could see him plain as day from the waist up."

MORE THAN four decades later, Moulden's eyes bore holes through that same rise in the terrain. He is temporarily silent. The only sound comes from the rushing river nearby. Finally, he speaks.

"I remember thinking, 'Well, I wonder what's he gonna do?' Is he gonna come out here in the road and we go fist-to-fist?' That would've been fine with me. I was a boxer, and I knew he'd been drinking. I was sure I could take care of myself.

"Then I thought, 'Is he gonna throw a rock? Bring a stick?' The wheels in my mind were just spinning.

"I knew some people hated me for the color of my skin. Even though they didn't know me or know what I did or anything, they were just mad at me for my color. Still, it never crossed my mind that he'd shoot me. So I sorta lowered my head and kept walking."

ONE SECOND, Moulden was striding confidently. The next, his left leg blew backward just as his right leg was coming forward. His body crashed into the roadbed.

"Ain't it funny?" he says. "I remember crushing that can of corn as I fell. Corn spewed out all over the road. My fishing pole broke. My knuckles were bloody."

He struggled back to his feet and began looking for that imagined "mad hornet stinger." The assailant stepped into the road, re-aimed, launched a second (albeit errant) round, pointed the muzzle of his pistol skyward, fired twice more into the air and vanished into the woods. It was over in an eye-blink.

Moulden tried to walk, but his legs betrayed him. He fell again and began crawling toward the only cover available: a steep bank to his left.

"I didn't know if maybe he was coming back around to shoot me from above," Moulden recalls. "I just remember lying on my back and looking up through the trees, trying to find him."

At that very moment, the heads of two young boys popped up from the river. Moulden shouted for them to get down. They vanished, only to reappear and run by him seconds later.

"I don't think they had anything to do with the shooting," he says. "Maybe they were upriver somewhere, fishing with their dad. That's the last I ever saw of them.

"My buddies had taken cover. They were hollering: 'Charlie! Charlie! Did he just shoot you?'

"I said, 'Yeah!'"

Moulden gathers himself once again as the shocking event replays in his mind. He chooses his words deliberately, every syllable punctuated by the anger and pain he felt that day:

"I YELLED real loud back over my head, toward the woods: 'Yeah, that SON OF A BITCH just shot me!'"

He adds in retrospect: "I guess that wasn't the smartest thing to say, knowin' he was probably right above me. But honestly, I was hurtin' so bad by then I didn't care if he came back around and killed me."

The next few minutes are a blur.

Moulden's friends were afraid to come to his aid for fear the shooter was perched above. Waiting. Pistol cocked. Aiming. Who knew?

Summoning what was left of his strength, Moulden crawled back across the road and down to the parked truck. He opened the passenger door, pulled himself into the floorboard and pushed the clutch pedal with one hand. The truck rolled rearward a few feet.

"They kept telling me how to cut the steering wheel," he says. "I'd turn the wheel and push the clutch and move closer to them."

Eventually the distance closed enough for his friends to sprint from hiding.

"Arvilee climbed over me and got hold of my belt," Moulden says. "He pulled me inside. The others jumped into the bed. Arvilee cranked the engine and sped around the curve."

About that time "a government man" pulled up in his car. Moulden doesn't know if it was a game warden or a Forest Service worker. He does know the man wasn't armed.

"My buddies kept yelling, 'Give us your gun!' The guy kept saying, 'I ain't got one!' But at least he called an ambulance."

For all the good that would do.

As soon as the situation was explained and radioed to civilization, rescue workers said no way were they coming into the national forest to pick up a black man who'd been shot by a white man—especially one who might still be hidden, poised to attack again.

"They had to drive me down to Tellico Plains (a distance of 18 miles)," says Moulden. "Once they got me loaded into the ambulance, the rest of the boys took off for Sevierville.

"I WAS RIDING along in that ambulance, begging them to give me a shot for pain. Nobody would. I finally asked where we were going. The only hospitals I knew were Baptist and UT.

"The driver said, 'We're going to Blount Memorial.' I asked, 'Where's that?'

"'Maryville,' he said."

Moulden can't help but laugh at his memory of that moment, terrifying as it was.

"Maryville was 10," he says, referring to the numeral 10 on Blount County license plates back in the day.

"Ten was where the Klan was! I used to see '10' on cars whenever there was a cross-burning. I kept thinking: 'Oh, Lord! I'm out of the frying pan and into the oven!'"

Happily, no ill will came Moulden's way at Blount Memorial. "They treated me real nice," he says.

He remained hospitalized five days and was discharged on crutches. The bullet was still embedded in his thigh.

It still is.

"The doctors told me it had fragmented into at least six pieces," he says. "They said they'd have to do a lot more damage to the muscles in my leg than the bullet itself. Those pieces cut me. They hurt me for a long time. Sometimes they still do."

MOULDEN WAS married with one daughter. He couldn't work. His wife applied for welfare.

"I hated that," he says. "I'd never been on welfare.

"After I could finally get up and move around on crutches, I asked Arvilee for some work, any work. I said I'd even hose out the wheelbarrows, whatever I could do to make some money. He had just gotten the job to pour the foundation for a motel between Pigeon and Gatlinburg, so he hired me.

"I taped a board to my leg. That way, I could get down on one knee and stick that leg out. I was able to start finishing concrete again.

"The going wage back then was $16-$18 a day. At the end of the first week, Arvilee paid me $20 a day. I told him he didn't have to do that, but he said I was out-working everybody else on the crew."

In 1971, Moulden was hired at K-25 in Oak Ridge. He stayed at the government facility until it closed 14 years later. He worked a variety of masonry jobs after that, even had his own construction company for a while.

He retired at age 66, only to be subsequently hired by Summit. The crews he supervises have built more than 75 Dollar Tree stores all over the United States.

"The first thing I did after Arvilee paid me was to go downtown and get off welfare," he said. "Bullet or no bullet, I wasn't gonna be on no welfare."

Getting in the game

It wasn't big news—literally—on August 30, 1963, when Charles Moulden introduced East Tennessee to racially mixed high school football.

The event was groundbreaking in social context, but earned minuscule mention in the media.

His contribution appeared the next day, on Page 6, in the second-to-last paragraph of News Sentinel sports writer Ted Riggs' story detailing Sevier County's stunning 13-0 upset over traditional Knoxville powerhouse Young High.

"Charles Mouldin (sic), reserve Sevier halfback, became the first Negro to play against a KIL (Knoxville Interscholastic League) team when he entered the game shortly before halftime," Riggs wrote. "His lone carry resulted in a four-yard loss."

"MOULDEN" OFTEN appeared as "Mouldin" in sports stories of that era.

"People were always trying to spell my name wrong," laughs Moulden, 70, who lives in Oak Ridge and travels throughout the U.S. as a construction superintendent. "With my brother Hubert (two years younger), they always got it right, with an 'e'."

Misspelled or otherwise, the name quickly became familiar with coaches and players—especially those on the opposite side of the line of scrimmage. Within weeks, it was rising higher on the page. All the way to headlines and opening paragraphs.

"Mouldin Sprints for Bears" read a News Sentinel keyline on Saturday, September 28, 1963, Page 8. Beneath it flowed the main headline: "Sevierville Deals Carter 1st Defeat."

"Sevierville's Charles Mouldin, first Negro to play football in the KIL, finally got a chance to show his speed at Carter," proclaimed the lead.

"The result: an 87-yard touchdown run that led to a 26-7 triumph over the host Hornets."

"It was the first touchdown I ever scored that actually counted," recalls Moulden. "Anytime I crossed the goal line, it always seemed a penalty flag had been thrown somewhere up the field. That's how it was back then.

"When I got into the end zone at Carter, the first thing I did was give the ball to the official. He placed it down for the extra point. I looked back up the field. No flags.

"Next thing I knew, my teammates were swarming me."

No doubt about it. In the end zone or on the sideline, Charles Moulden had landed in the right place at the right time.

Racial barriers were falling in East Tennessee schools, and he was able to take advantage of this sweeping change.

Just barely.

AS A YOUNG teenager, Moulden and other Sevier County blacks had been driven daily into Knoxville for junior high and high school classes. He finished at Vine Junior, then progressed to Austin High.

"All I'd ever played was sandlot football," he says. "I tried to play at Austin. I even got into a couple of games at Evans-Collins Field. But it was too much of a hassle.

"By the time practice was over and I'd get a ride back to Sevierville, it might be midnight; then I had to be up at 6 the next morning to catch a ride to Knoxville."

Two other factors also weighed heavily. One was beyond his control, the other his own fault.

"I never really felt welcome at Austin," he says. "Being from Sevierville, I was always an outsider, a hick. The other students called me 'Country'."

That, however, was the lesser of his woes.

Early in his senior year at Austin, Moulden was arrested for shoplifting.

"I was at Watson's (a Knoxville discount store) and stuck a $2 shirt under my shirt and tried to walk out. They caught me. I had a pretty bad reputation for fighting back then. The Austin principal even said so to the judge in court.

"I'll never forget what the judge told me: 'Young man, since you like to fight so much, we'll just put you in a place where there's lots of fighting.' I got 60 days in the Knox County workhouse."

IT'S STILL embarrassing for Moulden to discuss the incident.

"That's something I'm not proud of to this day," he admits. "It really tore my mama and daddy up. But Daddy never complained (about the harsh sentence). He said, 'Son, you did it; now you gotta do your time'."

Released after two months, Moulden was through with regimentation. He dropped out of school and began working full time as a brick mason with his uncle.

"I'd been layin' brick on the weekends and summers since I was 14," he says. "That's what I figured I'd do the rest of my life."

MOULDEN WAS busy with mortar and stone one morning in early August 1963 when two cousins showed up at the job site.

"They said they were gonna try out for football at Sevier County," he remembers.

"I was like, 'What?!?!'

"They said, 'Yeah, they gonna let us play at their school this year'."

Moulden didn't realize it at the time, but his cousins were pulling his leg—at least about trying to make the team themselves. For them, this was nothing but a practical joke.

Unbeknown to everyone, however, was the fact that yes, indeed; all candidates were welcome.

Says Moulden: "I kept talkin' about it and talkin' about it. Finally my uncle had heard enough. He wasn't happy. He threw half a brick over at me. It landed at my feet. He said, 'Boy, all you wanna do is play football! Git on outta here!'

"I ran all the way home and took a shower, then ran to the (high school) field house," says Moulden. "When I opened the door, everything got real quiet."

He chuckles.

"You know the ol' saying 'quiet as a mouse peein' in a bale of cotton'? Yeah, that quiet."

Assistant coach Pete Stafford approached and asked Moulden his intentions. Stafford listened, then told the youngster nobody could play football unless they were enrolled in school.

"That," Moulden exclaims with a broad smile, "is when I lied through my teeth!

"I told him my paperwork was on its way over from Austin. Wasn't true, of course. But I knew I could get it done and that it'd be six or eight weeks before everything got switched from Austin to Sevier County. By then, I'd be in school."

Done. And done.

IT WASN'T necessarily love at first sight for the white players. Yet as soon as pads and helmets went on, skin color ceased to matter.

It became readily apparent that Moulden had the size, speed, agility and passion for the game. All he lacked was a grasp of the fundamentals.

"I didn't even know which holes were odd and which were even," he says. "But they taught me real quick."

Before long, the team bonded closely. In late August, Sevier County traveled to Kingston for a scrimmage. Soon as the Roane Countians discovered the other team had a black player, they balked.

"We held a team meeting, and coach (Tom) Bass explained everything. He said, 'It's up to you, Charlie.'

"I told 'em: 'You boys go on out there. I'll stay here in the field house'."

Several team leaders—Moulden cites Tom Williams and Tony Atchley among them—then spoke up. No way, coach. We either play as a team or we don't play at all.

Moulden can hardly contain his pride about that defining moment: "We got on the bus and came back to Sevierville."

The same Tom Williams and Tony Atchley were two Sevier County Smoky Bears mentioned as strong leaders and powerful players in Ted Riggs' "Prep Chatter" column in the News Sentinel on Sunday, October 13, 1963, Page C-6.

In the same piece, Riggs quoted coach Bass about another excellent athlete on his team. Here's an excerpt from that column: "'Charles has done a fine job for us,' Bass remarked.' If I had him another year, the boy would be a real standout. This, you know, is his first season of football. He went out twice at Austin and had to drop off the squad each time because of transportation difficulties'."

Moulden participated in his last high school game on Thanksgiving Day, a 35-0 victory over Knoxville Rule in the Little Smoky Bowl. He graduated the following spring and went back to laying brick.

But perhaps there would be one more opportunity to show his skills on the field.

By the late 1960s, semipro football had come to East Tennessee in the form of the Knoxville Bears. Moulden landed a tryout for Saturday, April 13, 1968.

On Wednesday of that week, though, he had one other engagement: The opening of trout season in the Cherokee National Forest. By the end of that day, he would be lying in a hospital bed, a .38 caliber bullet buried in his left thigh.

Football was over forever.

AS THE YEARS went by, Moulden's interest in other sports expanded widely.

A shade-tree mechanic since childhood, he soon became enamored with speed. He built a Camaro dragster and competed in International Hot Rod Association races all over the United States, both as a driver and crew member.

He took up karate. He played amateur softball. He boxed in a Fraternal Order of Police program. And he continued to fish.

"After I moved from Sevierville to Oak Ridge, I bought a bass boat and really started hitting Watts Bar," Moulden says. "It became my favorite lake."

What about trout?

"No," he replies. "I've never been trout fishing again since that first day."

Escaping Justice

MADISONVILLE, Tennessee—If there were any doubts in Charles Moulden's mind about prejudicial feelings, they were settled the morning of September 4, 1968, as he limped into the Monroe County Courthouse on crutches.

"When I came in, there was this white lady standing in the hall," Moulden recalls. "I smiled and said howdy to her, how are you doing?

"She said: 'I'd be doin' a lot better if you wasn't here. We don't want no niggers down here. He shoulda killed you.'

"I told her, 'Well, he didn't.' I wasn't smiling by then."

Out on the courthouse lawn, rib-poking good ol' boy commentary was even more blunt, more biting. Moulden still has a vivid memory of those humiliating statements:

"Some of 'em were saying stuff like, 'You know Fred didn't shoot at that nigger. Fred's a better shot than that. If he'd shot at that nigger, he would've killed him.' Then they'd laugh."

Little wonder, then, why the jury reached a quick verdict.

Testimony in the case lasted a little more than half the day. In just under a half-hour—3:25 p.m. until 3:50 p.m.—the all-male, all-white panel came to a unanimous decision:

"Not guilty, your honor."

Forty-five-year-old Fred William Ellis—a previously convicted killer already infamous in the East Tennessee backcountry for frequent brushes with the law—was free to go.

Accordingly, Judge James C. Witt dismissed all charges and sent a smug and smiling Ellis on his way.

"Ellis was always acting nonchalant (on the stand)," said Moulden. "My attention was on him all the time. Whenever he looked at me, I could see the anger in his eyes.

"I will tell you this: I tried to make as much eye contact as possible, just to make him mad. I thought, 'Surely they won't let him shoot me here'."

By one measure, Moulden says today, he was surprised by the decision.

By another, it was nauseatingly predictable.

CASE NUMBER 3030 appeared airtight. The state had four eyewitnesses on its side.

There was 24-year-old Moulden, the victim who was black, along with his three white fishing buddies: Bill Williams, Arvil Lee Parton and Leroy Parton, all from Sevierville.

On April 10, Williams and the Partons had watched and listened as Ellis, a lifelong resident of the nearby Coker Creek community, cursed and angrily threatened their friend on opening day of trout season in the Cherokee National Forest. Later that same day, they had seen Ellis' car roar past their fishing party and then Ellis appear seconds later in a bend of the road ahead.

Agreed, only Moulden—cut down as the first shot was fired—had actually watched the assailant re-aim his pistol and squeeze off a second round. By then, the three others had ducked for cover.

Still, it was pretty strong evidence, especially considering that an intoxicated Ellis had been arrested at Tellico Lodge shortly after the assault occurred. He was charged with attempted murder and jailed under a $5,000 bond.

Officers believed Ellis sprinted up the ridge from the site of the shooting, hid his gun, dropped into a low gap and emerged where Bill White's rustic hunting and fishing resort was located.

It's a quite plausible theory. Anyone familiar with these hills and hollows could eclipse the distance in a matter of minutes.

"RIGHT BEFORE the trial started, the sheriff had us walk through the courtroom, one at a time, and look around," said Moulden. "Then he had us walk out through another door and describe what the shooter looked like.

"All four of us identified Fred Ellis. I thought this was going to be a slam-dunk."

It was a slam-dunk all right. Just 180 degrees in the other direction. Which underscores why Moulden wasn't surprised by the outcome.

"The whole thing was a farce, a dog and pony show," he said.

Leroy Parton, 66, who still lives in Sevierville, remains as bitter in 2014 as he was in 1968 when the not-guilty verdict was announced.

"They should've hung that son of a bitch," he said. "Instead, they let him go free."

Veteran criminal court reporter Jack Harrill recorded the spellbinding testimony on Edison Voicewriter vinyl discs, cutting-edge technology in its era but audio antiques today.

"That jury wasn't going to convict Fred Ellis of anything," he said grimly.

Moulden concurs: "It was either because I was black or all of us were outsiders from Sevier County. Or maybe everybody was afraid to testify against him. It didn't matter."

Just how poisonous was this atmosphere?

The Sevier Countians received so many threats, veiled and direct, they had to be driven to the courthouse by deputy escort.

THE DEFENSE, led by Knoxville attorney Calvin N. Taylor, planted seeds of doubt in the jury's mind at every turn. Such as:

How could Moulden and the Partons distinguish Ellis' black 1952 Chevrolet from other possible black 1952 Chevrolets on the road that day?

How could they identify Ellis from 50-75 yards away and yet not be able to describe the kind of gun he used?

Had it not been foggy?

Was there not enough emergent vegetation to obscure the shooter?

Who knows if "this colored boy" was even telling the truth about being shot? Why was there no doctor to testify about the extent of his injuries?

Ellis himself took the stand and repeatedly denied any involvement.

He swore he didn't own a pistol. He insisted he had only pulled his car off the road to consume "a half-pint of bonded whiskey some feller give me up on North River." He said he ran into the woods in fear for his own life when he heard shots being fired down the road.

Attorney General Tom J. Taylor of Cleveland re-examined often, allowing the victim and his friends to reiterate their eyewitness versions.

It was during his closing argument to the jury, though, that the prosecutor cut to the chase.

"You gentlemen are not stupid," his voice can be heard on the scratchy recordings, recently found in the Monroe County Courthouse's archives.

"You know what happened. You know what this case is really about.

"I don't know how you feel about mixing colored and white," Taylor continued, his voice rising with emotion. "But if you are so prejudiced (as to turn Ellis free), you might just as well put a badge on him and let him go back to terrorizing whoever he wants!"

"What if it had been your own (son) who'd been shot?" he pleaded with the panel. "How would you feel then?"

The attorney general's final sentence to the jury, delivered in the politically correct jargon of the day, reverberated through the courtroom like a fire-and-brimstone sermon: "You might let (Ellis) go free because he 'just shot a Negra,' but I tell you, it might not be a Negra next time!"

It wasn't.

ALTHOUGH ORIGINALLY accused of attempted murder, Ellis was ultimately tried for felonious assault. On May 6, 1968, the Monroe County grand jury had returned a true bill on that charge.

His first trial was held May 24. The outcome was a hung jury.

On September 4, as soon as the second jury announced its not-guilty verdict, Moulden saw no further use trying to beat the system.

"The attorney general told me it was my duty to come back and we'd fight this thing in federal court," Moulden remembered. "I said, 'No, sir. I've had enough. I wasn't comin' back no more. The only way I'd do that was if they gave Fred Ellis a fishing pole and me a pistol.

"I told him, 'These people want this man down here more than they want me down here. A person with no more intelligence than that, he'll probably never leave this area.

"Besides, my friends had a concrete-finishing business in Sevierville. They were losing money every time we came to Madisonville. I couldn't ask them to keep doing that."

Moulden's final message to the prosecutor proved hauntingly prophetic: "Now you've got to contend with him. Who's he gonna shoot next? He's already showed he doesn't mind pulling the trigger on another human being."

ELLIS BELONGED to a hillbilly family with a reputation for "law-bending"—mostly hunting and fishing violations, as well as making and drinking moonshine.

"I never personally arrested Fred," said former Monroe County Sheriff Frank White, 82, who still works as a courthouse officer when his health permits. "But it seems like my deputies were picking him up all the time, mostly for drinking. I remember he could really aggravate you."

By all accounts, the clan's patriarch, Ben Ellis, was a soft-spoken mountain man who supplemented his meager farm income as a bear-and-boar hunting guide—"in season or out," the late News Sentinel staff writer Willard Yarbrough once quipped in print.

As Ben's sons came of age, however, they turned to violence.

Two of them, Ed and Benton, died in separate outbreaks of gunfire. A third, Roy, was wounded in another shootout. Roy died at age 75 in 2008, although it is not clear whether those injuries contributed to his death.

TO RETIRE? OR NOT TO RETIRE?

By far, Ed Ellis' death attracted the greatest media attention. He was a major player in a 20th-century, East Tennessee version of the Hatfields and McCoys.

TROUBLE BEGAN brewing when another Coker Creek native, Korean War veteran Myles Witt, returned to Monroe County and started a construction business. Witt hoped to develop some of the region into vacation homes and retreats. He attracted outside investors, formed the Unicoi Mountain Corporation and set up operations.

Anger, jealousy, confrontation and retribution—"mountain justice" in local parlance—quickly followed.

The common denominator was a clear liquid dispensed in Mason jars.

The licensed making of corn liquor became legal in Tennessee in 2009; it has blossomed into a lucrative tourist attraction. But for two centuries prior, this art was practiced on the sly throughout these rough, misty highlands.

In the 1960s and '70s, the notion that flatlanders might start prowling around where stills were located—let alone take up residence—was a recipe for disaster. Here's what Yarbrough wrote about the situation in an analysis from September 8, 1974:

"The Ellis and Witt clans have been involved in court actions for the past 2½ years, both civil and criminal—ranging from allegations of cabin burnings and shooting into buildings owned by the Witt interests, damage suits and earlier bloodshed.

"The saga is complex," Yarbrough noted, "but it involves moonshining and little law enforcement, which at times is non-existent."

The conflict smoldered back and forth before exploding savagely. On August 17, 1974, Ed Ellis was killed in a rural road shootout with Myles Witt and two of his associates.

Witt and his men were charged with murder. Three trials resulted in hung juries. Prosecutors pushed for a fourth. But in November 1978, the Tennessee Supreme Court ordered all charges dismissed because "the probability of any future jury reaching a verdict of guilt or innocence is almost non-existent."

THE DEATH of Benton ("Babe") Ellis was even more grisly and mysterious.

On April 13, 1988, his body was found in the woods about one mile from his house. He had been struck at close range by a shotgun blast to the back of his head.

Months passed with no arrest, prompting investigators to attempt loosening lips another way. On August 5, 1988, the News Sentinel reported that a $2,500 state reward had been posted for information about the killing.

Still nothing. Money may be an effective lubricant for solving crime in some settings. Not here.

It wasn't until 1997 that a suspect was brought into custody. He was a Kentuckian, Roy E. Browder. He also was Babe Ellis' nephew.

Browder's trial was postponed several times. Finally, on April 19, 1999, he pleaded guilty to voluntary manslaughter and was sentenced to three years in prison. He was paroled on Christmas Eve of that year and returned to Kentucky on probation.

IN THE mid-1960s, long before the Moulden case, Fred Ellis had served 17 months in North Carolina for voluntary manslaughter. A decade later, he continued to be implicated as the Monroe County feuding, arson and gun battles raged.

In 1977, he received a two-to-five-year prison sentence on attempted murder charges—this time involving a shootout with Myles Witt and his wife, Dixie—but was granted probation after serving 60 days. During that same era, he racked up a litany of other arrests, everything from public drunkenness to attempted jailbreak.

Many longtime employees of the Tennessee Wildlife Resources Agency also recall a brief—albeit terrifying—standoff near Waucheesi Lookout between the Ellises and the late game warden John French.

"The way I heard the story," says retired wildlife biologist Dick Conley, "the boys had been drinking when John stopped them. One of 'em got out of the truck and started to point a shotgun at him. John grabbed his own pistol and stuck it in one of Ellis boy's ears and hollered, 'If you mother——s shoot me, I'll shoot him!' Everybody backed off pretty quick, but it rattled John to the day he died."

Ironically, on September 4, 1969—one year to the day after Fred Ellis was declared not guilty in the shooting of trout fisherman Charles Moulden—he was found guilty of possessing moonshine and fined $10 and court costs, a total of $69.85.

Despite his lengthy association with violence, Fred Ellis did not die at the end of a gun. He passed away October 3, 1986, at Athens Community Hospital.

Some say due to heart attack, others cancer. The Tennessee Department of Public Health would not release the cause listed on his death certificate. At any rate, he appears to have been a very old man at the relatively young age of 62.

MOULDEN HAS paradoxical feelings about the person he believes wounded him that spring day nearly half a century ago.

"Don't get me wrong. It took me well over a year to get rid of my worst anger," he says.

"I was one mad man. I kept saying to myself and my friends, 'That's fine if he stays down there in Monroe County. But if I ever catch him in Sevier County, I'll plant him'."

The years have softened his attitude and refocused his perspective.

"Fred was a product of his environment, his culture and the times," said Moulden. "That's just the way it was. I'm sure he was saying (in court) what his lawyer told him to say.

"Of course, he was a coward who hid behind a gun. I would have been happy to fist-fight him, man to man. But I do have a strange kind of respect for him. He told me to my face how he felt about me and what he was going to do to me. I was just young enough and dumb enough to believe it never would actually happen."

At this point, Moulden can't help but inject some gallows humor: "You know, Fred was a pretty good shot, wasn't he! When I went down, he probably thought he'd killed me. It was 50-75 yards between us. Maybe he had aimed for my chest and the bullet dropped and hit me in the leg. I'm just glad he missed the second shot."

RACIAL PREJUDICE still exists today, Moulden acknowledges. Instead of being expressed openly, though, bitter feelings often are veiled.

"What's worse?" he asked, "for somebody to come right out and say they hate you for the color of your skin? Or to smile at you and be polite and then say bad things as soon as you turn your back?"

If given the chance, what would Moulden say in 2014, not only to his attacker but the jurors who set him free?

He thought for a moment. Sighed deeply. His gray-bearded face finally settled on a resolute countenance: "If they were willing to shake my hand and say they were sorry, I'd shake theirs. If the Good Lord can forgive them, surely I can, too."

What's his opinion of the current social and political climate sweeping America, a stance that advocates carrying concealed weapons and stand-your-ground resistance?

"I certainly understand it," he answered, "and I suppose if anybody oughta be carrying a gun, it's me. But I don't.

"Think about it: Nobody announces he's going to shoot you.

"They didn't at that movie theater in Colorado or at that school in Connecticut. They just started shooting, the same way I got ambushed. By that time, it's too late to reach for your gun."

Then Moulden was asked what he would have done if he had had a gun that day.

"Hmmph," he responded, a grim smile on his lips. "You know the answer as well as I do.

"In 1968, it wouldn't have mattered if Fred Ellis had put six holes in me and I only returned one shot in his general direction. A black guy shootin' at a white man back then?"

He shakes his head wistfully.

"They would've strung me up to the nearest tree."

Making progress

MADISONVILLE, Tennessee—A stroll around the Monroe County Courthouse speaks volumes about the past.

At all four corners of the lawn, as well as on street-side utility poles, there are memorials to soldiers from this area who died in service to their country.

The street banners, complete with color photos and pertinent personal information, honor men who have fallen in Iraq and Afghanistan.

Those who perished in the Korean and Vietnam wars are listed alphabetically, including the date of their death.

Something stark, however, stands out on the memorials from World Wars I and II.

The warriors commemorated here are separated. On each granite face, there's a long, main list. Then a smaller one beneath.

Under "colored."

Such an observation should not be construed as New Age, politically correct judgment of Monroe County. Nor of small towns throughout America, particularly in the South, that continue to divide the memory of military service in this manner.

This practice is understandable. It is accurate. It is historical fact.

U.S. armed forces were segregated during those wars. So were many of the societies whence these brave men lived, worked, raised families, were drafted or volunteered their last measure.

They grew up separately, served separately, died separately, are memorialized separately.

Some communities have erased these old lines by posting new plaques that combine the victims into a single group. Some communities have not chosen to do so. To each its own.

Nonetheless, it does strike the casual visitor ironic that at this very courthouse, race—not damning testimony—determined the outcome of a long-whispered-about criminal trial.

On September 4, 1968, jurors decreed a local white man not guilty of felonious assault in a heinous, cowardly attack. In so doing, they disregarded the testimony of law enforcement officers and four eyewitnesses.

Eyewitnesses who were "not from around here." Including the victim, who happened to be "negro," in the language of the day.

Life is neither fair nor perfect. It won't ever be. Here or anywhere else.

But, locals say, if nothing else positive came out of the trial of Fred Ellis, accused in the shooting of Charles Moulden, it did spark a social awakening.

"Nobody is proud of that trial," says 89-year-old Charles Hall, revered businessman and historian who served 16 terms as mayor of Tellico Plains until stepping down from office in 1990. "Attitudes have changed immensely since then. Tellico Plains has made a lot of progress. So have communities all around here."

Hall recalled a high school basketball game, not long after the trial, pitting Tellico Plains against a Knoxville team with a lone black player.

"I met with our boys before the game and said, 'There aren't going to be any problems, are there?' They assured me no. And there weren't. They just played basketball."

Marty Cook, longtime Monroe County Circuit Court clerk, was in high school when Jim Crow-era restrictions fell by the way.

"I don't remember it being a big deal for any of us students," she said. "If there were any concerns, it was among a few adults. Everybody else got along. They still do."

"Yes, I remember those times," says Monroe County sheriff Bill Bivens, "but I can assure you it's not like that now. It's changed a lot."

A black deputy, Chris Francis, serves on Bivens' staff.

"Chris is as fine an officer as you'll find," said the sheriff. "He came here from the Sweetwater Police Department. He has great respect in this community.

"I've also had a couple of black female deputies. One retired, and one moved on to another job."

"I came to Tellico Plains in 1968," said Pennsylvania native Dick Conley, a retired biologist for the Tennessee Wildlife Resources Agency who now lives in Madisonville.

It didn't take Conley long to realize he had moved into a hotbed of bigotry: "Honest to gosh, I thought I'd stepped back in time. But it's not that way now," he emphasized. "Things certainly have changed for the better."

To illustrate, Conley cited Leon Tillman, who serves Blount and Monroe counties as a representative for the USDA's National Resource Conservation Service.

Tillman, who is black, frequently calls on farmers and timberland owners deep in the wilderness. This is the same remote territory where his skin color would have invited inevitable trouble in years gone by.

"One time I asked Leon if he wanted me to ride with him on some of those calls," Conley says with a laugh. "He shrugged it off. He didn't need any help. It was sort of like, 'Why?' He'd never had a problem."

Fifty-six-year old Monroe County Mayor Tim Yates recalled "a few" racially charged incidents from his teenage years.

"It's sad things used to be like that," he said. "It's sad the way the Indians were treated long before that, too. But that's in our past. It's history. I hope that's where it stays."

All of which brings the casual visitor back to those courthouse monuments. Specifically, the one memorializing veterans of the Civil War.

No individual names are listed here. Just the battalions, regiments and companies to which they belonged.

It is not lost on the observer that a single stone now blends these combatants from opposite sides of a bitter, four-year campaign dividing the nation.

They are divided no more.

One sculpted side of the monument reads: "Monroe County Confederate." A few inches away, the script says: "Monroe County Federal."

This stone was erected in 2004, a full 139 years after hostilities ceased. Who knows?

Perhaps after sufficient time, all of the Monroe County soldiers who lost their lives in World Wars I and II finally will be memorialized as one.

Burying the lead

As has been the case since humans began communicating with written words, "news" is defined by the era in which it occurs.

This is true with rare exception.

Just because an event commands blockbuster attention today doesn't mean the same occurred before. And vice versa. Consider coverage of Super Bowls "I" and "XLVIII"—and then try to imagine what might, or might not, be generated by the time S.B. "C" rolls around.

Be that as it may, the racially motivated shooting of an unarmed fisherman in 1968 in the Cherokee National Forest attracted so little media attention as to boggle the mind.

Only one newspaper in East Tennessee is known to have reported the incident when it happened. Perhaps others did; if so, the Tennessee State Library and Archives in Nashville could find no record.

On Thursday, April 11, 1968, the Knoxville News Sentinel carried a five-paragraph account. It was buried on Page 23—above an ad for Ronco spaghetti and sandwiched between a local story about funding for an industrial park in the Karns community and a UPI dispatch describing a plane crash in Mexico.

The one-column headline read, "Sevier Man Is Shot in Tellico Area."

The requisite who-what-where-when were duly reported—some accurately, others not so much.

The victim's name, age, address and (important back in the day) race were correctly listed in the News Sentinel's article: Charles Moulden, 24, Rt. 3, Sevierville—"a Negro who had gone fishing in Tellico River with a friend."

Beyond that, the short article is rife with errors, likely due to the fact that it was based on second- and third-hand information phoned into the newspaper's state desk.

It quotes then-Monroe County Sheriff Kenneth Davis identifying the crime scene as "the middle of Ball Play Road." That's off by approximately 20 miles.

This is understandable because Ball Play Road is near the spot where an ambulance picked up Moulden before delivering him to Blount Memorial Hospital. Moulden's fishing buddies had been forced to drive their wounded partner from deep inside the national forest into downtown Tellico Plains because rescue workers were afraid of being attacked by the shooter.

What's more, the sheriff was quoted as saying the victim was struck in the right leg. Just the opposite is true.

The story does accurately report: "Fred Ellis, 45, of Coker Creek community was charged with attempted murder and today was still sitting in Monroe County jail in Madisonville in lieu of $5,000 bond."

Arrested near the scene when he emerged from the woods behind Tellico Lodge, Ellis denied any knowledge of the attack.

This was a contention to which he clung in Criminal Court months later, despite four eyewitnesses who testified otherwise. Ellis' insistence ultimately freed him of felonious assault charges.

There were three telling sentences toward the end of the story, however:

"Bill Williams, Rt. 3, Sevierville, who was with Moulden at the time, said no words were passed before Moulden was shot. 'First thing I knew, I heard a shot and saw Charles fall down,' said Williams."

Also: "Sheriff Davis today said Ellis 'had been drinking'."

Given this much advance notice, not to mention the explosive nature of the story, surely the News Sentinel closely followed the two trials of Ellis— first on May 24 (hung jury), then September 4 (not-guilty verdict).

Right?

Wrong.

Not a single word appeared in any edition.

In fact, the only press coverage given to the acquittal was a two-sentence, two-paragraph brief.

It showed up September 11, 1968, on Page 1 of the Monroe County Democrat (motto: "What The People Don't Know Will Hurt Them") and was dwarfed by an up-page story and photograph highlighting the selection of a Madisonville girl as "Fairest of the Fair."

Here's the article in its entirety: "William Fred Ellis of Tellico Plains, charged with felonious assault in connection with the shooting of a negro (sic) in the Cherokee National Forest several months ago, was found not guilty by a Criminal Court jury here Wednesday.

"A previous trial for Ellis ended in a hung jury."

Once again, mistakes. Plus a major journalistic omission.

The Democrat (now called the Advocate and Democrat) had Ellis' first name and middle name reversed, perhaps because they were reversed on the official court record. Yet, incredibly, the paper didn't include any mention of the victim.

Perhaps it's just as well.

As Moulden—formerly a standout football player at Sevier County High School—used to laugh about how his name frequently appeared "Mouldin" in sports stories:

"People were always trying to spell my name wrong."

Getting it right

I didn't know Charles Orlando Moulden by name until early January 2014. But I'd known of him—and the many injustices he suffered—for a mighty long time.

Hard to pinpoint when Moulden first came to my attention.

When the crime perpetrated against him occurred in April 1968, I was a junior at the University of Tennessee and a fledgling reporter for the old Knoxville Journal.

By the time his case concluded in the mockery of a trial that September, I was a senior and covering my first major, ahem, newspaper assignment: the Tennessee Valley Fair. This historical nugget revealed itself by coincidence as I searched microfilm, fruitlessly as it turned out, for any Journal interest in the Moulden affair.

Perhaps someone in the Journal newsroom had mentioned it to me. Perhaps I heard it a year later during my brief stint at the old Chattanooga News-Free Press. Perhaps it was at the start of trout season 1970, the first one I covered (this was front page sports news back in the day) in my new job as News Sentinel outdoors editor. Perhaps it was on one of my frequent hunting-fishing ventures into the Tellico woodlands.

I simply can't recall.

I do, however, remember a casual gathering of personnel from the U.S. Forest Service and Tennessee Wildlife Resources Agency (1975-ish, I'm guessing) at a Tennessee Conservation League convention. That's where I met Bob Lusk.

Lusk recently had come to the Cherokee National Forest as supervisor. During the meeting, somebody brought up the story of how a fisherman got shot by one of the local yokels simply because of skin color—and how easily the assailant beat the charges.

Lusk was furious. Not to mention incredulous.

Yes, he said, he understood it occurred long ago. Yes, the case was closed. Yes, everybody knew it was a gross miscarriage of justice. No, there wasn't anything more do to about it.

Yet in my mind I can still see Bob Lusk, slowly shaking his crew-cut head and wondering aloud how a racially driven crime like this could occur on federal property and civil rights charges not be filed.

Nobody had an answer. Other than, "Hey, that's the way things used to be around here."

AS YEARS became decades, I thought about the case from time to time. Even picked around at it now and then. Nothing dogged, I'm ashamed to say in retrospect. But in self-defense, there wasn't a lot to go on.

"Everybody" in the Tellico Plains-Madisonville area remembered "something." Just no details.

"Fred Ellis got away with trying to kill a black guy" is as definitive a statement as I ever got.

"When?" I would ask.

"I dunno; sometime in the '60s, I think," was the standard reply.

TO RETIRE? OR NOT TO RETIRE?

Once, I even placed a few phone calls to some Coker Creek references that had turned up. Yes, I was told; they remembered. But when I pressed for particulars, amnesia inevitably—and not surprisingly—returned.

News Sentinel clippings were of no use. The only information we had on file involved the Ellis-Witt family feuds that frequently erupted in bloodshed more than 30 years ago. Same with records in the McClung Historical Collection of the East Tennessee History Center.

On more than one occasion, I even resorted to needle-in-a-haystack scrolls through newspaper microfilm. But with no hint of a specific date, they always dead-ended.

EVERYTHING changed not long after Christmas when I thought about resurrecting the old story for an upcoming Martin Luther King Day column. I was certain everyone involved in the case was dead. Still, I drove to the Monroe County Courthouse in hopes of finding something. Anything.

Circuit Court clerk Marty Cook was very helpful. Also apologetic for the condition of materials she placed in my hands.

Cook had managed to excavate these ancient, musty documents, but they were water-damaged and bug-eaten from years in storage. It's a miracle they existed at all. Separating some of the pages was like peeling dead skin after a sunburn.

Nonetheless, I found important elements that previously had eluded me: the victim's name, plus dates of the attack and subsequent court appearances.

Bingo.

That information in hand, I was able to use microfilm and finally locate the News Sentinel's lone account of the incident. Staffers at the Monroe County Advocate and Democrat then were able to track down their newspaper's single, short story from oh-so-long ago.

Turns out I was correct about most everybody being deceased.

Judge James C. Witt is dead. So is district attorney Tom J. Taylor of Cleveland, Tennessee, and his assistant, Ken White. Ditto defense attorney Calvin N. Taylor of Knoxville. Plus Sheriff Kenneth Davis. Also many of the individuals, on both sides, who were subpoenaed to testify—including two of Moulden's three fishing buddies who saw the attack.

Then there were the 12 jurors. The vast majority are long in the grave. Three may be alive, but I was unable to locate them.

Except for one. I found him through a relative and requested he contact me. Twice. No call ever came.

A few of the peripheral players were around, though; enough who could help fill informational gaps.

Amazingly, it also appeared there was a chance, albeit slight, that the man who'd been shot so long ago was still of this orb.

I MILKED the Internet for information, cross-referencing at every turn. After that came Shoe Leather Journalism 101, unchanged since I got into this business nearly half a century ago.

You make cold calls. Leave messages. Follow road maps. Knock on doors. Ask questions. Approach total strangers, identify yourself and say, "I wonder if you could help me with a story I'm working on."

If you're lucky, these efforts sometimes pay off.

When I arrived at the News Sentinel the morning of January 17, the red light on my telephone was flashing. I picked up the receiver and punched the requisite buttons.

"This is Charles Moulden," a quiet voice spoke. "I understand you're looking for me."

I listened, slack-jawed, as the message rolled.

He was on a job in Columbia, Tennessee, but driving to Oak Ridge for the weekend. My hands shook as I reached for a pencil to scribble his cell number. That is not hyperbole.

Twenty-four hours later, Moulden was sitting at my dining room table, speaking into a tape recorder.

Forty-eight hours later, he and I were in the Cherokee National Forest, retracing his 46-year-old steps toward a hidden gunman.

Seventy-two hours later, I was meeting with editor Jack McElroy and his senior news team, outlining what I'd learned. Drop whatever else you're working on, Jack said; run with this thing.

The next three weeks became a montage of telephone calls, interstate miles, legal pads, Q&A's, fast-food meals. Plus untold hours at the keyboard.

Humor has always been my medium of choice, whether I'm writing newspaper columns or books or performing stand-up comedy on stage. Can't think of a better way to earn a living. But throughout my career, I don't recall ever being as driven and excited as when this deadly serious project began falling into place.

As more than a few of my colleagues have noted, it's about time ol' Venob did a little honest work.

COMPARING THE standards of one era to those of another is the epitome of generational apples and oranges.

They do not, will not, mesh.

By any measure, though, there's no question Charles Moulden was treated unjustly—as others have been, present and past. (Consider: What chance for a nonprejudicial jury would, say, an American Latino or Islamist receive today under similar circumstances?)

In 1968, the sheriff and prosecutor appear to have handled their jobs with diligence. Beyond that, everybody else dropped the ball.

The courts failed him.

The media failed him.

Society failed him.

That was another time. Another place. Another set of values. We move on.

Thank God.

I CLOSE with two personal anecdotes.

• Turns out Moulden and I once stood within shouting distance of each other.

This was August 30, 1963, at Duff Field in South Knoxville, where my Young High Yellowjackets hosted his Sevier County Smoky Bears in the opening game of the football season.

Young was heavily favored; Sevier County pulled off a 13-0 upset.

Charles and I were in uniform on opposite sidelines that night.

In the spirit of full disclosure, let me stress that he actually got into the fray, thus becoming the first player to break the color barrier in a Knoxville Interscholastic League game. Indeed, as the 1963 campaign progressed, Charles would develop into a major component of the Bears' formidable running attack.

I, on the other hand, did not play in the Sevier County game.

Or many others.

Venable's number never was called unless YHS was either so far ahead or so far behind, his bumbling efforts wouldn't affect the outcome.

• I worked late the day Moulden contacted me. By then, I was well aware of the magnitude of this discovery. Driving home, trying to arrange everything into categories, my head was about to explode. That's when I thought of Big Sam . . .

My late father was among many good people in this region who aggressively pushed for desegregation of schools and athletics throughout the 1950s and '60s. A University of Tennessee professor and member of the old Knox County Board of Education, he knew the Jim Crow mantra of "separate but equal" was an ugly hoax that spawned a two-tiered society.

Here was no pie-in-the-sky academic. Quite the contrary. My dad had jock cred in spades.

Professor Venable wore a whistle and carried a clipboard. He was a Vol letterman, a basketball, football and track official, a member of the university's athletics board, an inductee into sports halls of fame all over this state. During halftime of the 1996 Tennessee-UNLV game, it was my honor to be selected by UT to wear his old jersey number and run onto Shields-Watkins Field during ceremonies commemorating 75 years of football in Neyland Stadium.

That kind of jock cred.

Thus, you can trust his eldest son: No person in the South was happier than Coach Sam A. Venable Sr. when archaic racial barriers fell and athletes of all stripes began to compete as one. Tragically, he didn't live long enough to see this evolution develop fully . . .

I was motoring along Interstate 40-W that night, just beyond the Papermill exchange, and happened to glance into the cold, starry heavens. Out there in the great beyond, I mused, Big Sam and Mary Elizabeth—separated much-too-soon by his premature death in 1972—were enjoying eternity together.

What reflexively happened next will follow me to the boneyard.

I raised one hand off the steering wheel, gave a thumbs-up toward the sky and winked.

"It may take a while," I whispered hoarsely, "but we eventually get it right. This one's for you."

And I tell you unashamedly that tears were welling in my eyes as I spoke.

A stunning moment of bonding

If you think silence can't speak volumes, you should have been with me on March 24, 2014, at the close of "Meet Charles Moulden Night" at the News Sentinel.

Charles was the subject of a three-day series we ran during Black History Month. It told how he'd been ambushed and shot in 1968 while trout fishing in the Cherokee National Forest—and how his white alleged assailant, Fred Ellis, was freed by a jury despite eyewitness testimony.

This evening was our opportunity to present Charles to the public and let them hear his riveting life stories firsthand. He did it top-notch style.

Even though Charles confessed before and after the event he was nervous about speaking on stage, he performed like a pro. In his calm, gentle voice, he delivered a message of forbearance and forgiveness the likes of which I've rarely heard.

Make no mistake: Charles Moulden's journey to inner peace was not immediate. As he related to 200-plus in the audience, voice quaking with emotion at times, there was a period after the shooting when "I hated all of you (white people)."

It is understatement to note more than a few eyes glistened as he continued.

But it was later—after the crowd departed, cameras stopped flashing, videos ceased recording and autograph pens were pocketed—that I witnessed a powerful moment of human bonding.

The last person in line was Monroe Countian Kenny Witt. He's the son of the late Myles Witt, a Coker Creek land developer who frequently feuded with the Ellis clan during the mid-1970s.

Kenny grew up amid this violence. He still suffers flashbacks. More than once, his family's home was torched or riddled with bullets. During one gun battle, Ed Ellis, brother of the man believed to have shot Charles Moulden, was killed. Kenny's father went to trial three times. Each ended in a hung jury.

"Mr. Moulden, we've never met," he said, tears rolling down his cheeks. "But both of us were victims back then."

Moulden's eyes welled, too.

Nothing else needed to be said. Moulden and Witt embraced. For 15-20 seconds, they stood there, black and white arms locked around each other's shoulders, reaching across the decades to share the pain each had felt.

"I'm sorry for letting my thoughts and emotions run away with me," Kenny emailed me the next day. "But when people who have faced great challenges get an opportunity to reflect with those who understand because they were brothers in conflict, only then can real sharing, sympathy and empathy take place."

No apology necessary. Instead, multiple thanks that I could witness it.

A trout trip 46 years in the making

Call it unfinished business.

On Wednesday, April 10, 1968, a 24-year-old black man, Charles O. Moulden, was shot during a cowardly racist ambush while fishing in the Cherokee National Forest.

On Sunday, May 4, 2014, Moulden, now 70, went back. And it sure didn't take him long to pick up where he'd left off.

On his first (I reiterate: first) cast into Tellico River, Moulden caught a fat rainbow trout. Four casts later, he did it again. Not bad for a gap of 46 years, during which he'd never been trout fishing.

"I've caught a lot of bass and crappie from Watts Bar and Douglas," he said. "I've caught salmon in the Great Lakes and red snapper in Florida. But this is the first time I've gone after trout since that day."

"That day" was the focal point of a three-day News Sentinel series, "Fragments of Hate." It ran during Black History Month in February 2014.

The stories told of the violence and skewed legal aftermath that occurred when Moulden, accompanied by three white friends from their hometown of Sevierville, traveled to Tellico for the start of trout season.

Early that morning, he had been accosted by an intoxicated local. Cursing and hurling racial epithets, the man ordered Moulden to leave immediately, "or the next time I see you, you're a dead (N-word)."

For Moulden—a former football running back who was in the first integrated class at Sevier County High School and the first black player in the old Knoxville Interscholastic League—such a crude pronouncement was nothing new. He brushed it off as just another of the many testy encounters he was forced to endure.

Hours later, the threat nearly came true.

Moulden was walking a Forest Service road beside the river, intending to try his luck in a long, deep pool that formed beneath broad cascades. Within seconds, he was face-first in the gravel, a .38-caliber bullet in his left leg.

The assailant touched off a second shot that missed. He then spun around, fired into the air and disappeared into the forest.

Rescue workers refused to enter the Cherokee. Instead, Moulden's friends were forced to drive him 18 miles into the town of Tellico Plains, where they met the ambulance crew that transported him to a hospital. Bullet shards remain in his leg to this day.

Fred W. Ellis, 45, a moonshiner, previously convicted killer and resident of the nearby Coker Creek community, was charged with attempted murder. His first trial, in May 1968, resulted in a hung jury. In a second trial four months later, an all-white, all-male jury quickly declared him not guilty of felonious assault. Ellis died of cancer in 1986.

That was then. This is now.

Our trout trip was not the time to remember such a dreadful era. Rather, it was a day to celebrate victory through physical healing and spiritual forgiveness.

The weather cooperated as if scripted by Hollywood. Greening vegetation glowed in brilliant sunshine. Warblers, thrushes and tanagers, unseen in the crowns of towering poplars, pierced the clear, cool mountain air with vibrant song.

Moulden laughed at how his steps are less steady than they were nearly half a century ago. Yet he waded the pools without so much as a stumble, casting accurately, working his bait through the runs with practiced hands. He smiled frequently.

"Fred Ellis may have slowed me down, but he didn't stop me," Moulden noted as he and I walked to the exact section of river where the shooting occurred. "I wonder what he'd say today."

It was lost on neither of us that we had just parked in the very pull-off where the shooter was poised oh-so-long ago.

"Right there," Moulden pointed with his spinning rod as he exited the vehicle. "That's where he was. Just up on that rise. He was standing behind a little bush."

He paused. "Even today I still can't believe it happened. Man! Just because of the color of my skin."

We fished the run for perhaps 20-30 minutes, each adding one rainbow to our tally. During that time, Moulden admitted he couldn't help but think back to 1968. Whenever a car or truck traveled through the curve above us, his gaze followed its progress. Then he returned to his fishing.

"This hole doesn't look quite as good down here as it does from up on the road," he yelled with a grin over the river's roar. "Maybe I should've let ol' Fred have it and kept looking for a better place!"

By noon, the forest was alive with visitors. Occasional campfire smoke curled skyward. In singles, pairs and threesomes, anglers crowded many of the popular pools. It was too cold for swimming, but kayakers—as foreign as black fishermen way back when—paddled in convoys through twisting runs of whitewater. As always, the mist-shrouded parking area at Bald River Falls was packed with tourists and sightseers, cameras in hand.

Downriver, Moulden and I took off our hip boots, shed our jackets and ate a sandwich on the tailgate of my truck. Anytime a vehicle approached, he casually nodded or gave a friendly wave. Often the gesture was returned with an out-the-window hand wave or "toot-toot" howdy.

Time passes.

Attitudes change.

It was just another day of trout season.

Made in the USA
Columbia, SC
25 April 2024

34592871R00163